Of Bread, Blood and *The Hunger Games*

Critical Essays on the Suzanne Collins Trilogy

Edited by MARY F. PHARR *and*
LEISA A. CLARK

CRITICAL EXPLORATION IN SCIENCE FICTION AND FANTASY, 35
Donald E. Palumbo *and* C.W. Sullivan III, *series editors*

McFarland & Company, Inc., Publishers
Jefferson, North Carolina, and London

LIBRARY OF CONGRESS CATALOGUING-IN-PUBLICATION DATA

Of bread, blood and the Hunger Games : critical essays on
the Suzanne Collins trilogy / edited by Mary F. Pharr and Leisa
A. Clark.
     p.   cm. — (Critical explorations in science fiction and
       fantasy ; 35)
[Donald E. Palumbo and C.W. Sullivan III, series editors]
Includes bibliographical references and index.

ISBN 978-0-7864-7019-8
softcover : acid free paper ∞

1. Collins, Suzanne — Criticism and interpretation.   2. Collins,
Suzanne. Hunger Games.   3. Young adult fiction, American —
History and criticism.   I. Pharr, Mary.   II. Clark, Leisa A.,
1968–
PS3603.O4558Z84 2012
813'.6 — dc23   2012022815

BRITISH LIBRARY CATALOGUING DATA ARE AVAILABLE

Front cover images © 2012 Shutterstock

Manufactured in the United States of America

McFarland & Company, Inc., Publishers
Box 611, Jefferson, North Carolina 28640
www.mcfarlandpub.com

To Joseph A. Dechert and Philip W. Pharr,
good men whose memory remains with us
and
To George and Phyllis Clark for your
encouragement, strength, and love.

Acknowledgments

All anthologies are the work of many minds and hands. We begin by thanking the contributors who have generously presented their analyses and insights within their essays. We owe special thanks to series advisor C. W. Sullivan. We are grateful as well to Florida Southern College for its technical support of this project. Jim Byrd, Peter Schreffler, Claudia Slate, Cat Eskin, and Kathy Kniffin deserve special mention. Equally important has been the help of the Humanities and Cultural Studies Department of the University of South Florida. We are particularly grateful to this department for allowing us to hold a number of our meetings within its confines. Thanks as well to Walter Danielak and Jennifer Melko for letting us spread out all over a shared office. Then there are those people who have sustained us in ways beyond counting during the months of working on this book. Among these friends and supporters, we are happy to acknowledge Amanda Firestone, Jessica Collard, René Llewellyn, Ruth Keyes, Cheryl DeFlavis, Cecilia Bolich, Gretchen Romilly Mueller, Marta Jones, and Mark Muncy.

Leisa would also like to give a special thanks to her ever-patient thesis committee: Dr. Annette Cozzi, Dr. Sara Dykins-Callahan, and Dr. Amy Rust.

Finally, we would be more than remiss if we did not acknowledge a debt beyond gratitude to Sally Gage for her love and encouragement in all ways during this process, and to Donald Pharr for his boundless support and immeasurable contributions.

Table of Contents

Preface

LEISA A. CLARK

In the 1980s, when I was employed by a major bookstore franchise in New York, I was given the daunting task of reorganizing the children's books to separate those designed for very young readers from those written for teen audiences. Although publishers had designated a distinct category for young adult readers as early as the 1960s, well into the 1980s books were usually still displayed together in one relatively small section of the bookstore — relegating teen literature to secondary status. Once I'd separated the children's books from those meant for adolescents, however, the new young adult section filled only four shelves on a wall unit situated in the back of the store. The new division was full of classic novels often assigned in schools, books such as *Silas Marner* and *Great Expectations*. These fine classics could arguably be described as literature not necessarily designed for adolescents but still good for them to read. There were also books by Judy Blume, Madeleine L'Engle, and Lois Lowry, books that explore the concerns and experiences of modern young adults — but such relevant books were few and far between.

Fast-forward to early 2012. At the time of this writing, a quick trip to any local bookstore shows a clear change in how young adult literature is marketed and respected: there are usually at least three entire shelving units, several end-caps, and multiple table displays prominently featuring young adult titles. Online, Amazon.com currently lists over 175,000 novels in the general "teen" category, which now includes multiple genres and subgenres, such as "love and romance," "manga," "fantasy," and "dystopian fiction." Moreover, although teenaged readers seem to have a great deal of buying power, as evidenced by the sheer number of books marketed to that age group, it is also clear that an increasing number of adults are buying books aimed at younger readers. My conversations with bookstore managers have revealed that the trend grows stronger each year. "We had to hire someone just to manage the young adult section," declared a manager I spoke to at a St. Petersburg, Florida, bookstore. "The books are outselling almost every other genre, and not just kids buy the books. We probably sell more YA books to adults than to teenagers these days."

Where literature goes, scholars follow. In March 2011, Mary Pharr and I were both presenting papers at the International Conference on the Fantastic in the Arts in Orlando. After attending several sessions on young adult literature, at which were presented a few papers on *The Hunger Games,* we began a conversation about how little scholarly work had been produced on the series at that point. We discussed the virtues of a recent nonscholarly publication on the trilogy but bemoaned the dearth of academic discourse on the subject. "Maybe we should put together an anthology," one or both of us suggested. Our research soon confirmed that, in spite of the upcoming films and the great success of the novels, the series had yet to garner the same level of scholarly attention as *Harry Potter* or *Twilight.* A review of the University of South Florida library's extensive database of journal articles demonstrated a particular interest in the series but few critical articles or books published about it. We set out to fill that gap by providing well-researched, analytical discussions of the series' key ideas, characters, and themes in one book.

Of Bread, Blood and The Hunger Games: *Critical Essays on the Suzanne Collins Trilogy* is the result of an extensive call for papers that produced more abstracts than we could possibly publish in one volume, thereby illustrating our point that academics want to talk about *The Hunger Games* and eagerly anticipate a venue in which to do so. Our contributors are primarily professional academics whose research affords them the experience and expertise to critically examine *The Hunger Games* series as a cultural and literary phenomenon. Spanning multiple disciplines, the contributors each bring a unique perspective to their chapters. Crucially, the essays within this anthology are not limited to a single critical focus. Our contributors use a range of evaluative tools, probing at the trilogy's meaning by using theories as varied as historicism, postmodernism, feminism, humanism, cultural studies, political studies, queer theory, and media studies. Like the readers of the books they study here, our contributors hail from a variety of regions within and beyond America. Ranging from graduate students to established faculty and writers, these scholars have a clear sense of the trilogy's complex layers: some see it as fundamentally tragic, while others find it hopeful at the last. Yet their diverse critical and intellectual perspectives have three elements in common: a deep appreciation of the work under consideration, a profound belief in its permanent value, and a need to share both appreciation and belief with fellow readers.

In a sense, then, this anthology is a celebration of value. But it is also a collection with a practical purpose: to enable students of the series to begin their research on any or all three of the novels with an anthology that is scholarly *and* readable. What you will not find in this volume is the last word on the series, because there is still so much more to be written, and we hope this book is just the first of many to follow.

The literary fire set by Suzanne Collins blazes on!

Introduction

MARY F. PHARR *and*
LEISA A. CLARK

Twenty-first-century American culture has often reimagined and popularized established narrative genres, a kind of vesturing of canonical material in postmodern clothing. Contemporary culture is, of course, also vested in the technological and/or the fantastic, much of our art and literature submerging the dilemmas of quotidian reality within the vision of another realm outside the familiar stressors of ordinary time and place. Indeed, pop culture repeatedly seems bent on confirming Harold Pinter's observation that there "can be no hard distinctions between what is real and what is unreal..." (11). Combined with the equally dominant tendency of the postmodern perspective to decenter traditional sources of power and authority in favor of multiple perspectives on just about everything, current popular culture invites an almost visceral response to its key works. Significantly, a number of those works can be found in the young adult genre.

Scholars have noted that the young adult genre began as morality books and "sugar-coated sermons" for Sunday school readers (Nilsen and Donelson 3). Initially, storytelling counted less than the teaching of Christian values and morals to young people. Tales focused on little boys and girls who either made the right choices or suffered the consequences of bad behavior. Late-nineteenth-century authors such as Horatio Alger wrote smarmy stories that the American Sunday School Union approved of and encouraged children to read. Eventually, perhaps inevitably, the Sunday school tomes gave way to more entertaining dime novels and domestic stories, and writers began to focus on the gender of their readers: boys were given adventure stories, while girls were encouraged to read tales emphasizing household virtues. By the early twentieth century, the Stratemeyer Syndicate was producing thousands of titles for young people over several decades. Not everyone was happy with the quality of the entertainment, however, and Stratemeyer books were sometimes challenged for questionable content (Campbell 67). A June 1917 article in *The English Journal* states that literature "must not shock the delicate sensibilities of either the teacher or the student" (Barbe 362) and further suggests that young people should be encouraged to read good novels filled with "wonder and marvel" (365). The author seems worried that youngsters might choose the wrong sort of books if they are not taught better — an argument still heard almost a century later.

After World War II, the publishing industry produced mass paperbacks, just as children found themselves with more access to the pocket change needed to buy these inexpensive books. Schools continued their concern with the quality of such readily available reading material. Starting in the 1950s, many groups of concerned educators and parent-teacher organizations began to review books for young people, trying to ensure that youths were not exposed to stories of questionable taste and dubious literary value (Cole 70). Such reviews did not stop the youths in question from buying supposedly immoral books, especially in the burgeoning paperback and comic book market. Many of the works in this market were science fiction, a genre that appealed to adults as surely as to adolescents in the Cold War era. Fiction that focused on alien invasions and on the alien next door suggested the paranoia that rose with McCarthyism, when Americans feared that Communists would infiltrate the U.S. and destroy it (Mann 50). An "us versus them" mentality took hold of Americans of all ages and informed a genre that had previously concentrated on industrial anxieties, uncontrolled science, and historical paradoxes.

Fortunately, science fiction survived this age of anxiety since, as Errol Vieth suggests, SF is a malleable genre, its narratives "like pieces of clay" that "can be reworked into different shapes and dimensions," thus allowing readers a variety of perspectives (1). As a genre, science fiction is at least as old as Mary Shelley's *Frankenstein* (1818), and it may be significant that when she began writing her iconic novel, Mary Shelley was herself a young adult, still in her teens. From the beginning, scholars have been unable to agree completely on a standard definition of the genre, but most readers can agree with Justine Larbalestier, who also recognizes the genre's malleability when she notes that science fiction is "something that is published as science fiction and read as science fiction" (xvi). While this circular definition may not elucidate researchers seeking the particulars of SF characteristics, it does fit the general sense most readers have of knowing a genre when they see it. More precisely, perhaps, most readers also know that science fiction challenges the boundaries of what a society perceives as normal or familiar. Often, SF writers present this challenge by reimagining the present as a future or alternate reality. Casual readers may associate SF with outer space, robots, technological wonders, and/or aliens. But at its core, science fiction is about conjecture. As imaginative as it is scientific, SF ponders our reality by speculating about possible other worlds, other times, other beings. At its best, it demands plausibility since it focuses on "actions and events that have not yet occurred within the realm of human experience but conceivably might" (Weedman 6). This plausibility separates it from works of pure fantasy.

Authors writing for the contemporary young adult audience recognize that their readers are used to speculative narration, readily apparent in such popular works as *The Adoration of Jenna Fox* (2008) by Mary E. Pearson, *The Forest of Hands and Teeth* series (2009–2011) by Carrie Ryan, and *Matched* (2011) by Ally Condie. Authors also understand the market for YA science fiction. Young adult novels that can justly claim to be science fiction may include elements of horror and cyberpunk, but they need at least a grain of plausibility. Among such novels are Neal Shusterman's *Unwind* (2007), in which (absent of legal abortion) parents may choose to have their unwanted teenaged children "unwound" and their body parts reused for organ transplants, and *Skinned* (2008) by Robin Wasserman, which takes the opposite approach to genetic and body manipulation through the downloading of minds into organic-looking android bodies that feel no pain and can never die. The dystopian misuse of science is a key component of many young adult novels set in the near future, and the plots often rely on extant technologies to create fear and anxiety in the characters and readers alike. Suzanne Weyn's *The Bar Code Tattoo* trilogy (2004–2009) offers an alternate United States where everyone over age sixteen is marked by a bar code containing relevant information, access to bank accounts, and data about genetic anomalies and possible illnesses that could affect one's quality of life. As corporations and the government begin using the bar code tattoos to determine suitability for employment and standard of living, those who suffer as a result of the tattoos begin to rebel.

This theme — the sudden realization that advanced technology may do more harm than good — is as old as *Frankenstein,* but contemporary young adult novels often take such ideas to the next level by showing what a world dependent on advanced technologies might look like. Novels such as Lauren DeStefano's intriguing *Chemical Garden* series, Veronica Roth's *Divergent,* and Lauren Oliver's *Delirium* (all initially released in 2011) reveal worlds in which dependent technologies have either vanished — having done more harm than good — or have been manipulated in such a way that the protagonists are unaware they are living with the after-effects of technological advances that have broken down. Readers in the twenty-first century are more than likely aware of the scientific and technological possibilities posited by these novels, so novels that suggest a failure or even a reversal of progress may seem particularly frightening to young audiences.

Thus, it seems only fitting that within the last decade, dystopian and postapocalyptic fiction has come to the forefront of science fiction written for the YA audience. In addition to and beyond the fear of technological catastrophe, the rise in dystopian and postapocalyptic fiction may be linked to America's response to the events of September 11, 2001. Dystopian and postapocalyptic novels seem both to evoke and relieve the mind-set of fear and isolation felt by many real-world people after the attacks on the Pentagon and the World Trade Center. Certainly, many children growing up after 9/11 may feel less confident about their personal safety than the generations who came before. And even those who have strong personal support may sense parallel erosion in confidence within the adults who, presumably, control the world. In 2003, in the *Journal of Future Studies,* Wendell Bell expressed the fear that America's course within the next decade would "undermine civil liberties in the United States, erode our electoral system, and threaten social programs affecting the environment, education, and health," even as it failed to deal effectively with "future attacks on America by nonstate terrorist groups" (79). As the second decade of the new millennium struggles with national and international recession amid political scandal and gridlock, Bell's dire predictions seem even more ominous. Bombarded by bleak forecasts from both reliable sources and electronic posts that are seldom securely fact-checked, Millennial adolescents are especially open to postmodern interpretations of reality as reimagined in fiction — no matter how grim those interpretations may be.

Earlier YA dystopian/postapocalyptic novels tend to be single-minded tales of survival, whether against oppression, aliens, or the environment. The post–9/11 novels in this genre are somehow different, focused more on personal *and* social change. Most are concerned with fighting totalitarian governments that only the young adults in the stories recognize as such. Adults are often portrayed as either ineffectual or indoctrinated. The former group may recognize the evils within their society, but having lived through those evils and seen what happened to those who did not survive them, these ineffectual adults are too afraid to dissent. The indoctrinated, on the other hand, are so embedded with the ideologies of the dystopian regime that they have become "true believers" in its actions and dogma. Thus, Marena's father in James DeVita's *The Silenced* (2007) conforms completely to the Zero Tolerance Party after his wife's execution for speaking out against the new regime in its early days, while Martin's parents in Clare B. Dunkle's *The Sky Inside* (2008) willingly allow themselves to be part of a city of lies. It's left to the young to do what their parents cannot or will not do. Like the *Swingjugend* (Swing Kids) of the 1930s, who defied Hitlerian culture at great personal risk (many were arrested and sent to work camps), the young in post–9/11 YA novels often seem more daring than previous generations — no matter the cost.

More and more, however, contemporary YA readers accept and even expect a dark, dystopian view of existence in their preferred literature — but a view of an existence that, while plausible, is still presented as an "other" time, place, or reality: not the dreary diurnal reality that may be defeating their parents. In this respect, *The Hunger Games* reflects the postmodern fears that things are not going well for America and that the United States may eventually fall like the Roman Empire. The world of the trilogy projects a possible future of fear, anger, violence, and misery; yet Suzanne Collins also gives that future the possibility of hope through the creation of a hero whose job it becomes to redeem her world — even if she does not know it and cannot see it as her fate. Unlike the highly romantic *Twilight* series, Collins's trilogy is both plausible enough and speculative enough to serve as science fiction, attracting its core YA audience and an ever increasing cluster of older readers.

Thus, *The Hunger Games* (2008), *Catching Fire* (2009), and *Mockingjay* (2010) serve as proof that young adult literature can transcend the "adolescent" label that so often limits its critical reception among scholars and mature readers. Folded into the truly epic scope of this series are multiple, sometimes contradictory narrative genres: a war story that is as well an antiwar treatise, a romance that is never unreservedly romantic, a science fiction adventure that also serves as grim social satire, an identity novel that is compellingly ambivalent about gender roles, and — like other great epics — a tragedy depicting the desperate human need for heroes and the terrible cost of heroism. Even its futuristic location is evocative: the dystopian Panem is built on the ruins of the continent we call North America, its inhabitable land drastically reduced through a cascade of natural and man-made disasters. The setting is painfully easy to imagine. As a pure story, *The Hunger Games* trilogy has a cultural significance that moves through and beyond the postmodern world — all this in a series that may be the fastest page-turner in publishing history.

Suzanne Collins was already an established writer when she began *The Hunger Games*. The daughter of a military historian, she traveled abroad as a child with her Air Force family. Years later, after receiving a graduate degree from New York University in dramatic writing, she worked first in children's television; then in 2003, she published *Gregor the Overlander*, the initial book in the five-part Underland Chronicles. Popular with both readers and reviewers, the Underland books marked a milestone for Collins as a children's literature writer. Yet nothing could have prepared her for the response to her next set of novels.

In 2006, Underland's publisher, Scholastic, acquired the rights to *The Hunger Games* manuscript, along with its anticipated sequels, and the work in progress soon became "an in-house favorite" (Sellers 19). Initially, the publishing house expected a *Hunger Games* first printing of no more than 50,000 copies, but early enthusiasm quadrupled the initial printing (Sellers 19). That enthusiasm turned into elation as the book came out in 2008 to laudatory reviews and strong sales. John Green called it "an exhilarating narrative," its strength coming from "Collins's convincingly detailed world-building and her memorably complex and fascinating heroine" (30).

In 2009, *Catching Fire* was published in both print and audio versions. Reviews were mixed, even contradictory, regarding the second novel's pacing — a result, perhaps, of an inevitable comparison to the breakneck speed of *The Hunger Games*. Virtually all critics did, however, find this second book a worthy addition to the series. Citing her admiration for protagonist Katniss Everdeen's increasing sophistication and observational acuity, Gabrielle Zevin even called *Catching Fire* "a sequel that improves upon the first book" (13). Michelle Kerns amplifies this focus on the heroine by noting that the sequel "moves the story from the oppressed, under-duress phase to the full-blown rebellion phase: it's the final transitional stop for Katniss as she morphs from trapped bird to lovebird to mockingjay" ("'Catching Fire'"). As a transition, the book left readers wanting more.

And they got what they wanted. *Mockingjay,* the final novel in the trilogy, was published in the summer of 2010, with a first printing of well over one million ("Scholastic Increases"). Sarah Hutton, a Washington state bookstore manager, predicted it would be "the biggest book in the Y.A. section, probably for the entire year" (qtd. in Bosman C1). The prediction was accurate, *Mockingjay* selling some 450,000 hardback and eBook copies in the U.S. during its first week of release ("*Mockingjay,* The Final Book"). Reviewer Sue Corbett called the book "a powerful, emotionally exhausting final volume" (69). As a novel in its own right, *Mockingjay* confirms the depth of its author's narrative genius and social perception. As a conclusion to the series, it certifies the trilogy's epic status as well as its place in both young adult literature and postmodern culture.

Even concluded, the series continues to sell. In January 2012, Brooks Barnes and Julie Bosman reported "23.5 million books [from the trilogy] in print in the domestic market" (B6). As of February 2012, *The New York Times* had listed the trilogy on its "Children's Best Sellers" Series list for seventy-five weeks (BR 26). As telling is the way the series has helped to redefine the YA audience. Both *Hunger Games* and *Mockingjay* appeared on *The Chronicle of Higher Education's* list of best-selling books in college bookstores, with the first book reaching number one in 2011 ("What They're Reading"). Clearly, as Susan Dominus has noted, *The Hunger Games* trilogy is now part of "a kind of publishing holy trinity, taking its place alongside J. K. Rowling's 'Harry Potter' series and Stephenie Meyer's 'Twilight'" (32).

Being part of this postmodern trinity brings controversy as well as fame. Thus, *The Hunger Games* made the American Library Association's list of "most frequently challenged" library books, coming in fifth on the 2010 list.

The ALA reports three objections presented by challengers to Collins's work: it is "sexually explicit" and "unsuited to age group," and its plot contains "violence" ("Top Ten"). The unintended irony in the first of these charges against the author's discreetly poignant depiction of adolescent romance is, perhaps, less significant than the challengers' misunderstanding of the plot as it relates to the characters and their audience. Violence is, indeed, seminal to that plot, which requires that blood be spilled as a means of both sustaining life and controlling it. But so, too, is hunger a seminal element within the story, the need for bread serving as a corollary to blood, again a means of sustaining *and* controlling life. Of the three mega-selling series, *The Hunger Games* trilogy has the most open and profound presentation of the complexity within a society whose needs are brutally contradictory yet inextricably linked. While the novels' detailed environment, relentless action, and compelling lead characters may help to explain how Collins conveys this complexity to Scholastic's target audience, the series has a still greater appeal: a reach that moves among readers of all ages, an epic reach that forces, without force, its audience to ponder adult issues at their most intense. Ultimately, what makes *The Hunger Games* unique among the "Big Three" series is that its fantasy-filled plot somehow eschews wish fulfillment. So do *Gilgamesh* and the *Iliad*. No one can predict which postmodern works will last even a fraction of the time the oldest and greatest of literary works have lasted, but it's not hubris to suggest that *The Hunger Games* series is remarkable not just as a young adult phenomenon but as a literary masterwork in its own right.

As with any work of art, the thematic core of *The Hunger Games* lies somewhere within its origin; yet as is also often true of memorable works, the trilogy has taken on a thematic life and cultural resonance of its own. In the beginning, however, the basic inspiration for the first book came to Collins as she flipped television channels. Motivated by her father's Vietnam experience, Collins found the nucleus of a story in the unsettling conflation of a reality-TV competition and real-war coverage. The embryonic story's details were soon enhanced by her interest in the Greek myth of Theseus versus the Minotaur and in the rebel subject of a favorite movie, *Spartacus* (Blasingame 726–27). Collins has said that she decided to write "an updated version of the Roman Gladiator games" (qtd. in Margolis), one that would delineate her fear that "today people see so many reality shows and dramas that when real news is on, its impact is completely lost on them" (qtd. in Blasingame 727). From the first chapter of *The Hunger Games* through the epilogue in *Mockingjay,* Collins succeeds not only in updating classical mythology and common-era history through contemporary science fiction, but also in explicating her anxiety about the dangers inherent in the postmodern confusion of "acceptable" fantasy and "unacceptable" reality. In so doing, her books speak to and for millions of readers of all ages.

Such shared contemplation is a remarkable enough accomplishment for any set of novels, let alone a set labeled as young adult. But what fundamentally propels this particular YA set toward postmodern epic status is its scope: however personal it may seem during a first reading, the plot actually hurls both characters and readers through an apocalypse that engulfs every part of Panem — a wide reach within a trilogy that posits Panem as the future of all that once was North America, if not the world. Thematically, the trilogy's reach extends to some of the most controversial aspects of current American culture, most especially the conflation of "bread and blood" within the larger social perception of basic human needs. Probing inwards as well as outwards, the series touches issues of history and culture, identity and gender, ethics and aesthetics under duress, and of resistance to an increasingly pervasive atmosphere of high-tech surveillance and control. Above all, *The Hunger Games* trilogy touches a root human fear, common at any age but most especially terrible for the young: the fear of not knowing what to do, how and when to act in an ever-more-dangerous world. Ambiguity dominates the arena, embracing Katniss Everdeen with an intensity that neither Peeta Mellark nor Gale Hawthorne can match. And like Achilles, that greatest and most tragic hero of the Trojan War, Katniss must accept the consequences of this embrace.

As almost every critic of the trilogy has noted, it's Katniss herself who first grabs a reader's attention. She is both the classic reluctant hero from the science fiction and fantasy genre described by Stuart Voytilla (259) and a contemporary female protagonist, struggling to find independence in an uncertain world. Like Han Solo in *Star Wars* and Wolverine in the *X-Men* series, Katniss has virtually no initial interest in playing the hero role forced on her first by the Capitol and then by the rebels. Born into poverty but also born with the natural instincts of both a survivor and a hunter, she is unwilling — inherently unable — to give up and die when she is placed in the arena of the Hunger Games. Like many protagonists in the speculative and science fiction genres, Katniss has always lived in the space between the ordinary and the extraordinary, though she enters another level of that hell when she chooses to take her sister's place at the Games. Only in the arena, under the relentless gaze of all Panem, does Katniss find the resources within herself and her district partner that allow them first to survive the survivable, then to become the heroes in fact that they have earlier just pretended to be as part of their pragmatic survival plan. Yet Katniss is always more comfortable with her role as survivor than hero. She knows how to act but never with the certainty that people want in their heroes. Even when costumed as the all-important Mockingjay, even at the close of the war against the Capitol, she remains plagued by doubt — but she is also inherently incapable of giving up: she is a survivalist down to her genes. Crucially, however, her survival ensures the continued existence of whatever is left that offers hope to Panem. In truth and in spite of herself, Katniss *is* the epic hero Mockingjay.

She is also an ambiguous figure in a world that exhibits some frightening similarities to our own. From the perspective of history's dire tendency to repeat its worst moments, *The Hunger Games* trilogy can be read as a cautionary political tale as well as an epic — a glimpse into an alternate but ever possible reality. Panem is corrupt, its civilization so unbalanced as to be in danger of collapsing. The world that Collins has created is a paradigm of decadence, its facade of inane elegance supported by a framework of human suffering and social inequity. History attests to the fall of regimes, sometimes even nations, when governments exhibit no concern for the mass of humanity within their own borders. So it was with Imperial Rome, Bourbon France, the Soviet Union; so it is with Panem. In this alternate future, the United States has long disappeared, its land now occupied by a nation whose government-sanctioned inequalities leave most of the population living desperate lives of poverty, while a "lucky" few have nothing better to do than waste resources and their lives in the most jejune way possible. What makes its protagonist ambiguous and what particularly links this series to so many of its readers is that while Katniss knows what is wrong with Panem, she has no clear sense of what to do about it, no all-embracing plan to save her world. In that sense, she's easy for a Millennial audience to identify with. Her ultimate heroism may give hope — but never simplistic answers.

Nothing in fiction is ever entirely new, of course. Prototypes of and parallels to Katniss can be found in other YA dystopian/postapocalyptic novels where a downtrodden, oppressed young girl becomes a hero and an inspiration. Among these prototypes are Tia in H. M. Hoover's *Children of Morrow* (1973) and Lisa in O. T. Nelson's *The Girl Who Owned a City* (1975). Like Katniss, Tia and Lisa both have a younger sibling to protect, and both fight tyrannical leaders for the sake of that sibling; however, neither becomes the symbolic representation of rebellion as Katniss does. Later characters, like Tally Youngblood in Scott Westerfeld's *Uglies* series (2005–2011), come closer; but Tally is never as powerful as Katniss, even when, like Katniss, Tally is used by the government to control others. Most recently, Katniss's strength, intuition, and focus on staying alive can also be found in Saba, the heroic teen in Moira Young's *Blood Red Road* (2011), the first volume in the Dust Lands trilogy; and in Beatrice Prior, the protagonist of Veronica Roth's *Divergent* (2011), also the beginning of a series. Yet none of these characters has the innate charisma and overt ambiguity of Katniss Everdeen.

Because readers of all ages and backgrounds can empathize with Katniss's personal anguish, the implications of her story more than merit scholarly discussion. Conferences like the International Conference on the Fantastic in the Arts and the Annual Meeting of the Popular Culture Association have already held sessions focused on *The Hunger Games* trilogy. In 2010, a group of writers who specialize in children's and young adult literature contributed essays to Leah Wilson's *The Girl Who Was on Fire*. Other companion books have followed. Now, *Of Bread, Blood and* The Hunger Games: *Critical Essays on the Suzanne's Collins Trilogy* hopes to make a distinctive contribution to this emerging study by presenting a group of scholarly essays to an audience of both young adults and older students. Our anthology makes no pretense of being all inclusive, but it does offer a wide range of scholarly perceptions and research to those who want to know more about its subject. Many *Hunger Games* readers may have begun the first novel while in high school, while others discovered it in college. Today, both groups, along with increasing numbers of older adults who have also been captivated by the series, want to delve further into its characters, themes, and theory. To that end, we have divided the essay portion of this book into four parts, each focusing on critical elements that make *The Hunger Games* trilogy both memorable and meaningful.

Part I, "History, Politics, Economics and Culture," opens with Bill Clemente examining the trilogy in terms of its relationship to crisis economics and political engagement. Seen in this light, the novels become an activist series, warning readers about destructive political and economic currents in our own world. In his essay, Anthony Pavlik has a different perspective on the misuse of political power within the novels. Working from Umberto Eco's analysis of fascist ideology, Pavlik believes that the trilogy suggests that the destruction of fascist evil requires violence in pursuit of ultimate good — thus leaving open the question of whether the trilogy also reveals a gradual acclimatization to the ideology Collins seeks to show as intolerable. Gretchen Koenig next sees Collins engaging with the idea that history is always political, rewritten by those in power who use it to shape cultural memory. Only when Katniss disengages from public/governmental narrative can she find her own personal power.

The final three chapters in Part I look at the way Collins's work reflects American culture. Valerie Estelle Frankel finds that the world of *The Hunger Games* mirrors real-world artificiality at its worst. Both the Capitol and the Games are artificial constructs, their superficiality revealing the dangerous waste and false values of contemporary America, a media-driven society unable to draw the line between entertainment and reality. Tina L. Hanlon considers a very different aspect of American culture in her essay: the specific Appalachian community that is the real-world equivalent of District 12. Exploring the sociocultural parallels between Appalachia as it is and as it is reimagined as District 12, Hanlon finds that the "coal-town" environment Collins uses within her futuristic story both demonstrates the human cost of industrialization and makes the story recognizable to today's readers. The use of an economically marginalized area of America as home of the Mockingjay also suggests the value of home itself and the possibility of reclamation. In the final chapter in this group, Max Despain studies Collins's use of food — its absence *and* abundance — as central to discontent in Panem. Despain notes that the metaphorical complexity of food within the series links Panem and America, which also has a mixed response to food, associating it with both abundance and indulgence. With food centralized both literally and metaphorically, Panem's own cultural identity is portrayed through different kinds of hunger, variously satisfied.

The essays in Part II review issues of "Ethics, Aesthetics and Identity." Guy Andre Risko begins with a consideration of the ethical complexities within Collins's narrative. Drawing on the work of Giorgio Agamben, Risko finds that the series argues for a complicated version of decision making that moves past dichotomous thinking. By resisting encapsulation by either Capitol or rebels, Katniss becomes a threshold figure, constantly attempting to avoid totalizing discourses as she acts. From a very different perspective, Tammy L. Gant examines a related issue stemming from the seeming dearth of spirituality in Panem's postapocalyptic world. Noting that the arts can serve a spiritual need in the absence of religion, Gant finds that the music of revolutionary Panem provides the kind of transcendence that religion traditionally offers and so helps Katniss to act ethically. Katheryn Wright then examines the way the series critically engages with the aesthetics of contemporary popular culture through its "reality television" format. The ultimate meaning of such a narrative format proves to be beyond anyone's complete control, as the Games shift from affirmations of Capitol power to demonstrations of revolutionary art. But *Mockingjay* shows that even revolutionary art is uncertain, with the ambivalent symbolism of the Mockingjay image representing what aesthetics has become in our world.

Part II continues with Sharon D. King's analysis of Panem's penchant for monstrosity, conflating both aesthetics and nature with identity. Hybridity is everywhere: the mutated birds, the killer animal mutants, the elite denizens of the Capitol with their self-inflicted mutations — even Katniss and Peeta, whose identities prove as impermanent as everyone else's. King finds that the series as a whole describes a society where the liminal and the monstrous have triumphed. Examining hybridity with a different lens, Ellyn Lem and Holly Hassel first observe that *The Hunger Games* challenges gender stratification by appealing to both sexes equally. Finding Katniss a "male-identified" female character, Lem and Hassel further conclude that the narrative threads within the first novel deliberately complicate binaries of masculine and feminine as Collins weaves a new tale from the generic traditions of war stories and heterosexual romance, effectively creating a hybrid genre in YA fiction. Jennifer Mitchell also looks at identity, noting that as Katniss develops within the series, she comes to perform a variety of gender roles. In particular, her inconsistency in negotiating between the staged girly romance she is required to accept and the traditionally masculine hunter's survival instinct that has long defined her suggests the performativity inherent in both roles. Arguing that Katniss's mobility is quintessentially queer, Mitchell finds that Collins's text is a celebration of the insubstantial relationship between self and gender.

Part III examines "Resistance, Surveillance and Simulacra," each a key element in the trilogy's position in postmodern literature. Amy L. Montz notes that the transformation of Katniss from girl into symbol is based on style as surely as on action. Master stylist Cinna understands that pleasing spectacle presented upon a female body can be a crucial component of resistance, and the creation of the ever-fashionable Mockingjay becomes a visual site for resistance to the Capitol. Montz further notes that the series problematizes this use of fashion when Katniss realizes that it's her stylized image rather than her living body that matters to the rebel leaders. Kelley Wezner also examines transformation, noting that the Capitol uses a panoptic system of surveillance to control and modify those under its power. Gradually, Katniss becomes aware of ways to negotiate these panoptic mechanisms, only to find rebel District 13 even more challenging, since its controlling mechanisms are less obvious than those of the Capitol. Expanding on the idea of the all-seeing eye, Shannon R. Mortimore-Smith scrutinizes the voyeuristic elements within the Hunger Games themselves. Critiquing the relationship between the viewer and viewed in both the arena and in its counterparts in contemporary television, Mortimore-Smith notes that while the viewers gain privilege through the act of viewing, the viewed must negotiate their survival by holding the "gaze" of the privileged masses watching them. Closing out this section, Helen Day investigates a line of fiction that demonstrates the increasingly sophisticated manipulation of image in relation to audience. Starting from Jean Baudrillard's theories of simulacra, Day analyzes Stephen King's *The Running Man,* Koushun Takami's *Battle Royale,* and *The Hunger Games* trilogy, each featuring a dystopian society that functions through electronic surveillance and that uses a national game as a means of creating terror, diversion, and division.

Part IV, "Thematic Parallels and Literary Traditions," acknowledges some of the works related to *The Hunger Games* novels by subject, characterization, theme, and/or tradition. Catherine R. Eskin opens by considering Collins's series in light of Shakespeare's second Henriad. Rather than argue for an analogous interpretation of Katniss and Prince Hal, Eskin focuses on the ways an early modern and postmodern bid for political power may be parallel in execution but dissonant in outcome — with both bids dependent on public relations. Next, Rodney M. DeaVault finds that concepts of femininity and maturation are questioned and negotiated in both Robert A. Heinlein's *Podkayne of Mars* and *The Hunger Games* trilogy. Podkayne's repositioning of her initial goals in favor of more-traditional ones remains controversial, but Katniss, allowed more personal and perceptual development than Podkayne, transitions within the trilogy from a manipulated girl to an insightful woman. A different perspective on maturation can be found in Sarah Outterson Murphy's essay, which posits that Collins's trilogy subverts the hero myth of violence as progression toward maturity. Murphy finds support for her reading of the series as an allegory of the adolescent child's encounter with a self-destructive adult world in Orson Scott Card's *Ender's Game*. Both Katniss and Ender Wiggin become disillusioned with violence, eventually allowing them to interrupt its self-perpetuating cycle. Amanda Firestone then examines the heroines in Stephenie Meyer's *Twilight* and Collins's *The Hunger Games*. Moving past the popular tendency to see Katniss as the positive antithesis to Bella Swan's passive heroine, Firestone looks at the differing literary traditions that lie behind each novel, traditions that can shed light on just how much Katniss and Bella can and should be compared. In the final essay in this collection, Mary F. Pharr reviews the correlations and distinctions in the development of Harry Potter and Katniss as epic heroes. If the iconic Harry Potter can be read as a hero for contemporary children, then Katniss can be seen as a hero for contemporary adolescents, less lovable and more tragic than Harry — but also potentially more consequential in terms of real-world issues.

The much anticipated Lionsgate quartet of cinematic adaptations of *The Hunger Games* novels is now under way, guaranteeing that Panem will remain in the public eye for the foreseeable future. While the movie versions are beyond the scope of this anthology, we are confident that the films will only add to the general fascination with and critical appreciation of the novels. We also believe that even in an age of image, Collins's words are the narrative foundation of a story that deserves to be assessed as more than just compelling young adult literature. This book assesses the Panem novels as a paradigm of Millennial anxieties and human complexity set within a cross-genre, cross-generational narrative that is itself proof of the validity of human creativity in a seemingly inhumane world. The experience of finding such proof has meaning for readers of any age, and we hope that the essays in this anthology will serve to deepen that experience.

WORKS CITED*

Barbe, Waitman. "Literature, the Teacher, and the Teens." *English Journal* 6.6 (1917): 361–71. Print.

Barnes, Brooks, and Julie Bosman. "'Hunger Games' Book Sales Bode Well for the Film." *New York Times* 23 Jan. 2012, nat. ed.: B6. Print.

Bell, Wendell. "How Has American Life Changed Since September 11?" *Journal of Future Studies* 8.1 (2003): 73–80. Print.

Blasingame, James. "An Interview with Suzanne Collins." *Journal of Adolescent & Adult Literacy* 52.8 (2009): 726–27. Print.

*Citations for YA novels referenced within this Introduction can be found in the Core Bibliography.

Bosman, Julie. "Booksellers Brace for 'Mockingjay' Landing." *New York Times* 24 Aug. 2010, NY ed.: C1. Print.

Campbell, Patty. "Trends in Young Adult Literature." Cole 66–69.

"Children's Best Sellers: Series." *New York Times* 19 Feb. 2012, nat. ed., Book Review sec.: 26. Print.

Cole, Pam B. *Young Adult Literature in the 21st Century.* Boston: McGraw-Hill, 2009. Print.

Corbett, Sue. "Mockingjay." *People* 13 Sept. 2010: 69. Print.

Dominus, Susan. "'I Write About War. For Adolescents.'" *New York Times Magazine* 10 Apr. 2011: 30–33. Print.

Green, John. "Scary New World." *New York Times* 9 Nov. 2008, NY ed., Book Review sec.: 30. Print.

Kerns, Michelle. "'Catching Fire,' Suzanne Collins' Sequel to 'The Hunger Games': From Lovebird to Mockingjay." *examiner.com.* Clarity, 1 Sept. 2009. Web. 1 June 2011.

Larbalestier, Justine. *Daughters of Earth: Feminist Science Fiction in the Twentieth Century.* Middletown: Wesleyan, 2006. Print.

Mann, Katrina. "'You're Next!': Postwar Hegemony Besieged in *Invasion of the Body Snatchers.*" *Cinema Journal* 44.1 (2004): 49–68. Print.

Margolis, Rick. "Suzanne Collins's 'The Hunger Games' Has Plenty of Blood, Guts, and Heart." *School Library Journal* 1 Sept. 2008: N. pag. *schoollibraryjournal.com.* Media Source, 2011. Web. 1 June 2011.

"*Mockingjay,* The Final Book in the Hunger Games Trilogy by Suzanne Collins, Tops All National Bestseller Lists...." Press Release. Media Room. *scholastic.com.* Scholastic, 2 Sept. 2010. Web. 11 June 2011.

Nilsen, Alleen Pace, and Kenneth L. Donelson. *Literature for Today's Young Adults.* 6th ed. New York: Longman, 2001. Print.

Pinter, Harold. "Writing for the Theatre." National Student Drama Festival. Bristol. 1962. Speech. Rpt. as "Introduction: Writing for the Theatre." *Complete Works: One.* New York: Grove-Black Cat, 1977. 9–16. Print.

"Scholastic Increases First Printing of Mockingjay, the Final Book of The Hunger Games Trilogy, to 1.2 Million Copies." Press Release. Media Room. *scholastic.com.* Scholastic, 1 July 2010. Web. 11 June 2011.

Sellers, John A. "A Dark Horse Breaks Out." *Publishers Weekly* 9 June 2008: 19. Print.

"Top Ten Most Frequently Challenged Books of 2010." *ala.org.* American Library Assn., 2011. Web. 5 Aug. 2011.

Vieth, Errol. "Science as Liberation: Women Scientists in 50s Science Fiction Film." Seminar Series. Central Queensland Univ. Queensland. 21 Apr. 1999. Web. 14 June 2011.

Voytilla, Stuart. *Myth & the Movies: Discovering the Myth Structure of 50 Unforgettable Films.* Studio City: Wiese, 1999. Print.

Weedman, Jane B. Preface. *Women Worldwalkers: New Dimensions of Science Fiction and Fantasy.* Ed. Weedman. Lubbock: Texas Tech University Press, 1985. 5–8. Print.

"What They're Reading on College Campuses." *Chronicle of Higher Education* 57.35 (May 2011): A25. Print.

Zevin, Gabrielle. "Constant Craving." *New York Times* 11 Oct. 2009, NY ed., Book Review sec.: 13. Print.

PART I.

History, Politics, Economics and Culture

1

Panem in America

Crisis Economics and a Call for Political Engagement

BILL CLEMENTE

In a critical piece about the recent surge in young adult dystopian titles, Laura Miller argues that "Dystopian fiction may be the only genre written for children that's routinely *less* didactic than its adult counterpart" (134, emphasis in original). She adds that unlike adult dystopian literature, with its rational warnings about present conditions that (if not corrected) will result in future horrors, young adult dystopias metaphorically reveal "what's happening, right this minute, in the stormy psyche of the adolescent reader" (134). Thus, the "arc" of a YA dystopian narrative "mirrors the course of adolescent disaffection" (135), the real world, apparently, at the center of young readers' restricted perspectives.

Many, of course, would take issue with the preceding statement about the aim of adult dystopian literature, with its emphasis, in Miller's reading, on prediction over reflection. On the other hand, Suzanne Collins's *The Hunger Games* trilogy certainly does connect with adolescent readers' psychological turmoil through the personal confusions and conflicts with which Katniss Everdeen contends (e.g., the love triangle involving Peeta and Gale, and Katniss's emotionally charged relationship with her mother). Miller's contentions, however, limit the scope of the trilogy, particularly with respect to the political and economic issues at the narrative's core. In addition, Collins's achievement with her young adult dystopian fiction transcends what Kay Sambell describes as the "creative dilemma for Children's authors using the dystopian narrative form" (164), the fabrication of an awkward happy ending at logical odds with the rest of the narrative's dystopian turn — a creative disjoint that waters down the narrative's impact. Collins's Katniss, however, confronts tragic issues and consequences that reflect on the political dissatisfaction and economic hardship that inform contemporary society. And while forcing her central character to grapple with what Sambell terms "dark truth" (164), Collins avoids the pitfall of trying to reconcile these alarming threats and horrific experiences with the impulse in YA fiction to provide a hopeful outcome. For Katniss, her world's future remains uncertain at the trilogy's conclusion, any happiness burdened always with painful scars both literal and figural.

As the three "Mockingjay" narratives underscore emphatically, the insular world that is the stormy psyche of an individual character like Katniss provides more than an attractive connection with a young adult reader's adolescent angst. The significance of the personal turmoil and of the actions in these books rises above individual psychological chaos and self-interested motivations. Instead, the Mockingjay's battle to bring about change in Panem's status quo grows to the point that her entire country becomes involved in collective action. In fact, through their thematic scope, the novels address specific political and economic forces that afflict not only Panem but also our contemporary society. The books argue for the necessity of increased awareness, despite the uncertainties and often painful consequences that engagement brings.

In this important sense, Collins offers readers something both uncommon and refreshing: progressive or radical fiction for young readers that involves collective action on a large social scale. The novels' scope includes economic and political struggles that undermine a nation, eventually uniting Panem's thirteen districts in the struggle for the justice the Mockingjay embodies. And while the last novel's conclusion does suggest some hope and the possibility of continued positive change, this outcome grows logically from the horrors experienced that stain the world and ultimately constrain the characters, who cannot escape the narrative's dark truths. In this important sense, *The Hunger Games* offers a version of progressive literature as described by Herbert Kohl: "What makes a book radical is both that it is partisan and that it presents a vision of solutions that are not merely individual but affect entire groups of people" (49). And the dreams of the past that haunt both Peeta and Katniss twenty years after the war's end, as well as the book that they hope will keep alive the rebellion's efforts and dreams, bespeak the continued sacrifice and requisite commitment necessary to prevent their world from slipping into that repeated dark past the trilogy chronicles. In this sense, the characters cannot escape the previous conflicts and experiences the novels detail.

The references to the past that inform and structure the trilogy provide revealing contexts. The frequent use of Roman names, such as the name Panem itself, references both the gladiatorial slaughters in the arena and the Silver Age poet Juvenal's satire on *panem et circenses,* "bread and circuses," Rome's empty form of appeasement that Juvenal condemned in his Tenth Satire. Here Juvenal warned of the price paid for the abdication of social responsibility by the Roman populace: "Only two things really concern them: bread and the

Games," an indifference connected to the news that "that many are to be purged" (80–81).

As Plutarch Heavensbee explains to Katniss, the people of the Capitol have relinquished their power, placated by "full bellies and entertainment" (*M* 223). Juvenal's works also point to ways in which politicians often offer short-term measures to placate, thereby masking complex and enduring problems; *The Hunger Games* uses the "bread and circuses" metaphor in similar ways. Indeed, what translator Peter Green identifies in his Introduction to *The Sixteen Satires* as one of Juvenal's central concerns applies equally to Collins's trilogy: "A governing class that lowers its standards and neglects its traditional duties constitutes a positive danger to the social structure over which it is set" (xxxviii).

The characters' names and other references do, to be sure, incline readers to interpret the story as a future repetition of Rome's inglorious past, but one made more brutal and spectacular through technological advances. This perspective has some merit. The list of names points to Roman extravagance and corruption straight from the more ostentatious descriptions found in Suetonius's *Twelve Caesars,* the source for Robert Graves's engaging novel *I, Claudius.* Collins populates the pages of the first two books, in particular, with these references, ranging from Caesar Flickerman and Claudius Templesmith, Flavius and Octavia, to Plutarch Heavensbee and Coriolanus Snow — and later, Alma Coin, once District 13 enters the conflict. Other borrowings thicken this context, from the mention of the twenty-year terms Peacekeepers serve to the purple robes in which the Gamemakers adorn themselves.

As previously noted, Juvenal used the term "bread and circuses" to chastise a Roman citizenry that had abdicated its political responsibility for the comforts complacency provided. And certainly the vomitory practices at the Capitol, as well as the rising inflection that punctuates the citizens' trivial conversation, point to both the wasteful consumption and vapid discourse that define the Capitol, itself the name of the chief Roman temple of Jupiter on Capitoline Hill. However, the name of Panem's ruler, that strange combination of classical and contemporary, suggests the way Collins uses the references to ancient Rome to provide commentary on contemporary American society. Snow's actions to maintain power — the poisonings of his potential competitors and his manipulation of tributes such as Finnick Odair (whom Snow prostitutes as a demonstration of the Caligula-like extremes and vulnerabilities that characterize life in the Capitol) — point to classical antecedents that find a comfortable fit with current practices. Thus, while the references to Rome provide the novels, especially the first two, with a compelling structure, Collins's trilogy as a whole points beyond this classical period. The Games themselves and the classical antecedents serve in the main to lay the foundation from which the narratives and related themes grow.

The prolonged term of President Snow's office, for example, reflects the modern concerns of many in the United States that elections serve the interests of the few instead of the many. In Panem, Snow need not bother with elections, for his media team keeps the fear of revolution and its consequences alive, necessitating a continued vigilance and requisite security that upholds the status quo. The last thing Snow wants is change, the country's stasis indicated by the looping images of District 13's destruction, reminders from the past presented as ominously present. Snow's manipulations reinforce a perception of continuity, an apparition of sameness supported by the familiar faces connected with the ubiquitous Hunger Games broadcasts that serve as entertainment and admonition and that fill screens throughout Panem.

That Snow poses as a president without election and that he uses a combination of roses and blood to convey his presidential persona do, I believe, bear on current political and economic problems. The vitriolic polarity that dominates current debate in American politics, for example, has in the minds of many, such as Matt Taibbi, resulted in what one might characterize as a politics of ignorance, especially in the country's current economic situation, with both major parties beholden to the Wall Street interests that seem to have caused the near depression that has hobbled the country. According to Taibbi, the winning of the presidential election has come to mean nothing in terms of anticipated change. Indeed, he characterizes this political event as a "beautifully choreographed eighteen-month entertainment put on once every four years, a beast called the presidential election that engrosses the population to the point of obsession" (Taibbi 9–10). These entertainments, in Taibbi's estimation, ensure an upholding of current practices that play to Wall Street financial interests — to which most politicians owe their positions. This situation maintains these institutions' hold on the country despite their deep involvement in the economic shell game that continues to threaten fiscal chaos.

In many respects, the complexity of the issues involved in the recent economic collapse guarantees Wall Street's relative impunity — and, ironically, creates a situation in which many of the victims of corporate fraud engage in a politics that attacks the government's attempts to regulate the very financial institutions responsible for the abuse. Consequently, in Taibbi's opinion, a presidential election has become "a drama that we Americans have learned to wholly consume as entertainment" (10), and winning carries little expectation of change. Taibbi describes the feeling that winning voters experience as equivalent to a home team's victory over the hated cross-town rival (10).

Snow's presidency suggests something of the unfortunate situation Taibbi describes. The sleight of hand that ensures continuity also upholds a system as corrupt as the odor from Snow's rotting mouth — running sores that result from his drinking poisons to cover his political murders. The smell is somehow made worse by the scent of the genetically altered rose that Snow wears to conceal the rot. Katniss detects this decay through her potentially deadly proximity with the man. His corruption and decomposition also find reflection in the Justice Building in District 11. Banners attempt to cover this rotting edifice of power, pointing to what Katniss discovers on her Victory Tour of the districts: a society overripe for the revolution for which she will become the symbol. The Hunger Games themselves play the same role as the elections Taibbi describes, media entertainments orchestrated to satisfy the ignorant population of the Capitol, who bet extravagantly on the bloody sport's outcome. In their turn, home districts attempt to raise money to support their candidates, especially the Career tributes who hail from the more economically comfortable districts that provide the support the Capitol requires.

A closer examination of the Games and their significance for both Snow and the Capitol indicates that Panem operates not so much like the Imperial Roman government many of the trappings suggest but more like a modern global conglomerate, a fully integrated industry, the complexity of which the media coverage of the Games hides. This grim reality escapes the great majority of the citizens of the Capitol, content with their ever-shifting fashions and unrelenting indulgences. Those who work in the surrounding dozen districts, however, suffer the consequences, for they are the price paid to uphold an illusion Katniss will help reveal.

The Games serve a double purpose. On the one hand, they entertain a frivolous crowd in the Capitol, which revels in the conspicuous consumption the system provides, the fruit of a muscular capitalism that feeds on the twelve districts. At the same time that the media turn the Games into a commodity, their broadcast reminds those in the districts of the Capitol's relentless power. The dual-use technologies that make this spectacular entertainment possible and with which the Games experiment — from animal mutations to fabricated climatic disasters — likewise identify the horrific technologies of menace with which Snow threatens the increasingly restless population of the Panem below the Capitol's heights. Indeed, Snow eventually unleashes a number of the powerful weapons tested in the Games against the rebels. Ironically, the same dual-use technologies of terror that create the spectacular visual effects in the Games also produced the mockingjay, an animal weapon become song and symbol turned against its original creators.

For most of Panem's people, the Games represent the near-starvation they suffer owing to the Capitol's policies. The Games likewise serve as a reminder of the rebellion in Panem that the Capitol brutally put down some seventy-five years ago, the rebellion that culminated in the destruction of District 13 and the signing of a treaty of complete submission. The television screens throughout the country regularly play stock footage of District 13's destruction, a fraud Katniss and others eventually discern. The treaty likewise inaugurates the Games to remind everyone of their inherited guilt, endlessly expiated through the reaping ceremony. The word *reaping* reinforces the extent to which the Capitol has turned the people into capital, a commodity harvested for the Capitol's appetite. In addition, individuals eligible for the reaping can avail themselves of a "tessera" (*HG* 13), equal to one year's supply of grain and oil; however, each tessera requires recipients to add their names multiple times over the years to the lottery, increasing significantly their chances of being chosen for the Games. Thus, the system disadvantages the poorest citizens, who must improve their chances of getting harvested by "cashing in" their odds for meager foodstuff.

This commodification resembles in organization and scope a corporate takeover that turns the twelve districts into production centers in a fully integrated economic system that bleeds the people of their potential power and wealth to sustain itself. In *The Shock Doctrine*, Naomi Klein argues that corporations take advantage of a crisis to privatize government functions and exploit wealth to the disadvantage of the majority. She writes, for example, that "The ultimate goal for the corporations at the center of the complex is to bring the model of for-profit government, which advances so rapidly in extraordinary circumstances, into the ordinary and day-to-day functioning of the state — in effect, to privatize the government" (14). Thus, the Capitol treats the catastrophic aftermath of the rebellion as what Klein terms "an exciting market" opportunity (6). This disaster capitalism results in a system of control that victimizes an increasingly destitute population, such as the 8,000 people who live in District 12.

To punish District 12 for excesses that Snow blames on the Mockingjay, the Capitol takes advantage of the crisis to cut rations and further squeeze economically all the residents of the area, sending the coal miners ever deeper into the mines but without necessary and costly safeguards. This exploitation also affects the shrinking middle class in District 12: e.g., the family-owned bakery whose products the family cannot afford to eat. As Klein points out — and as the situation in District 12 underscores — this system of privatization results in "an ever widening chasm between the dazzling rich and the disposable poor and an aggressive nationalism that justifies bottomless spending on security" (18). Snow clearly plays this tune, recruiting men and women from the Capitol and District 2 (which manufactures weapons) to join the government as so-called Peacekeepers, district guardians whose debts are often forgiven for their service. The debt into which this corporate system drives people ensures a continued flow of volunteers, and the Capitol reminds Panem constantly of the internal danger that requires formidable security forces. Those who have been identified as threats to the nation, such as the former Peacekeeper Darius, become voiceless "Avox[es]" (*HG* 77): the government cuts out their tongues and makes them slaves — grim reminders in the Capitol of the penalty for breaches of security.

The Capitol's pervasive surveillance even uncovers a kiss Gale and Katniss share in the forbidden forest. Ironically, Peeta reveals the extent of Snow's obsessive concern for security and control when he notes that he wants Katniss and him to share the truth and avoid "*falling into snow* every time there's a camera around" (*CF* 51, emphasis added). In addition, fences that surround each district, ostensibly to protect people from wild animals, actually work to contain the human inhabitants. Crossing the fences to visit other districts is forbidden, a law Katniss and Gale break regularly until Snow electrifies the fences that had previously worked only sporadically. And once the Mockingjay's actions galvanize rebels in all the districts, Snow orders the total destruction of the coal-producing District 12, an area perhaps perceived by the Capitol as of little consequence other than as a symbol of sedition punished.

Despite its political call to action, *The Hunger Games* trilogy is no left-leaning polemic against corporate abuse. While I characterize the novels as progressive, Collins eschews a simple or shrill partisan attack against current economic or government policies. As the reemergence of District 13 reveals, the books offer much more than a Main Street-against-Wall Street conflict. After Katniss and the other surviving tributes escape the Quarter Quell arena, she finds out that District 13 has survived underground for the past seventy-five years. Weakened by a poxvirus that killed many and left others infertile, in need of the infusion of people the growing revolution provides, the district now determines to take advantage of the rebellion in other districts and the Capitol itself. A provider of the graphite essential for the refinement of weapons-grade uranium, District 13, with its stockpile of nuclear missiles, had fought the Capitol to a stalemate — mutual destruction assured. Now an apparent ally in the fight against the Capitol, District 13 strikes the reader at first blush as the moral opposite of Snow's regime. If the Capitol epitomizes capitalist extremes, District 13 reveals a regimented communal organization of Spartan discipline structured for survival, a controlled economy. Given the ostensible differences between the two societies and the manner in which the possession of nuclear weapons produces a stalemate, these two poles of Panem bring to mind the duration of the Cold War, which dominated American and Russian politics from 1946 until 1991, chronicled in books such as Stephen J. Whitfield's *The Culture of the Cold War* and Paul Boyer's *Fallout*. These studies relate how paranoia-motivated fictions in the United States led not only to an obsession with security (a fixation that the Capitol and District 13 share) but also to increased spending on security. This obsession led, for example, to significant expenditures on military hardware during the Kennedy era to shrink an imaginary missile gap and to the creation of deterrents such as the Space Defense Initiative, an abhorrently expensive boondoggle from the Reagan years.

Viewing the two areas as representative of the Cold War, however, puts readers in the ironic position of siding with District 13 and its communist structure against the shallow capitalist Capitol. But Collins's strategy ultimately asks the reader not to take sides but to appreciate the manner in which a long-lasting confrontation between two powers — e.g., the Capitol and District 13 (seventy-five years) or the USA and the U.S.S.R. (forty-five years) — will plunder their populations' wealth to finance unnecessary armaments and proxy wars. As Richard Rhodes argues, the Cold War bankrupted both the Soviet Union and the United States: "Far from victory in the Cold War, the superpower nuclear-arms race and the corresponding militarization of the American economy gave us ramshackle cities, broken bridges, failing schools, entrenched poverty, impeded life expectancy, and a menacing and secretive national-security state that held the entire human world hostage" (308). In *The Hunger Games* trilogy, Collins portrays both the Capitol and District 13 as equally bankrupt, unable to sustain themselves in the long run. And as in the actual Cold War, the people caught in the middle in Panem pay the price, especially after District 13 joins the other districts in a war that engulfs the entire country.

At first, however, Collins's narrative portrays District 13 as a refuge for exiles from the various districts, as when factory workers Twill and Bonnie escape to a District 13 that Katniss does not yet believe exists. After the escape from the last arena, Katniss and her fellow tributes initially view District 13 as an ally. The final volume of the trilogy, however, gradually reveals the truth. As Katniss notes soon after her arrival, District 13 can be "even more controlling than the Capitol" (*M* 36). In many respects, Katniss falls again into snow in District 13, for as Alma Coin's name hints — something along the lines of "dear" or "nourishing" money — she exploits power in a manner that aligns her with Snow. The computer codes on the wrists of the inhabitants of District 13, for instance, resemble the bar codes on commodities purchased in grocery stores today, making the people of the district seem often more like automatons than humans. Coin's inhumane treatment of Katniss's prep team, in addition, is a weak imitation of the tactics Snow employs to punish. Just as Snow dispatches adversaries with poisoned drinks, Coin works to have the Mockingjay eliminated; she also brings the war to a pointlessly bloody conclusion by using Al-Qaeda-like terrorist tactics that not only kill Primrose Everdeen and other noncombatants but also add to the grievous wounds the Mockingjay sustains. Coin also wants to keep the Games going, using them, one assumes, to control her enemies, real and imaginary — just as Snow did. The joining of Coin and her flip side, Snow, becomes vividly apparent when the rebels break into the Capitol's electronic transmissions to Panem, and Snow's image dissolves to reveal Coin's: "it's not President Snow but President Coin" (*M* 294) who now addresses the country.

In the final analysis, the similarities between Snow and Coin allow no easy distinctions between just and unjust systems. This situation has a good deal in common with the alienation from government felt by increasingly large numbers of young people — a distrust that includes both of America's major political parties. In *Wingnuts: How the Lunatic Fringe Is Hijacking American Politics,* John Avlon argues, "Political parties are held hostage by the most extreme voices, while the rise of partisan media pumps up political divisions" (221). This situation leaves many young people feeling helpless as "extreme voices" perpetuate the divide and further drive the vitriolic discourse that presently infects political debate. But Avlon, like Collins, sees some hopeful possibilities if people reject the extreme choices that promise more of the same — much as Coin and Snow did — and organize themselves across party lines. Avlon believes that "we can determine who wins elections" that will actually mean something and "move our country not left or right, but forward" (241). Collins's progressive novels urge this difficult commitment to avoid the repetition of past errors.

Despite being physically and emotionally wounded from the Games and the war, Katniss and Peeta wed and eventually have children. They also keep the past alive. This embracing of hope despite an uncertain future emphasizes Katniss's greatest asset: courage, including the courage not to hate despite her injuries, sacrifices, and losses. Her suffering suggests both the cost of all commitment to bring about social change and the necessity of this engagement. In the end, Katniss and Peeta enjoy a life hardly characterized by unqualified happiness, for their sacrifices do not culminate in the fulfillment of their greatest desires. This emphasis on suffering also points to the author's achievement, for the book argues against complacency, against giving in to pervasive discouragement, against succumbing to the temptation of surrender in the face of odds that seem insurmountable. The novels argue that a refusal to become involved equals an abdication of the responsibilities freedom requires; such a refusal often results in leaders such as Snow and Coin.

The Hunger Games trilogy embraces the spirit of Avlon's argument about getting involved in politics to move the country forward — especially at the trilogy's conclusion, when the future remains uncertain. And while Katniss and Peeta do not appear to take an active role in Panem's politics, they work on a book that clearly bears on the future. To document the past and the people they and their colleagues knew, the book includes vivid details that Katniss believes "would be a crime to forget" (*M* 387). While neither Katniss nor Peeta nor their collection of memories embraces a specific political movement, the three combine to insist on the need to remember. This emphasis has parallels with what Bernard E. Harcourt argues in defense of Occupy Wall Street's refusal to articulate a specific political agenda. He labels the movement's actions political disobedience, which "resists the very way in which we are governed: it resists the structure of partisan politics, the demand for policy reforms, the call for party identification, and the very ideologies that dominated the post–War Period." Katniss's project is politically disobedient in the sense that the details included do not articulate a partisan position on government or offer policy statements; instead, the pages underscore the need to live a good life to give meaning to those who died to provide Panem this time of freedom. By implication, the Mockingjay's book will sew seeds of dissent if circumstances threaten the sanctity of this newfound hope for a better future; thus, the book calls for constant vigilance fortified by memory, for as Harcourt writes, "what matters to the politically disobedient is the kind of society we live in, not a handful of policy demands."

WORKS CITED

Avlon, John. *Wingnuts: How the Lunatic Fringe Is Hijacking America.* New York: Beast, 2010. Print.

Boyer, Paul. *Fallout: A Historian Reflects on America's Half-Century Encounter with Nuclear Weapons.* Columbus: Ohio State University Press, 1998. Print.

Collins, Suzanne. *Catching Fire.* New York: Scholastic, 2009. Print.

_____. *The Hunger Games.* New York: Scholastic, 2008. Print.

_____. *Mockingjay.* New York, Scholastic, 2010. Print.

Harcourt, Bernard E. "Occupy Wall Street's 'Political Disobedience.'" Opinionator. *New York Times.com.* New York Times Co., 13 Oct. 2011. Web. 2 Nov. 2011.

Juvenal. *The Sixteen Satires.* Trans. and introd. Peter Green. New York: Penguin, 2004. Print.

Kohl, Herbert. *Should We Burn Babar: Essays on Children's Literature and the Power of Stories.* New York: New, 2007. Print.

Klein, Naomi. *The Shock Doctrine: The Rise of Disaster Capitalism.* New York: Holt, 2008. Print.

Miller, Laura. "Fresh Hell: What's Behind the Boom in Dystopian Fiction Readers?" *New Yorker* 14 June 2010: 132–36. Print.

Rhodes, Richard. *The Arsenals of Folly: The Making of the Nuclear Arms Race.* New York: Knopf, 2007. Print.

Sambell, Kay. "Presenting the Case for Social Change: The Creative Dilemma of Dystopian Writing for Children." *Utopian and Dystopian Writing for Children and Young Adults.* Ed. Carrie Heintz and Elaine Ostry. New York: Rutledge, 2003. 163–78. Print.

Taibbi, Matt. *Griftopia: Bubble Machines, Vampire Squids, and the Long Con That Is Breaking America.* New York: Spiegel, 2010. Print.

Whitfield, Stephen J. *The Culture of the Cold War.* Baltimore: John Hopkins University Press, 1991. Print.

2

Absolute Power Games

ANTHONY PAVLIK

The presentation of ultimate power and supreme governmental control in *The Hunger Games* trilogy offers an implicit understanding that the downfall of totalitarian political systems requires people (here, young protagonists) to engage in violent and military actions for a supposed ultimate good: the just war. This picture of oppressive systems and what constitutes the right response to them can be considered through Umberto Eco's notion of Ur-Fascism, for Eco lived through the fascist excesses of World War II, and his comments on the nature of fascist ideologies and practices emerge from both firsthand experience and theoretical considerations. As such, they offer a way both to assess the trilogy itself and its place within a wider social context, and to question whether or not the series actually subverts itself by working within political assumptions that have produced a gradual familiarization with, and even adoption of, the very principles the series presents as unacceptable.

The trilogy portrays oppressive violence as a primary political tool. This is not, in itself, a new departure, for fantastic fiction is full of violent responses either by or towards perceived enemies. From *The Lord of the Rings* (1954–1955) to the Harry Potter series (1997–2007), there is little arbitration or conciliation when dealing with enemies, but much combat and battle. Here, through Katniss's eyes, the reader is privy to the Capitol's atrocities and oppressive machinations, the most omnipresent and overt being the Hunger Games themselves, as both a symbol of an ideology of oppression and a means of controlling the populace through a stylized act of violence. According to official doctrine, Panem emerged from what had been North America, rising out of devastating natural disasters and a "brutal war for what little sustenance remained" (*HG* 21). Panem — the Capitol and thirteen districts — was supposedly at peace until the districts rose up against the Capitol, only for twelve of them to be defeated and the thirteenth apparently destroyed. To punish the uprising, which Katniss refers to as "supposed crimes committed generations ago" (*CF* 90), thereby questioning the nature of events that have become integral to Panem's official history, the Hunger Games were instituted as an annual reminder that rebellion against the Capitol should never again be considered.

The Games are the ultimate in terror tactics because they are played with the lives of innocents: two children from each of the districts are pitched into an arena where they must all fight and kill one another until only one remains alive. Any temporary alliances in the arena are ultimately dissolved, for, just as with the Capitol itself, there can only be one victor, one overpowering champion, and all others must be suborned (and, in this case, killed) in order to achieve that end. Even the Victory Tours—forced celebrations of the Games—reinforce the message in the districts that the Capitol has an "iron grip" (*CF* 4), one that makes the Games both a weapon against the districts and a symbol of the power the Capitol holds. The Games and Victory Tours are compulsory television viewing, with television a propaganda tool for the Capitol. Even the arenas are preserved and turned into tourist spots, popular with Capitol residents, and are thus sites that reinforce the foundational myth that the institution known as the Hunger Games preserves.

Pitting district against district in a death match also reflects the way each district is dislocated from the others, through a political strategy of divide and conquer that maintains the Capitol's elite position. People in the districts are herded and shepherded within areas surrounded by tall electrified fences, making the districts akin to animal pens. Even without the cruelty of the Games, the Capitol regulates Panem through its control over electricity supplies and, more importantly, food resources. People in the districts are constantly close to starvation, yet hunting for food is a crime, and families are compelled to bargain their children's involvement (in effect, their lives) in future Hunger Games in exchange for extra rations. The Capitol's total dependence on the districts for resources makes its position somewhat precarious, but all dissent is met by excessive force. After Katniss's actions in the Quarter Quell instigate open revolt, the Capitol obliterates her home district, killing more than 7,000 people and laying waste to the land. Even before this, however, public punishments and summary executions—carried out by the ironically named Peacekeepers—have maintained day-to-day social control. Some people even have had their tongues removed as punishment, becoming "Avox[es]," speechless Capitol slaves (*HG* 94).

Reigning supreme over the Capitol (and, therefore, Panem) is President Snow, a man who has achieved and kept power by poisoning his enemies and rivals. Snow even drank poison *with* his victims to avoid suspicion of complicity in their deaths falling upon him. Strongly contrasting with life in the districts, the Capitol, where Snow's government resides, is the epitome of multicolored decadence, extravagance, and self-indulgence. Residents sport their excess in their clothing, makeup, and hairstyles. It is a place where even bulimia is fashionable. The Capitol is also the seat of a sociopolitical system that will use any and all of the means available to a military power with a stranglehold over its dominions to preserve its rule.

Indeed, when President Snow tells Katniss that any revolution against the Capitol would mean that "the entire system would collapse" (*CF* 25), there is some sense that Snow understands and knowingly authorizes great wrongs because he intrinsically believes in the rightness of his actions, the notion of the greater good of the Capitol, and the preservation of the (peaceful) status quo. Nevertheless, in preserving this system, Snow's administration displays the hallmarks of authoritarianism: antidemocratic actions; political and economic rule by an elite; monopolistic control of the mass media, military forces, and weapons; and a policy of systematic violence and terror against those depicted as enemies. Indeed, when Katniss imagines Snow as being backed by "marble pillars hung with oversized flags" (*CF* 21), the picture and the social reality behind the image are so redolent of those of Nazi Germany that the term *fascism* springs readily to mind as a descriptor for the Capitol and how it operates.

Umberto Eco's comments on fascism in his essay "Ur-Fascism" come from a 1995 speech given at Columbia University for the fiftieth anniversary of victory in Europe in World War II, a time when the events of the Oklahoma bombings were still echoing throughout American society. Although Eco does note the "fuzzy" nature of fascism (73), his outline of the elements of Ur- (or eternal) Fascism would certainly strike a chord with anyone who was describing the nature of the Capitol's administration. Eco cites, for example, "*the cult of tradition*" (78, emphasis in original) as one element of Ur-Fascism and notes its syncretic nature whereby, despite the mix of different and often contradictory belief systems, "Truth has been spelled out once and for all, and we can only keep interpreting its obscure message" (78). Another element, says Eco, is the principle of "*actions for action's sake*" (80, emphasis in original) and a sense of irrationality in those actions, along with a lack of self-analysis since, for Ur-Fascism, he says, "*dissent is betrayal*" (81, emphasis in original). Everyone must follow the party line or suffer: witness, for instance, Peeta's beatings and torture after he publicly warns District 13 about an imminent attack, or Cinna's savage beating in front of Katniss after he uses his designs to express anti–Capitol ideas.

Eco also notes that Ur-Fascism seeks to win popular support through an appeal "against intruders" (81), taking advantage of people's natural fear of the Other. The appeal of this focus is not to the masses as a whole, says Eco, but rather to the middle classes, who fear lower social groups and thus live obsessed with plots — creating a feeling of being "under siege" and an "*obsession with conspiracies*" (82, emphasis in original) against their continued well-being. Underlying this is a utilization of a "popular elitism" (83) and a "*scorn for the weak*" (83, emphasis in original). Such contempt exists even though the fascist elite knows that, underlying its power base, its force relies upon the ultimate weakness of the population it hierarchically rules over, whereby, says Eco, "Having lost their power to delegate, the citizens do not act" (85). This form of rule includes the use of Newspeak, even if that form of linguistic control takes only "the innocent form of a popular talk show" (84). It is easy to see how these elements form a foundation for the way Snow and the Capitol hold sway over the districts. Capitol citizens are more concerned with their appearance, food, and entertainment (such as the slick, semi-scripted televising of the Games — a highlight of the Capitol's year) than with politics or the fate of the districts that they consider beneath them.

In opposition to the Capitol, District 13 provides a rallying point for rebel sympathies. Long believed destroyed, the district had survived the earlier rebellion through a nuclear standoff with the Capitol and through a social regimen that requires the citizens of the district to share all resources on an equal basis, maintain a disciplined lifestyle, and remain constantly alert to threats from the outside. District 13 continues an underground existence that remains unknown to the other districts and to all but a few in the Capitol. Had it not been for the ravages of disease, 13 would, indeed, have been a powerful force on its own. Katniss describes District 13 as "militaristic" and "overly programmed" (*M* 34), operating like a "well-oiled machine" (*M* 70); however, in seventy-five years, it has turned self-sufficiency into an art form. In the process, it has developed an army of citizens, where children start at the lowest level of the military when they turn fourteen, within a society that is uniformly gray in color (doors, civilian clothing, military uniforms, even President Coin's hair). With its constant security drills, strict discipline, and daily routines tattooed onto people's arms, this is a constrained social system of self-denial, again supposedly for the greater good, with efficiency and precision as its watchwords.

Here, too, is a strong president, Alma Coin, who, like Snow, distrusts others and works to ensure that those she oversees are kept on a tight rein, ostensibly for their own safety. The residents of District 13 cannot come and go as they please, movement above ground is forbidden, and rations are strictly regulated. Worse, while torture and crimes against humanity are expected of the Capitol, Coin's own regime is not above such practices, and she is not beyond her own brand of ruthlessness. Katniss's old prep team, for example, abducted from the Capitol against their wishes, is found barely recognizable, imprisoned in squalid conditions for trying to take more bread than the regulated allowance. Their treatment seems tame in comparison to the torture meted out in the Capitol, but the prep team's treatment is still evidence that, in District 13, no individuals (particularly outsiders) are to be trusted, and that failure to follow the strict regulations will invoke a harsh response. Ur-

Fascism, says Eco, can be found "in the most innocent of guises" (87) and in what are seemingly caring governmental systems.

Later, when the rebel forces encounter the mountain stronghold of District 2, still holding out in defense of the Capitol, Katniss's friend Gale determines to neutralize this obstacle by trapping or killing everyone inside the mountain; as a rebel leader, Gale has no compunction about such murderous action. Then, with rebel troops in the Capitol, Coin plots Katniss's death at the hands of the brainwashed Peeta. A dead Katniss would still maintain her symbolic value to the rebels, while a living one could be a rallying point for groups that might oppose Coin once the war is over. Even the symbol of the revolution is disposable in pursuit of other ends, in this case Coin's continued leadership. Soon, rebel troops indiscriminately fire on civilians; adults and children alike are stuck down. The violence climaxes after Snow uses children as a human barricade set in front of his mansion: a hovercraft bearing the Capitol's seal drops a set of bombs — some time-delayed and all disguised as gifts — on the children. Katniss's sister, Prim, is killed in one of the ensuing explosions. The implication is that this bombing is a last desperate act of depravity on Snow's part, but he tells Katniss that Coin instigated this horror to end all Capitol allegiance to his government. Even without proof beyond Snow's words, Katniss knows the kind of military tactics that rebel leaders like Coin and Gale are willing to deploy in pursuit of their own supposedly justified ends.

After the war is over, an emerging understanding of Coin's true nature is sharpened by the lesson Snow gives Katniss in *realpolitik:* that the plan all along was for the districts and the Capitol to destroy one another, leaving District 13 in control. Subsequently, Coin suggests that, rather than killing all the remaining Capitol inhabitants, the children of important Capitol citizens should be forced to play the Hunger Games. This final turn in the arena, Coin opines, would be both punishment and retribution, providing a perverse form of closure for the people in the districts who have suffered so much. All she is truly offering, however, is the same thought pattern and rationale for the Games that the Capitol itself had used: renewed appeals to tradition and a popularist political outlook. Katniss's conclusion about the state of affairs is understandably pessimistic: "Nothing has changed" (*M* 432). Worse, she fears that this will forever be the case; the system will repeat and sustain itself in an endless circle. Mindful of all that she knows, it is no surprise, perhaps, that Katniss chooses to assassinate Coin rather than execute Snow.

Clearly, some of Eco's elements of Ur-Fascism relate, broadly, to both the Capitol and District 13; the remaining elements that Eco sets out have a specific link to the rebels in particular. There is, says Eco, a feeling of humiliation brought on by "the enemy's vaunted wealth and power," enemies that must simultaneously be seen as both *"too strong and too weak"* (83, emphasis in original) and that must be attacked in pursuit of a final victory. In tandem with this is a principle that pacifism is "*collusion with the enemy*" and that "*life is a permanent war*" (82, 83, emphases in original). In such an atmosphere, Eco notes that "heroism is the norm" because "everybody is trained to become a hero" (84). Both sides, then, display elements that Eco identifies, but Eco is also clear that not all of the elements of Ur-Fascism have to be simultaneously present within a system: "all you need is one of them to be present, and a Fascist nebula will begin to coagulate" (78). The narrative of the trilogy thus works to confirm that there is little difference, in reality, between the political games of repressive control on the one hand and manipulated consent on the other.

Both Coin and Snow, then, wield essentially fascist control despite being opposed to each other. Both display elements that Eco outlines in their control of submissive citizens whose energies are organized and directed by the state's call to action. Both are also, in their leadership style, representations of the famous 1887 pronouncement from John Dalberg-Acton (Lord Acton) that "absolute power corrupts absolutely" (364). Consequently, the rebel victory and Coin's death might suggest that one form of absolute power cannot be used to replace another. Indeed, at one point, when Gale asks who would be in charge of government once the Capitol is defeated, Plutarch Heavensbee responds that everyone will be in charge because the plan is to set up a democratically elected, central government, just as their ancestors had done. Cynically, but probably correctly, however, Katniss surmises that the rebels' victory will bring Plutarch, a former Head Gamemaker and so a former part of the Capitol's oppressive elite, certain expected benefits within a new ruling elite.

The trilogy thus offers the idea that, although both Coin and Snow's systems are repellent, the eventual institution of democratic social order should be good, regardless of the means used to achieve it. Consequently, the final picture in *Mockingjay* is of a new social order, where District 12 produces medicine not coal, and where Panem's children are no longer sent to die but rather sent to school to learn from their nation's violent history. This suggests that, by teaching children about the mistakes of the past, the same awful pattern of events will not happen again in the future. As such, it sounds a note of optimism. However, the words of Plutarch Heavensbee, the arch manipulator, work to undermine this glimmer of hope. While Plutarch does note that people might recognize that the horrors of the past should not be repeated, he also understands that humans are "fickle, stupid beings" possessed of "poor memories" and with "a great gift for self-destruction" (*M* 442). The future, it seems, may not necessarily be so bright.

As an aside, in response to the question as to whether such a situation could develop in North America, Suzanne Collins replied that "You'd have to allow for the collapse of civilization as we know it, the emergence of Panem, a rebellion, and seventy-four years of the Hunger Games. We're talking triple digits" ("Author Profile"). Intriguingly, here Collins does not say "no" to this question; she simply suggests that it would not be likely today. Her response is not necessarily a prediction, but it is not to be dismissed either. Robert Sutherland has observed that "The values which shape a book are the author's politics. The promulgation of these values through publication is a political act" (157). Certainly, a literary work is no less political in its ideological baggage than any other medium of communication.

In an interesting contrast to the solution offered in the trilogy, 2011 witnessed largely peaceful uprisings and regime changes in the Middle East and North Africa by populations that had long lived under totalitarian governments, governments that very much mirrored the Capitol in terms of authoritarian oppression. What has been termed the "Arab Spring" saw people take to the streets, armed only with a belief in the need for a better social order, and many have attributed the start of the movement to a very real person on fire: the self-immolation of Mohammed Bouazizi in Tunisia in December 2010, in protest against the unwarranted confiscation by police of his vegetable cart. Across television screens, generally peaceful rebellion successfully played out alongside other images of the Western powers' ongoing military actions against the enemies that have been identified in less-developed countries such as Afghanistan. The trilogy is not so much an allegorical warning about the future as it is a portrayal of the nature of current times and the way the same scenario is constantly played out in both domestic and international politics.

Violent response to situations may well be universally condemned and recognized as harmful to social systems, yet it remains an everyday part of global culture. Televised wars inure the public to the horrors of death and at the same time present them, through a discourse of the Other, as permissible in certain circumstances for the greater good or for a just cause. Media coverage sets up an enemy and thereby dehumanizes "others," which in turn allows for soldiers to kill them without guilt and for ordinary citizens to support these actions without guilt. The trilogy can be said to espouse a point of view, through Katniss, that nobody gains from living in a society where such terrible events are allowed to take place. Yet how effectively can such a message be communicated to, and taken up by, readers exposed to a social discourse that itself works with Eco's Ur-Fascist principles at times even as it pits Western nations against enemies such as radical Islam? Western governments have projected terrorism as a "war" to be fought and have simultaneously enacted draconian legislation that limits individual freedoms at the same time as it speaks to protecting the population. As Jacqueline Rose observes, "[T]here is nothing like war for engendering a spurious and temporary psy-

cho-cultural unity which rallies everyone to the flag" (62), whether it be in
a literary text or in real life.

The resort to war as a solution in the world also resonates with Richard
Maxwell Brown's understanding of a uniquely American view of self-defense
whereby, when faced with a deadly threat, there is an inalienable right to
stand one's ground and fight; there is no duty to retreat. For Brown, this
right developed out of frontier attitudes with the push westward and has been
enshrined in United States law since the nineteenth century. It continues to
shape American politics, he argues, because no duty to retreat persists as a
central theme in American thought and character. In practice, says Brown,
"no duty to retreat is an attribute so deeply embedded in [the American]
national character" (173) that it remains largely unchallenged by the values
of peace-oriented social activism that opposes the kinds of military actions
overseas that have become a feature of American foreign policy.

In the trilogy there exists, therefore, an unresolved contradiction between
the values of pacifism and those of the American revolutionary heritage that
speaks to the necessity and justice of armed insurrection against the ruling
elite. Indeed, it does not take a huge leap of the imagination to connect the
thirteen districts with that heritage in the trilogy's echoes of the original thirteen colonies' uprising against an overbearing and distant colonial power across
the Atlantic, the monarchy of Great Britain (the Capitol), which taxed and
used the resources of the American colonies, offering little in return. The trilogy gives no indication that young protagonists should be mediators between
rival factions, as real-world peacemakers. Characters young and old adopt the
"either/or" mentality bluntly expressed by former President George W. Bush
on September 20, 2001: "Either you are with us, or you are with the terrorists"
(Speech to Congress). There is no middle way.

The trilogy is not simply offering an account of how a regime that resorts
to violence against its own people loses legitimacy. It provides a narrative that
asks the reader to recognize and resist authoritarianism, but does not wholly
escape the contextual proposition that might is right in pursuit of a higher
purpose — here, the overthrow of dictatorial government. In so doing, its own
message of peace is subverted by offering no logical or practical way to remove
oppressive regimes from power other than through militaristic means. This
reflects not so much a discourse of rapprochement but rather a reinforcement
of traditional armed responses to oppression. Importantly, too, as Eco notes,
fascism as an ideology cannot and must not be consigned to the annals of history because its manifestations are subtle and shifting and still with us today,
for "you can play the Fascism game many ways, and the name of the game
does not change" (76). It is the game that still surrounds the readers of *The
Hunger Games*, the game of absolute power.

WORKS CITED

"Author Profile: Suzanne Collins." *Teenreads.com.* Book Report, Aug. 2010. Web. 28 Aug. 2011.

Brown, Richard Maxwell. *No Duty to Retreat: Violence and Values in American History and Society.* New York: Oxford University Press, 1991. Print.

Bush, George W. Speech to Joint Session of Congress. Washington, D.C. 20 Sept. 2001. *cnn.com/U.S.,* 20 Sept. 2001. Web. 2 Sept. 2011.

Collins, Suzanne. *Catching Fire.* London: Scholastic, 2009. Print.

_____. *The Hunger Games.* 2008. London: Scholastic, 2009. Print.

_____. *Mockingjay.* London: Scholastic, 2010. Print.

Dalberg-Acton, John Emerich Edward [Lord Acton]. "Acton-Creighton Correspondence." *Essays on Freedom and Power.* 1948. Boston: Beacon, 1949. 357–73. Print.

Eco, Umberto. "Ur-Fascism." *Five Moral Pieces.* San Diego: Harvest, 2002. 65–88. Print.

Rose, Jacqueline. *States of Fantasy.* 1996. Oxford: Clarendon, 2004. Print.

Sutherland, Robert D. "Hidden Persuaders: Political Ideologies in Literature for Children." *Children's Literature in Education* 16.3 (1985): 143–57. Print.

3

Communal Spectacle

Reshaping History and Memory through Violence

GRETCHEN KOENIG

A young girl rises from bed in a clearly impoverished house, walks out past a disheveled cat, then goes through a strip of land that barely passes as a meadow to a barbed-wire-topped fence that encircles District 12, her home. In theory, the fence exists to keep wild things out of the district, but it also keeps the girl trapped, even watched. So she escapes to the open wildness of the land beyond the fence to find a sense of autonomy and freedom on a rock that gives her a view of the entire valley: a place to be herself. She escapes to find food for her family, but the escape also gives her a unique view of the nation that holds her hostage to poverty and hunger. The opening scenes of Suzanne Collins's novel *The Hunger Games* subtly demonstrate that Katniss Everdeen knows how to find her way to a place of vision, a place overlooking her prison of a home, but also a place where she determines the path of her own story. Throughout the trilogy, Collins engages the notion that victors write the script of their own history as she uses Katniss to question who holds the pen that creates, shapes, and defines cultural memory.

The cultural context that is Katniss's daily life matches significant moments in recent real-world military history. From the draft and other voyeuristic elements of the Vietnam War to the national rhetoric of the Israeli response to the Holocaust, those in power shape the cultural memory of significant events as a means of invoking their citizens' loyalty. Collins's trilogy imagines a world set in what had been North America, a world where power resides in the hands of the physically weak but positionally strong Capitol. The power it wields throughout the districts relies primarily on observation fueled by violence. The Capitol projects the idea that it can see everything in Panem, leaving citizens bereft of privacy. Michel Foucault contends that power exists in what he terms "observing hierarchy" and "normalizing judge-ment" (184). Through these techniques Foucault suggests that power derives from the process of differentiation and judgment as examination combines "the ceremony of power and the form of the experiment, the deployment of force and the establishment of truth" (184). Panem's Capitol holds the power of differentiation and judgment while its citizens have limited or no access to that power, so they are at the (dubious) mercy of the Capitol. Worse yet, the Capitol couples surveillance with actual violence in the highlight of its year, the annual Hunger Games. Through random selection, district tributes arrive in the Capitol, parade in costumes, and proceed to die in what amounts to a cage, all as a reminder of who holds the reins in Panem.

Collins's first chapter centers on the power of forcing citizens to partic-ipate in reshaping their own history as we observe the ritual of reaping day, when tributes are selected from each district to participate in the involuntary Games. Those watching the footage are ready to devour the reaping's emo-tional imagery. American citizens during the Vietnam and Iraqi wars engaged with coverage that we did not ask for but that was provided by our own com-mercial media. In Panem the overt sense of control is emphasized as the mayor of District 12 reads the country's history: a tale of catastrophe and failed rebel-lion. Katniss interprets the message of the "history" as the Capitol telling the locals it will "take your children and sacrifice them" (*HG* 19), reminding the populace of rebellion's costs (19). Thus, the Capitol's dominance does not end with the present power of observation; instead, it reaches back into Panem's collective memory and tells the districts what to think of their own history. Whether in Panem or our America, this process of reobserving and re-creating history is dangerous as it leads citizens to develop a violent, nor-malized narrative of their country's past.

Foucault illustrates the historical move from public discipline, which focused on spectacle, to the modern prison system, which focuses on obser-vation and the creation of introspection until prisoners assume the mantle of their own guilt. Collins's work engages both paradigms of control and pun-ishment. In the reaping, Collins evokes the effect behind public execution as laid out in Foucault: "In the ceremonies of the public execution, the main character was the people, whose real and immediate presence was required for the performance" (57). Foucault continues by claiming that the goal "was to make an example ... by arousing feelings of terror by the spectacle of power letting its anger fall upon the guilty person" (57–58). In this case, the Capitol has chosen to select random children to represent the "guilty persons" who treasonously fought against the Capitol more than seventy years before. We see the public spectacle at work as Katniss and her sister make their way to the reaping. Capitol camera crews sit "perched like buzzards" around the square, preying on this most gut-wrenching day for the districts (*HG* 16).

The children become a living embodiment of historical evil; they become a living metaphor of the past. And the Capitol chooses to reenact an execution in the most public form possible: televised death games.

In an interview, Suzanne Collins acknowledges that the power of memory and the tragedy of war were ever-present realities in her childhood. Her father was an Air Force officer who served in Vietnam, and other relatives fought in each world war. While her father was not drafted, the reality of war for families was a constant topic of conversation (Dominus). The reapings in *The Hunger Games* include hints of the draft, so predominant in the war that shaped Collins's own childhood. Panem's families watch the reaping either in person or on television, waiting for the fate of their friends and loved ones, their children, to be determined by a drawing. Americans watched the televised lotteries in the Vietnam era for much the same reason. The reapings resemble the draft even more when statistics show that those drafted for Vietnam "were more likely to see front-line action" than those who enlisted (Modell and Haggerty 210). For Collins's draft, there is only front-line action leading to virtually certain death. In addition, Vietnam was the first televised war where producers focused on combat footage since those "scenes tended to be more dramatic, more exciting, and therefore — and this was the primary consideration — more likely to attract viewers than other kinds of coverage" (Mandelbaum 159). Viewers become desensitized to the brutality, normalizing the horrific images, perhaps unaware of the cost. Collins seems to turn our own historical memory of the Vietnam War into a comment on our own capacity for, and attraction to, violence.

After Katniss volunteers to take her younger sister's place in the Games when Prim's name is drawn in the reaping, Katniss's biggest concern is how she will appear as the cameras hone in on her. As Effie Trinket, the Games' District 12 liaison, acknowledges Katniss's sacrifice, the crowd bands together, silently acknowledging her courage. When she feels as though she cannot keep her emotions in check any longer, District 12's only living victor, Haymitch Abernathy, drunkenly staggers about, pulling the eyes of the Capitol after him. Katniss recognizes the reprieve his actions give her and pulls her emotions together. She begins to understand that her success or failure in the Games depends upon her image, her ability to shape public perception. Katniss represents a soldier in the employ of the Capitol and, as such, she must project the stalwart soldier image that we as consumers prefer to the less-polished realities. Today, uniforms, codes of conduct, quality-controlled public statements, and screened or prohibited images of caskets returning to U.S. soil project a deliberately crafted image of control. A generic military member must follow orders, remain physically fit, execute extreme violence if directed to do so, and yet emotionally continue to "soldier on." Interestingly, movies shape many Americans' notions of the ideal soldier, a blatant form of revisionist history affecting reality. Much the same as our modern vision of an ideal soldier, Katniss at once recognizes her role and conforms to that image.

Katniss learns that the Capitol doesn't simply want to use her for present power; it wishes to appropriate her past, present, and future image. It wants to reinvent her story and limit her power. Alternately, Katniss takes control of her story, as much as a pawn can, in her relationship with Cinna, her stylists, and Haymitch. Cinna unleashes the power of her appearance on camera, and Haymitch attempts to mold her interviewing tactics, to soften her social image. The conversation revolves around who her audience is and what her attitude should be. Katniss is not initially cooperative with Haymitch because he wants to change her identity. When she shouts that the Capitol may own her now and forever, but it cannot have what "mattered to me in the past" (*HG* 117), she rebels against the Capitol's attempt to rewrite her personal past, just as it has rewritten Panem's collective past.

What she understands is that the Capitol is not simply interested in controlling future rebellions but also in shaping the public memory of the past. President Snow engages in perpetuating "political amnesia," a term Michael Rogin uses when he discusses the political ways that U.S. presidents have used the language of popular films (103). What Rogin claims about U.S. presidents applies to Panem's president as well: "Political amnesia works, however, not simply through burying history but also through representing the return of the repressed" (106). Snow replaces history with a myth of the past. Rogin continues, "Spectacle is the cultural form for amnesiac representation, for specular displays are superficial and sensately intensified, short lived and repeatable" (106), everything the Games themselves represent. Rogin claims that "the concept of amnesia points to an identity that persists over time and that preserves a false center by burying the actual past" (107). The story of Panem's past never truly emerges in the novel. Instead, readers must attempt to interpret the "rebellion" through the Capitol's vision. The fabricated reenactment of the rebellion played out in front of Panem every year masks the actual events. The Capitol shapes the rhetoric and internalized perception of history through present spectacle.

Arriving in the Capitol, outsiders Katniss and Peeta react to the city's colors and pageantry, even brighter than what they have "seen on television" (*HG* 59). The sight takes their breath away for its cleanliness and opulence, at stark odds with existence in the districts. They recognize the Capitol's focus on the concept of the visual. The Capitol's physical distinctions, from architecture to the bodily features of its residents, purposely mark outlying districts as inferior. This definition of "other" and "inferior" allows the Capitol to justify government violence against the districts. Collins's use of children as tributes for a long-ago crime comes into sharp focus when we realize that they, like every district resident, show their distinction in their flawed skin. The bodies of the Capitol residents are nourished, polished, even colored. The children cannot even be worthy tributes until approved Capitol technicians reimage them for television consumption by "superior" Capitol residents. The government's fabricated narrative of Panem's past requires the modification of all the present-day actors to fit the fictionalized versions of their real-life identities.

According to Foucault, a vital part of physical punishment is the role of the body itself: "[P]ower relations have an immediate hold upon [the body]; they invest it, mark it, train it, torture it, force it to carry out tasks, to perform ceremonies, to emit signs" (25). The Capitol insists that the tributes' bodies be turned into signs of its own superiority. The tributes must submit themselves to the Remake Center to have their bodies embellished for Capitol ingestion. The production of the Games necessitates reshaping impoverished children from the districts into healthy, vigorous weapons. In a sense, the Capitol must manufacture the identity of the unwilling tributes who tell the Capitol's narrative reenactment of the rebellion. Collins exploits the spectacle of punishment in the physical difference between the free Capitol population and those who must physically bear the memory of the districts' past. The tributes know that even with their modified bodies, Panem sees them as imposters and so watches their every move. Peeta must take Katniss to the roof, where the wind will drown out their words, because they "might be under surveillance" (*HG* 80). The Capitol succeeds in projecting dominance through violence, observation, and cultural memory.

As we watch Katniss mature through the Games themselves, there are two distinct moments where she intentionally turns the gaze away from the tributes as entertainment to pawns in a game of cruelty by the Capitol. Her actions reflect political and militaristic moves against the power of the Capitol, reinforcing her position outside Panem's hierarchy of power. The first incident is Rue's death. When Katniss finds Rue tangled in the nets with the spear in her stomach, her first reaction isn't to wonder who is watching her. Instead, she mourns for her friend. However, as she turns to walk away, she realizes that the cameras will have to show the hovercraft picking up the girl's body. Only then, as she realizes the power of vision, does she visibly honor the slain child to mark the "injustice" of the Games (*HG* 236). The flowers Katniss wraps the young girl in represent innocence, youth, loss, and human compassion, all things President Snow does not want his people to acknowledge. He needs Panem to see the Games as a necessary reminder of a not-so-forgotten past to protect a precarious future. Katniss's second intentional act of visual defiance comes in the final moments of the Games. When announcer Claudius Templesmith says the Gamemakers have retracted the revision allowing two victors, Katniss has another moment of clarity. Her power does not reside in her bow, her tenacity, or even her supposed love for Peeta. Her strength resides in the ability to shape what people see and feel. She forcefully appropriates the political narrative as she turns a fistful of poisonous fruit into an act of defiance and forces the Head Gamemaker to allow two victors after all.

Katniss's on-camera defiance shifts the balance of power because it shifts the arc of the cultural narrative. President Snow targets her because she lifts the veil on the historical amnesia he has imposed on Panem; she dares to rewrite the script he owns. She reminds the people of the districts that they are simply humans suffering for a rebellion none of the children participated in. Her moves are reminiscent of Vietnam veterans who bore the brunt of a political situation created by an older generation unwilling and unable to participate in the war personally. Like hippies, draft dodgers, and rioting college students, Katniss strips Snow's power away by changing Panem's script.

The balance of power stays in Katniss's favor briefly, until the Victory Tour in *Catching Fire*. Before Peeta and she head out on their tour of the districts, she receives an ominous visit. When Katniss sees Snow in her room, she has an image of him standing "in front of marble pillars hung with oversize flags" (*CF* 18). Snow is not simply a president coming to warn Katniss against her behavior; he is the bodily representation of oppression, violence, and fear — all couched in patriotism. His very presence reeks of blood, perhaps the blood of his own people. He comes bearing a warning before she embarks on the tour designed to make the districts both remember who holds the power *and* to make them "celebrate it" (*CF* 4). Despite Snow's threats against Katniss's loved ones, she manages to retain the balance of power momentarily by taunting him. She cuts to the heart of the Capitol's tenuous grasp on power as she notes that a fistful of poisonous fruit could "bring it down" (*CF* 22). While her words are bold and truthful, she does not understand either their power or the power of the districts' changing memory. Instead of simply reenacting the antiquated Games, Katniss's actions ask the residents of Panem to remember the children's sacrifice rather than the arena's entertainment.

Throughout the Victory Tour and subsequent Quarter Quell, Katniss becomes ever more aware of the surveillance imposed upon her. She notes the likely presence of cameras watching everywhere, marking a maturity in her understanding of the Capitol's visual power. In addition, she learns to gather information about the other districts with whom she is supposed to have no communication. She uses her prep team's vanity to extract information as she encourages them to talk about hard-to-find products, translating that information into knowledge about which districts are beginning to rebel. Meanwhile, the Capitol ratchets up the violent messages, using bodies as memory. Katniss and Peeta's new servant is Darius, once a friendly Peacekeeper who turned a blind eye to Katniss's transgressions, now a maimed reminder that those who transgress lose their tongues because the Capitol sees everything.

In addition, Cinna's death at the moment Katniss enters the arena for the Quarter Quell is a bodily reminder that the Capitol sees and hears everything. Not content simply to kill the man who turned Katniss into the fiery figure of rebellion, Snow uses Cinna's body as a spectacle of power to invoke terror in Katniss just as he thrusts her into the ocean arena. Snow's message is clear: he will douse the fire of revolution.

Governments have a history of using collective memory as power in creating a sense of national identity, much as the Capitol does. Dr. Idith Zertal, a recognized figure in Israeli history, speaks to the concept of memory, violence, and nationhood in her article "From the People's Hall to the Wailing Wall: A Study in Memory, Fear, and War." This article looks at the Israeli-Arab conflict though the history of the Holocaust. Of particular interest is Zertal's discussion of cultural memory in the years leading to the Adolf Eichmann trial and David Ben Gurion's manipulation of his country's emotions. Zertal charts Ben Gurion's use of his people's Holocaust memories, beginning with silence, then moving to an all-out assault on the Israeli memory through televised violence. Ben Gurion used Eichmann's trial to incite a culture of fear, comparing Nazi atrocities of the past to current Arab nations' actions, thus moving Jews from victims to "victimizer" (98). Zertal asserts that the result of Ben Gurion's rhetoric was the "juxtaposition of the past revived, of politicized memories and present politics, and the images of the Israeli brutality toward Palestinian civilians projected daily on Israeli television and around the world" (98). Collins demonstrates this exact turn of victim and visualization through the results of the Quarter Quell. When the Quell ends abruptly and Katniss wakes attempting to get her bearings, she realizes that the Capitol isn't the only one using her. She understands that her image, her story, her love, and her loss have all been "[u]sed without consent, without knowledge" to turn the victims, districts, into something stronger (*CF* 385). The new power regime conspires to distract the Capitol's vision through its own spectacle, which it uses to usurp the Capitol's power and rebel.

Collins's second novel illustrates the way the rhetoric of national pride shifts from the dominant Capitol to the scattered districts. As readers, we want to see the oppressed rise up and take back their autonomy, their dignity, and the lives of their children. However, Collins suggests that what is to come in *Mockingjay* will not satisfy either our desires or those of the districts. Finnick, winner of the Sixty-fifth Annual Hunger Games and tribute again for the Quarter Quell, attempts to soothe Katniss's fears and anger against the manufactured image the rebellion leaders need her to embrace; but his words hauntingly suggest he knows where the story ends. As he and Katniss think of those they love stuck in the grasp of the Capitol, Finnick claims to wish them "all dead and [us] too" (*CF* 389). While Finnick certainly does not want to feel the pain of knowing those he loves suffer, his death wish indicates a larger issue. When he wishes he were dead, his weariness suggests that he recognizes how the districts have traded the terrible power of the Capitol for another manipulative power.

In his essay on spectacle as amnesia, Rogin argues that in order for political amnesia to work, several myths must be in play, three of which are relevant in this trilogy. The first is "redemption through violence, intensified in the mass technologies of entertainment and war" (107). Collins's narrative demonstrates this element as Alma Coin, president of District 13, pushes Katniss into representing the new regime, promoting violence against the Capitol in her televised promos. The next of Rogin's myths at play is "the belief in individual agency, the need to forget both the web of social ties that enmesh us all and the wish for an individual power so disjunctive with everyday existence" (107). Katniss as the Mockingjay embodies individual agency giving hope to others that they, too, can metaphorically rise above. The last of Rogin's myths is "identification with the state, to which is transferred the freedom to act without being held to account that in part compensates for individual helplessness but in part reflects state weakness as well" (107). Much the same as Ben Gurion's use of Adolf Eichmann's trial, Coin rallies a disenfranchised people who have been on the receiving end of the spectacle of violence, leading them to retaliate with equally brutal violence. Coin's tactics finally mirror the Capitol when she suggests holding a final Hunger Games using "Capitol children" (*M* 369). The new government brings the power of observation, spectacle of violence, and national rhetoric full circle. Coin's cruel suggestion attempts to wrench the Capitol's ultimate weapon into the districts' arsenal. The rebels will return violence and punishment to the aggressors, thereby becoming fully entrenched as aggressors themselves: Rogin's political amnesiacs.

For a brief time, Katniss upholds the new state as she takes on the role of Mockingjay. She relishes a new feeling: "Power" (*M* 91). The authority she holds is the influence of visible identity. Residents of the districts feel a sense of connection when she is present, suggesting that she is the literal embodiment of the new regime. But her sense of power is short-lived. The Capitol sacrificed twenty-three children each year in the Hunger Games so that the districts would not forget their past atrocities. President Coin sacrifices numerous soldiers, citizens, and children to shift the balance of power. Eventually, Katniss realizes she has traded one violent regime for another. "Did you find what you were looking for?" asks Commander Paylor when Katniss emerges from her final conversation with the incarcerated Snow (*M* 359). The answer is yes. Katniss finds the truth through memory — but not a remembrance tainted by the rhetoric of cultural identity or rebellion, and not one of the staged presentations of history. Rather, the truth is an un-fabricated memory of events and people. And with that recollection, she recognizes that she cannot live in a world that "sacrifices its children's lives to settle its differences" (*M* 377). Katniss refuses to tolerate a new state built on the same foundation as Snow's Capitol.

In his discussion on the purpose of public executions and the ensuing terror, Foucault suggests that at times the visual spectacle of punishment led to situations in which the watching crowd would "express [their] rejection of the punitive power and sometimes revolt" (59). In essence, the voyeurs became overwhelmed by the sense of euphoric ownership of the spectacle, leading to a rebellious rejection of unpopular verdicts. The public venue of violence and punishment led to further violence through revolt. Foucault's scenario speaks directly to the powerful warning *The Hunger Games* trilogy offers young readers. Collins admits that she first thought of the narrative's premise while she "was channel-surfing and flipped from a reality-television competition to footage from the war in Iraq" (Dominus). Her experience turned the story into "[a]n overt critique of violence ... forcing readers to contemplate their own roles as desensitized voyeurs" (Dominus).

Essentially, the trilogy reveals the uncomfortable truth that our national narratives construct for us. When Plutarch (the new Secretary of Communications) and Haymitch travel with Katniss as she returns to the remains of District 12, Katniss asks Plutarch if he thinks there is another war in their future. The man laughs, but wisely acknowledges the possibility because people are changeable and have "poor memories" (*M* 379). In other words, Panem's potential for amnesia means its citizens may not live in peace long. In light of Panem's poor memory, the true power of Katniss's revolt is not assuming the role of Mockingjay. Her power comes in disengaging from public vision and narrative as well as her separation from the visibility of the public and the strength of her memories. Despite being out of sight of the rest of Panem, Katniss does not begin to heal until she creates her own narrative of the past in the form of a book that records all that she "cannot trust to memory" (*M* 387). The book starts as blank sheets that Peeta, Haymitch, and Katniss fill with everything they know they cannot afford to forget: memories of loss, of individuals. The three are able to re-create a life of hope in the midst of the reality of memories that are not collective memories, or national memories, but personal memories that define human existence. Katniss gains power by extracting herself from the government's gaze and its reenvisioned, amnesiac history, into a place removed from public view but not from the truth of her own history.

WORKS CITED

Collins, Suzanne. *Catching Fire*. New York: Scholastic, 2009. Print.
____. *The Hunger Games*. New York: Scholastic, 2008. Print.
_____. *Mockingjay*. New York: Scholastic, 2010. Print.

Dominus, Susan. "Suzanne Collins's War Stories for Kids." *nytimes.com*. New York Times Co., 8 Apr. 2011. Web. 28 Aug. 2011.

Foucault, Michel. *Discipline and Punish: The Birth of the Prison*. 1975. New York: Vintage, 1990. Print.

Mandelbaum, Michael. "Vietnam: The Television War." *Daedalus* 111.4 (Fall 1982): 157–69. *JSTOR*. Web. 7 June 2011.

Modell, John, and Timothy Haggerty. "The Social Impact of War." *Annual Review of Sociology* 17 (1991): 205–24. *JSTOR*. Web. 7 June 2011.

Rogin, Michael. "'Make My Day!': Spectacle as Amnesia in Imperial Politics." *Representations* 29 (Winter 1990): 99–123. *JSTOR*. Web. 1 June 2011.

Zertal, Idith. "From the People's Hall to the Wailing Wall: A Study in Memory, Fear, and War." *Representations* 69 (Winter 2000): 96–126. *JSTOR*. Web. 3 June 2011.

4

Reflection in a Plastic Mirror*

Valerie Estelle Frankel

"I was channel surfing between reality TV programming and actual war coverage when Katniss's story came to me," Suzanne Collins comments. "One night I'm sitting there flipping around and on one channel there's a group of young people competing for, I don't know, money maybe? And on the next, there's a group of young people fighting an actual war. And I was tired, and the lines began to blur in this very unsettling way, and I thought of this story" ("Conversation"). In *The Hunger Games* trilogy, Katniss survives by playing the part she's been assigned, competing on the public screen to win her audience's support as star-crossed lover and political figurehead. But as she's forced to smile for the camera and the Capitol's frivolous, pleasure-seeking citizens, Panem with its Hunger Games begins to mirror another world — ours. This isn't just a dystopian future; it's the dystopia of present-day America.

From the first moment of Katniss's visit to the Capitol, she's stunned by its superficial society. Each person owns more clothes, shoes, wigs, and makeup than any ten people of her district. They swallow brightly colored pills with their morning coffee, reminiscent of our many drugs and vitamins. And they practice social bulimia, throwing up at feasts to make room for more, as the other districts starve. Katniss is appalled at the waste.

Embarking from her first train ride, Katniss appears much like a foreigner from a developing country. She gazes awestruck at the skyscrapers, glistening cars, and garishly dressed people who have clearly never gone hungry. The colors especially stand out for her: pinks, greens, and yellows impossible in nature, foreign to the forest-dwelling huntress. She has entered another world. Once within it, she longs to ride up and down on the glass elevator and marvels at the abundance of elegant food. The shower has a hundred settings

*Some of the concepts discussed in this essay have also been considered in the author's *Katniss the Cattail: An Unauthorized Guide to Names and Symbols in Suzanne Collins'* The Hunger Games (LitCric, 2012).

of massage, strange soaps, and warm air. And there's far too much light to see the stars.

Effie Trinket, guide to this world, condescends to Katniss and Peeta, dwelling on their table manners and the "barbarism" of their district (*HG* 74). She believes that anyone without a Capitol upbringing is sadly lacking. America today, of course, is often less than kind towards those who can't speak the language or blend in. As Katniss endures the criticism, she in turn considers how obtuse Effie is: her "civilized" society is preparing the new tributes for slaughter, all for a few episodes of live television. The Gamemakers, too, consider tributes beneath notice, and they ignore Katniss's demonstration of her combat skills in favor of stuffing themselves. When she shoots their dinner in true barbaric fashion, she also reveals their spoiled behavior, these bureaucrats who shrug off the death of others as entertainment.

Capitol citizens appear wasteful and gluttonous, especially to the near-starving Katniss. With one meal, she calculates how much hunting and gathering she would have to do to afford the chicken in orange sauce, even with thrifty substitutions. She's disturbed by how much the people take for granted. The true horror comes at the *Catching Fire* banquet held in honor of the new victors, when she discovers gluttony beyond her imagining. Everyone is expected to stuff themselves, vomit, and stuff themselves again. Delicate glasses of clear liquid are even provided for the purpose. Peeta condemns the citizens with horror, while Katniss can only think of the emaciated children back home. But American readers can see a parallel in bulimics, people who can afford to throw away food, binge and purge from dieting, and waste more meals than some people ever see.

While the Capitol citizens color their hair pink and green, dye their skin, and glory in cosmetic surgery, their fashions aren't much more extreme than those of Americans today. Katniss's stylists want to augment her breasts to make her more attractive once she's a star — a common practice in Hollywood. Her descriptions of Capitol citizens blowing up their lips and tattooing themselves with cult symbols (like the mockingjay) are popular in our own culture, as is their obsession with looking youthful. "Do they really have no idea how freakish they look to the rest of us?" Katniss wonders (*CF* 49). For those struggling for food and warmth, our garish lipstick, hair dyes, and unnecessary surgeries must seem ridiculous indeed, as we design exotic fashions out of boredom and waste money on luxuries so decadent they're outlandish. Our reality shows are filled with divas obsessing over their hair colors or the source of their next million. The first episode of *The Real Housewives of New Jersey* introduced Teresa, who loves shopping for her new multimillion-dollar dream home. On *The Real Housewives of Atlanta,* Sereé got nearly two million dollars in cash and property in her divorce. When she didn't receive alimony, she appealed to the Supreme Court of Georgia, explaining that she had few job skills and needed help to support herself and her children. Ramona on *The Real Housewives of New York City* sells her own line of jewelry through the Home Shopping Network and developed the skin care line TruRenewal, while her fellow housewife Heather owns the shapewear business Yummie Tummie. These "Real Housewives" our networks show off to the world are often spoiled, squabbling princesses with millions to devote to frivolous pet projects. Can they really spend so much on jeweled dog collars and big-screen TVs while the world goes hungry?

Katniss's prep team shaves off all her body hair and bathes her over and over, removing her objectionable "third-world" origins. Only her hairstyle gets to stay (though team members don't say "exotic primitive craftsmanship," they're likely thinking it). Katniss sees her groomed self as alien — a stranger in the mirror. The prep team themselves are notable for their alien nature, with strange piping accents, fashion affectations, and close-mouthed hissing. Katniss sees them as incomprehensible twittering birds rather than people. Their entire purpose for being — to make Katniss look appealing — is incomprehensible to her. In her life, she ignores all unnecessary luxuries in favor of simple survival. Ned Vizzini, in his essay "Reality Hunger," explains, "A world like the Capitol, where food can appear at the touch of a button and image is everything, does not seem real to Katniss, and *realness* — real emotion, real resolve, real fire — is at the heart of *The Hunger Games*" (83).

Katniss expects to be paraded around wearing a miner's getup or coal dust — not because this is who she is, but because it's how the Capitol views her district. She might as well be Miss Wisconsin, carrying a cutout of her state or a giant cheese. However, her stylist, Cinna, chooses to surround her with flame. Although this fire, like her later symbol of the Mockingjay, is an artificial construct, both echo the natural power inside Katniss, her strength and will for survival. "We've literally outshone them all," Katniss thinks after her dazzling display (*HG* 72). But what outshines the other tributes is Katniss's honest, blunt love for her family that fuels her determination.

The Miss America-style interviews, with high-heeled shoes, groomed nails, and heavy makeup, all mirror the pageantry of our culture — even among children. *Toddlers & Tiaras,* an American reality series, shows kindergarteners and two-year-olds wearing fake eyelashes, spray tans, and swimwear as they compete in "glitz" beauty pageants that judge their artificial, doll-like beauty. The names of various pageants, such as "America's Trezured Dollz" and "Precious Moments Pageant," only add to the stereotype. And it is just such a competition in which Katniss is trapped. To the Capitol, Katniss is not meant to be strong or independent — only appealing in a jeweled gown. She must giggle and smile to charm sponsors, who like her best when Peeta's proclaimed affection makes her look "weak" (as Katniss puts it) — a word Haymitch considers equivalent to "desirable" (*HG* 135). She is remade and objectified, perched on a stool as a lovely passive model for the audience to gape at. Beside her in line sit Rue, dressed as a tiny gossamer fairy, and Glimmer, in a see-through golden gown looking "provocative" (*HG* 125). On *Toddlers & Tiaras,* tiny competitors must present giant, fixed smiles, must blow kisses and flirt. Backstage, however, many have tantrums at the pressure of their parents' expectations, at the endless practice, at the irritating beauty treatments. Katniss, in her high heels and jeweled gowns, must perform in the same way. And Katniss certainly has her tantrums before Cinna and Effie, as she cries for hours and tears apart her room. With this, Collins portrays the misery of beauty pageants, since inside, Katniss feels murderous.

Katniss must also adopt an artificial persona — a platform to make viewers care for her. Adrianne Curry, former contestant on *America's Next Top Model,* gives advice to potential contestants that mirrors Haymitch's and Cinna's advice to Katniss. Curry suggests that aspirants find a persona like "drama queen" or "girl next door" or just be natural: "Just be yourself, and if being yourself isn't interesting, make up a character.... Everyone loves the bitch. Everyone loves the underdog. Everyone loves the diva" (qtd. in Robinson 229). Katniss attempts being spunky or sexy or sweet, but the forthright girl fails at all these. Only when Cinna coaches her to be herself and answer questions as if talking to a friend does she succeed. The audience comes to love her because of her lack of artifice. She shares a truth they find unusually appealing in the world of superficiality in which they exist. She's a genuine heroine, one who sacrificed herself for her young sister, one who hunts to survive, one who is honestly shocked when Peeta declares his love for her. And as such, she appeals to them and to us. "*The Hunger Games* presents us with the kind of hero that not only Panem but America likes best: the reluctant one, unexpectedly brilliant when challenged and then, once famous, desirous of a simpler life," says Vizzini (84).

The citizens of the Capitol, so used to their superficial lives, crave novelty, but they also crave genuineness. And there is nothing more genuine than a real fight to survive, fought by (mostly) guileless children from the more primitive districts. Nely Galan, creator of *The Swan,* explains, "Ultimately, the stars of reality TV are real people. I find it fascinating, because we spend so many years idolizing celebrities, and now real people get a shot at it" (qtd. in Robinson 85). Such is the appeal of allegedly unscripted television. When Peeta describes what the Games are truly like in an interview, there's a hush across the room, as everyone is entranced by the tale of unadulterated terror and the fight for survival. Suzanne Collins notes:

> The Hunger Games is a reality television program. An extreme one, but that's what it is. And while I think some of those shows can succeed on different levels, there's also the voyeuristic thrill, watching, people being humiliated or brought to tears or suffering physically. And that's what I find very disturbing. There's this

potential for desensitizing the audience so that when they see real tragedy playing out on the news, it doesn't have the impact it should. It all just blurs into one program [qtd. in Hudson].

While there are parallels with celebrity makeover shows, wedding shows, and talent competitions, the Hunger Games themselves are closest to *Survivor.* As Matthew Robinson describes the show in his book on reality television, contestants are "dumped into a remote location and made to fend for themselves.... If having no food, water, or shelter wasn't bad enough, these 'survivors' also have to figure out how to connive and manipulate one another in order to survive the voting-off ceremony at each week's tribal council. Oh yeah, and sometimes they also have to eat rats" (173). The disturbing part as the contestants suffer through starvation and injury in fetching bikinis is that their scenario is no more real than the environment of the Hunger Games: they are trapped on their island purely to entertain the masses with their misery.

Mitchell Olson, a contestant on *Survivor: Australia,* revealed that all the laughter and campfire sing-alongs got edited out: "I guess because it's not as dramatic — it doesn't show us being stressed out and starving" (qtd. in Robinson 182). The Gamemakers share this attitude as they throw in firestorms and traps just to raise the level of action. Granted, *Survivor* is more likely to have challenges of racing through an obstacle course to collect puzzle pieces than fleeing a firestorm. But even tests depending on teamwork feature cameras poised to catch the complaints and frustration. Scandal, tears, arguments, and recriminations are the lifeblood of reality shows, in which contestants are urged to share their frustration with viewers, to blame other contestants, to have tantrums onscreen. Even on this small scale, contestants undeniably suffer for viewers' amusement. "Evoking emotion from the casting department is the name of the game, so do whatever you can to up the tearjerker factor," Robinson advises (39). Whether deaths in the Hunger Games or momentary misery, the reality show must have drama.

One common protest against reality TV is the total lack of privacy for contestants. Intimate conversations and romances have been broadcast on national TV, often against the participants' wishes (Bilstereyst 93). In this way, Katniss's emotional talks with Peeta are offered to the camera in a performance she must knowingly put on for the masses. The Game makes even emotion artificial, as Katniss gives Peeta long kisses to entertain the cameras and sponsors. It's entertainment, and she knows her lines. She who is most entertaining will live longest, a rule in our society of *American Idol* and Miss America, as well as in Katniss's. While the sponsors' products don't come with brand names, they almost could, reminding viewers that Katniss survived by using Acme burn cream or Johnson's sleeping bags. The sponsors choose which tribute to support based on beauty and appeal, like today's advertisers choosing a spokesmodel.

A leading newspaper in Greece claimed that reality TV would bring to the surface of society the most repulsive and deplorable characteristics of human nature (Biltereyst 97). In the Hunger Games, these are evident in the Career Tributes, whom Katniss describes as "overly vicious" and the "Capitol's lapdogs" (*HG* 161). A past tribute turned cannibal in the Games, and even gentle Peeta resolves to kill other children to defend himself. Reality TV is fundamentally exploitative, as "the programme-makers exploit their subjects through 'manipulation' and editorial control, or the participants exploit the programmer in an entrepreneurial bid for media exposure" (Holmes 111). While Katniss is tortured for the entertainment of the masses, the Career Tributes try to exploit the Games in return, to become proficient killers in exchange for wealth and fame. Only in the final book do we discover that many media darlings of the Games like Finnick are still exploited, forced to be a source of entertainment and prostitution for the Capitol.

Reality shows "generate only a *faux* community, one that obliterates trust" (Cavender 169). They echo President George W. Bush's Homeland Security programs, which, like the policies of Panem, allowed the government to eavesdrop on its citizens without warrants. Being in such an environment encourages betrayal and blame shifting, as citizens fear to say what they really think. Katniss always knows someone is watching. Similarly, the Hunger Games tributes know they cannot work together, that any alliances must end with destroying one another. While Katniss's humanity prevails over the rules and she bonds with Rue, she fears the threat that they will be left until the end and forced to turn on each other. This is indeed the worst side of humanity, not its best.

Months after their triumphs, reality TV contestants appear on talk shows, in newspapers, and on the Web, informing bored fans about their lives. In the second book, Katniss and Peeta have the Victory Tour, a series of press events meant to entertain the masses and promote the Capitol's agenda. But Katniss finds it hard to stay herself as she slips into the celebrity persona the Capitol demands. Once more she's buffed and groomed, stuffed into perfectly designed outfits. Her romance with Peeta is owned and managed by the public, not by her. When their engagement, too, is staged, she models wedding dresses for her fans, who will log in to vote on her gown like so many *American Idol* groupies.

In *Catching Fire,* it's revealed that Katniss is expected to develop a "talent" (*CF* 39), as if her connection with Miss America wasn't clear enough already. Flower arranging and playing instruments are common choices. Peeta starts painting, a hobby for the rich. But Katniss's only "talents" are singing, which is too personal, and hunting, which doesn't count (if shooting a painted target won't make the cut, presumably Katniss is supposed to cultivate a purely friv-olous art in keeping with Capitol pursuits, rather than a practical or violent hobby). Katniss, worthless at time wasting, has Cinna help her pretend she designs clothing, while Peeta paints the Hunger Games, in a move both rebellious and therapeutic. These required talents not only reflect the foolishness of the Capitol, but also the "accomplishments" that ladies of quality once learned, such as dancing, foreign languages, and embroidery. They were designed to fill a day and add to one's refinement, rather than being useful chores to bring in money (such as laundry or weaving). They were the opposite of work, serious education, or higher thought, and were used to keep ladies useless and decorative, just as Katniss the spokesmodel becomes. They are also a means of ensuring that those with fame and success are too contented to question the government.

In *Mockingjay,* former Head Gamemaker Plutarch Heavensbee describes the Capitol's obsession with *"Panem et Circenses,"* meaning "Bread and Circuses" (*M* 223). This was a Roman concept, for the Capitol itself is a mirror of Rome, the founder of Western civilization's gluttony. With plenty of bread and circuses — food and entertainment — the citizens are kept spoiled and debauched, caring nothing for politics or the deprivation of others. The founders of Panem may have named the world after this philosophy (and if the Capitol is defined by bread, the rest of Panem and the Hunger Games themselves are certainly defined by its lack). Sadly, we Americans are also living in a world of bread and circuses, filled with more entertainment channels than news. We are kept amused, distracted, fed to the point of being overfed. We can obsess like reality shows' "Real Housewives" over new cars we must have and exotic fashions we must design. But at its base, this lifestyle is frivolous, wasteful, and thoroughly artificial. Perhaps that is part of what Suzanne Collins wants us to remember. In an interview, she explains that she employed the dystopian setting of her novels to explore "the power of television and how it's used to influence our lives" (qtd. in Hudson).

The Games themselves reflect this, fought as they are in a completely synthetic environment. When Katniss enters the arena, its artificiality is emphasized in every moment. The weather and temperature are designed to kill contestants. The very wasps and jays have been artificially bred to hurt people, leaving nature a deadly snare. As Elizabeth Rees says, "Nothing in Katniss' previous experience can prepare her for the calculated, psychologically brutal nature of the Gamemakers' tricks and traps" (47). Backpacks and night-vision goggles, spontaneous "feasts," and sponsor gifts are thrown in to add to the spice, mimicking the rewards on shows like *Survivor.* And like *Survivor,* every dramatic moment must be played for the camera. As television critic Christopher Dunkley points out, "the phrase 'reality television' ... is ultimately silly because ... it places groups of people desperate for fame in the most contrived and artificial situations" (24). The golden Cornucopia, overflowing with deadly weapons, is the perfect symbol of the Games.

Katniss and her friend Rue, each named for the natural environment they embody, succeed using the skills they learned out in the country: Rue's knowledge of berries and wasp-sting remedies, Katniss's hunting skills and plant lore. Even Peeta's camouflage, as he paints himself into the natural environment and becomes part of it, is essential to keep him alive. Their lifestyle of simplicity and economy contrasts with the Capitol's lifestyle at every turn. As Katniss reflects, she and Rue are used to living in nature, used to going hungry, so they're better prepared for this survival course than the Career Tributes, who pile up supplies from the artificial Cornucopia, building a pyramid of crates and land mines as Rue and Katniss fade silently into the trees. Finally, Katniss, who despises artificiality, blows up the pyramid of supplies, using — apples! "*Let the Seventy-fourth Hunger Games begin,*" she thinks gleefully, committing to take the Careers down, rather than just survive (*HG* 226, emphasis in original). Deprived of their unfair stockpile of supplies, the Careers must fight her on an equal footing. In fact, they must now suffer through the Hunger Games as she has been, rather than lording over her. And as a girl so attuned with nature, Katniss has a chance of winning.

Running off into the forest and staying there is Katniss's great fantasy through the misery of her life; it's her image of Eden. It's also an American fantasy, as literature by James Fenimore Cooper, Washington Irving, and Henry David Thoreau focuses on the retreat into the forest, the quest for a return to nature. It offers simplicity, endless bounty, and safety from the agendas of others. But the forest remains a fantasy or only a momentary sanctuary where Katniss can slip off with Gale or can remember her father. She is imprisoned in one Game, then a second, and then in the ultimate Game of the snare-filled Capitol.

The Quarter Quell arena in that second Game offers an environment shaped like a clock, whose deadly traps switch on and off artificially. Peeta envisions it ticking away his life, with "every hour promising some new horror" (*M* 22). There are no mockingjays here, only jabberjays who torture Katniss with the cries of her loved ones. The monkeys are mutated monsters, it rains blood, and poisoned fog shrouds the land. Ever present are the force fields, a teasing, deadly reminder of the real world just beyond. This time, however, the participants use the arena's artificial nature to crack it open and escape, breaking through the phoniness and destroying it. The setup of the Games reminds Katniss that real people are torturing her for entertainment, that every player's death must be laid at their feet. The enemy of *Catching Fire* is not the survival course but frigid, calculating President Snow.

After escaping from the second arena, Katniss arrives at District 13, an even more artificial environment than the Capitol. Indeed, as critic Elizabeth M. Rees notes, "The district proves to be a distorted mirror image of the Capitol itself" (55). For while the Capitol's citizens disdain nature in favor of entertainment, District 13 is all utilitarian and grey. The Capitol glorifies in waste and excess; District 13 forbids alcohol, drugs, and indulgence. Everything is carefully controlled, from measured food portions to the schedules tattooed on each forearm to the allotted bath times. Katniss, once again miserable, finds herself seeking nature in small ways, begging to hunt for fresh food and arranging to keep Prim's cat.

Worse yet, she must be the Mockingjay, television personality. The rebels try to film Katniss on a sound stage, a faux bloody bandage on her arm and a scripted slogan on her lips. It fails. Only the genuine Katniss — grieving, loving, sacrificing — can charm her followers. When she dances at Finnick's wedding, recovers in a hospital bed, and trains for action, all her reactions are captured for the camera. She must struggle to identify her own needs, buried as they are beneath everyone's desire to use her. Vizzini says, "She is forced to consider how much of her persona is real and how much is fashioned by her many handlers, from Cinna to Haymitch to President Coin — all of whom do not end up well" (84). At last, absent of her will, Katniss's hand writes the demand, "*I KILL SNOW*" (*M* 38, emphasis in original). With most of her spirit buried in others' needs, Katniss finds that revenge still flickers within.

Assigned to the Star Squad, Katniss is trapped in a unit used for publicity shots. When her staged battles prove uninteresting on camera, a real fight is set up against Capitol booby traps, in a mission that is designed to serve as a photo shoot, so much so that Katniss's camera director, Cressida, is the one to cry, "Action!" (*M* 275). However, an unexpected trap kills Katniss's commander, shattering the photo-shoot atmosphere. Real smoke and blood replace the special effects, and the staged scene turns very ugly. In this moment, Katniss takes charge through the skill at deception she believes she has slowly come to master. Lying to the squad about a secret mission, she leads them, now a general not a pawn, as they fight on. Her buried agenda takes over, and this core of will, which has simmered beneath orders, leads them all the way to the President's mansion. The squad's survivors later reveal that they saw through her lie but wanted to follow her anyway, their Mockingjay. All the fakery for the camera has become truth.

The violence ends ironically. Katniss seems to yield to new President Coin's demands, to do all she must to fire the last shot of the war. But this shot (in the form of an arrow) is aimed at Coin, the true manipulator, the one who murders children to steal popular opinion about the war. And so Katniss rebels at last, firing her final shot at the ultimate deceiver. The former Mockingjay heals from the war only when she settles in her old district, caring for the dead and memorializing the truth of their lives in a book. She retires from all forms of media attention, keeping only her true friends Peeta and Haymitch. She returns to hunting. District 12, no longer a dangerous coal mine, becomes an agrarian culture where children laugh and play in a meadow. By returning to nature, Katniss can return to simple village life, disdaining forever the superficial world of the Capitol. For her, there is a greater truth in the forest.

We in America still dwell among the artificial lights, wastefulness, and constant entertainment filling our screens. We prefer to watch others suffer and strive than to do so ourselves. Collins warns us that an obsession with bread and circuses can lead to a dark future of apathy and callousness regarding others' suffering, something we already see in American citizens as they laugh at people's misery on *Fear Factor* or *Survivor*. Worse yet, a lifetime of deprivation for those less fortunate can soon turn to anger and revolution. Thus, Collins shows us the potential downfall of corporate America, in danger of being destroyed by the nations we've oppressed and ignored as we barely make it off our couches to protest. Our obsession with luxury has turned to blindness and a startlingly naive political reality compared with those living in other countries. It's time, Collins reminds us, that we start paying attention to the world, becoming part of it rather than just watching. The important thing is knowing where to draw the line between entertainment and reality.

WORKS CITED

Biltereyst, Daniel. "Reality TV, Troublesome Pictures and Panics: Reappraising the Public Controversy around Reality TV in Europe." Holmes and Jermyn 91–110.

Cavender, Gray. "In Search of Community on Reality TV: *America's Most Wanted* and *Survivor*." Holmes and Jermyn 154–72.

Collins, Suzanne. *Catching Fire*. New York: Scholastic, 2009. Print.

_____. "A Conversation." *Scholastic.com*. Scholastic, n.d., Web. 10 Oct. 2011.

_____. *The Hunger Games*. New York: Scholastic, 2008. Print.

_____. *Mockingjay*. New York: Scholastic, 2010. Print.

Dunkley, Christopher. "Reality TV." *Financial Times* 10 Jan. 2001: 240. Print.

Holmes, Su. "'All You've Got to Worry about Is the Task, Having a Cup of Tea, and Doing a Bit of Sunbathing': Approaching Celebrity in *Big Brother*." Holmes and Jermyn 111–35.

Holmes, Su, and Deborah Jermyn, eds. *Understanding Reality Television*. New York: Routledge, 2004. Print.

Hudson, Hannah Trierweiler. "Sit Down with Suzanne Collins." *Instructor* 120.2 (2010): 51–53. *Academic Search Complete*. EBSCO. Web. 2 Sept. 2011.

Rees, Elizabeth M. "Smoke and Mirrors: Reality vs. Unreality in the Hunger Games." Wilson 41–66.

Robinson, Matthew. *How to Get on Reality TV*. New York: Random, 2005. Print.

Vizzini, Ned. "Reality Hunger: Authenticity, Heroism, and Media in the Hunger Games." Wilson 81–98.

Wilson, Leah, ed. *The Girl Who Was on Fire*. Dallas: SmartPop-BenBella, 2011.

5

Coal Dust and Ballads

*Appalachia and District 12**

Tina L. Hanlon

It's all that coal dust, from the old days.... It was in every crack and crevice.— Catching Fire [131]

Early in *The Hunger Games,* Katniss Everdeen notes that her home was once called Appalachia and that its mines are so deep because coal has been mined there for hundreds of years. Her past-tense verbs and comments about learning these facts in school suggest that old place names are no longer used. Although the trilogy has few specific references to the places and history of America as we know it (except for the Capitol being located in the Rockies), the distancing of this futuristic nation makes it all the more significant that Appalachia is named as the location of District 12, "the smallest, poorest district" (*M* 226). The focus on coal mining and the exploitation of miners and mountain families obviously link District 12 with Appalachian history. Katniss's accounts of the injustices and deprivations suffered by miners' families resemble countless stories, real and fictional, from Appalachia and other mining regions, illustrating the human cost of industrialization. Details about the coal-town environment, hunting and the black market, folk medicine, folk music, and propaganda spread by mass media make her futuristic world recognizable to today's readers because issues of employment, law, energy, food, health care, communication, and cultural traditions are fundamental to the structure of our society and our ideals of individual rights to "life, liberty, and the pursuit of happiness."

Appalachian history is certainly not the only frame of reference for Panem, as this dystopia is full of multilayered allusions to other traditions and events, ranging from ancient gladiatorial games in Rome, to poaching in

*Portions of this essay first appeared, in an earlier form, on the author's *App.Lit* website.

Medieval Europe, to wars and slavery throughout history, to contemporary popular culture. Suzanne Collins has acknowledged that the life of Spartacus influenced her story, along with the myth of Theseus saving children from being fed to the Minotaur as tributes (Dominus 33). The Hunger Games seem barbaric, but real armies still use children and young adults as warriors and victims today. Katniss's flashback to the life-altering moment when the boy Peeta left himself open to punishment in order to give a starving girl bread from his family's bakery — an encounter that ignited Peeta's love for Katniss — reads like a scene from Charles Dickens or Victor Hugo. Descriptions of starvation and persecution in Panem also resemble accounts of the Irish Potato Famine and devastated European and Asian communities during and after World War II. The firebombing of District 12 and returning of survivors to rebuild are especially reminiscent of countless scenes after World War II when refugees sought new lives. District 12's mass grave at the end of *Mockingjay* and Katniss's memory book to honor the dead also remind us of the Holocaust, the Soviet Union, and other occurrences of starvation and genocide under totalitarian regimes. And, of course, the Hunger Games themselves and excesses of life in the Capitol have many shocking similarities with American popular culture and politics today — with celebrity worship, the popularity of survivor games and voyeuristic programming on "reality TV," and other increasingly pervasive uses of advertising and electronic media in everyday life. But this essay focuses on sociocultural parallels between Katniss's home environment and Southern Appalachia, although many conditions and traditions that characterize Appalachian cultural history are shared with other regions as well.

Roberta Herrin has written about the dearth of fantasy fiction in Appalachian children's literature, theorizing that fantasies tend to use familiar, mainstream settings as their "jumping off place," not remote, marginalized regions (10). She and other scholars of Appalachian Studies have shown that Appalachia itself "is a fantasy landscape in the American imagination" (10). However, Herrin also recognizes exceptions that "spin one fantasy world out of another ... build[ing] upon the unique history, geology, mythology, and diversity of the region" (11). In southwestern Virginia, fantasy artist Charles Vess, while working on a new graphic novel with scenes in his real hometown and on the Blue Ridge Parkway, agreed that fantasy set in Appalachia is rare but there are new developments in recent Appalachian books. Herrin concurs that "the region offers fertile soil" for new kinds of fantasy fiction (11). For example, Ruth White (in *Way Down Deep*) and George Ella Lyon (in *Gina. Jamie. Father. Bear.*) have experimented with magic realism and parallel worlds in twenty-first-century novels about Appalachian families.

Since Collins's science-fiction trilogy is set in the futuristic remnants of America, where citizens in all districts are oppressed except for privileged classes in the Capitol, the Appalachian coalfields provide one of the best historical backdrops for a dystopian view of exploited workers, especially since that exploitation continues today. Elizabeth Baird Hardy of North Carolina has described eloquently how elements of coal-town history and stereotypes "slapped onto Appalachian people" by "mainstream media" apply to District 12. Katniss and her friends Peeta and Gale belong to a long tradition of folk heroes who arise from obscurity to become lucky and heroic survivors, leaders in struggles against injustice. As in many realistic Appalachian stories, the heroes emerge from and return to a marginalized home that is torn by conflict but never defeated or forgotten, where they choose to reclaim their traditions and rebuild their lives.

The death of her father in a mine explosion is the defining event of Katniss's life before the Hunger Games. The suffering and deprivations of her youth initially make Katniss a rebel in a brutal, oppressive society. Although he was compelled to work as a miner, Katniss's father, like many Appalachians, knew how to live off the land, and he taught his older daughter useful skills. In Panem, however, hunting and gathering plants mean breaking the law. As in early-twentieth-century Appalachian coal towns, Katniss's and Gale's families have few rights after the fathers' deaths in the mines. They received a small sum to cover six months of mourning and then nothing more. Katniss resents her mother's period of helpless depression, which required her, still a child, to care for her mother and younger sister. In Gretchen Moran Laskas's historical novel *The Miner's Daughter,* sixteen-year-old Willa faces similar challenges when her pregnant mother is ill and her family is destitute. As mines open and close in the 1930s, her father barely survives working away from home on a construction project that killed hundreds of laborers, West Virginia's Hawks Nest Tunnel. Willa struggles with hunger, grueling housework, her longing for books and schooling, and discrimination when she wants to work harvesting food as men and boys do in summer. When her family moves to Eleanor Roosevelt's utopian new town, Arthurdale, Willa questions the racism that prevents friends from living there and hopes to use her writing to protest against injustice in the future. Katniss's role in a more brutal dystopian world plunges her into more extreme forms of rebellion throughout Collins's trilogy.

The first chapter of *The Hunger Games* shows that Katniss and Gale are resourceful enough and rebellious enough to help their families by hunting, fishing, and gathering plants illegally, venturing into forbidden meadows and woods that are fenced in (supposedly for the protection of citizens). They trade on the thriving black market and sell goods to district officials who can afford to buy delicacies such as wild berries. Ripper, a woman who lost an arm in a mine accident, sells illegal liquor like many past and present moonshiners in Appalachia. Miners live in the Seam, a poor area where people with "hunched shoulders, swollen knuckles ... stopped trying to scrub the coal dust out of their broken nails ..." (*HG* 4). Katniss suspects that school isn't teaching about past rebellions; most of the education revolves around coal and what localities owe the Capitol. Periodically, Katniss mentions that coal dust drifts into everything in her district. When the black-market warehouse is burned in *Catching Fire,* she sees it oozing from the smoking ruins as black liquid. In *Mockingjay,* after District 12 has been destroyed by firebombing, she learns that Gale saved their families by taking them to a secret spot away from dust-filled wooden houses that burned to the ground, and his knowledge of hunting and fishing sustained the 800 survivors for three days.

Even before the firebombing, District 12 suffers as Panem collapses. After rebellions begin, the mines are closed for two weeks as punishment and people starve. Then miners are "sent into blatantly dangerous work sites" with longer hours and less pay while promised food supplies rot or fail to appear (*CF* 131–32). Katniss worries about Gale, who is now working in the mines, where he is at the mercy of those in power. Conditions during these times are reminiscent of periods of conflict over the organization of unions and strikes in twentieth-century Appalachia. James Still's novels *River of Earth* and *Sporty Creek* contain especially dismal views of Kentucky coal towns during the Great Depression, with employment in nonunion mines stopping and starting based on market forces and corporate decisions far away from the mines. Families in Still's novels wander back and forth between the coal camp that no one cares to maintain decently, with no job security, and their mountain home-place, unable in either location to feed their families well. The film *Matewan* is one of the most widely known accounts of a historical "mine war" in Matewan, West Virginia, with demoralizing and dangerous working conditions below ground while disputes above ground about strikes and unionization escalate into a bloody gun battle. In Panem, hunger and the Hunger Games are designed to hold all citizens hostage, to prevent another uprising against unfair working and living conditions. The trilogy and *Matewan* show not only that rebellion is inevitable, but also that those fighting for justice can find themselves torn by conflicting loyalties and pressured to make violent choices.

In *Mockingjay,* Katniss describes her father's death in detail, after Gale's proposal to bomb an army hidden in a District 2 mountain stronghold revives memories that make her question an action that would be like causing a devastating coal mine accident. Although she wants to declare that the people in the mountain should die, her District 12 origin makes her unable to condemn others to death in the way that President Snow does. Because of the mountain's history as a mine, she expects that anyone from District 12 would hesitate to kill those trapped inside, District 2 citizens in the service of the Capitol. Thus, the rebels decide to leave a train tunnel as an escape route. During the melee, Katniss impulsively tries to help an armed but wounded District 2 soldier because he reminds her of an injured miner. They are all pawns of the Capitol, she tells him — just before another soldier shoots her.

In the midst of this crisis, Katniss feels that her father is "everywhere today" (*M* 211). Missing him pains her because she is reminded of him in so many ways — by the fiery deaths in this old mine, by protective care from a man guarding her, and by hearing that her brainwashed friend Peeta responded positively to hearing one of her father's old songs. Her flashback describing the family and community vigil at the site of a coal mine disaster resembles many past and present stories from Appalachia and other mining regions. In Lee Smith's compelling novel *Fair and Tender Ladies,* for example, a similar scene in southwestern Virginia is a traumatic turning point in the life of Ivy Rowe in about 1920. It makes Ivy realize she loves a young miner who survives the mine accident. Together they leave the coal town that seemed like such a mecca of upward mobility to return to farming on the mountain where they were raised, while Ivy's newly widowed neighbor Violet goes away to spend years working for unionization, even leaving her daughter behind to be raised by Ivy after the mine disaster. Katniss's continuing nightmares about her father's death and memories of his many songs that she never sings illustrate how industrialization brings emotional as well as economic losses to exploited citizens. In Panem, the extreme contrast between living conditions in District 12 and the luxuries and technological marvels of the Capitol echoes old stereotypes about backwardness and poverty in rural Appalachia (where modernization sometimes lagged behind mainstream America); the contrast also reflects serious realities of our world in which the poor still do dangerous work while the rich get richer and enjoy luxuries provided by those workers. Miners still die, and Appalachian families today live in homes where dust from passing coal trucks damages their health even though technology could reduce those risks.

Those contrasts are especially dramatic in the area of health care, since District 12 has no modern medicine, at least not in the Seam. Katniss's mother, the daughter of an apothecary who left the merchant class to marry a miner, knows folk medicine and uses all kinds of healing methods to treat the sick and wounded who have no doctors. The trilogy's depiction of folk medicine links District 12 with the history of Appalachia and other traditional cultures where modern science has never completely displaced folk practices and society is reconsidering ways to blend the best of both approaches. Moreover, in Appalachia and other parts of the world today, many rural citizens have neither health insurance nor the means to travel to cities for medical care, creating a general lack of access to modern medicine. The folk medicine practiced by Katniss's mother is effective and has a human dimension lacking in the impersonal, high-tech treatments Katniss receives in the Capitol and District 13.

But folk medicine has limitations, and those who are seriously ill or injured have so little chance of survival that even artificial respiration is unknown in District 12. In *Catching Fire,* Katniss observes a tribute from another district using mouth-to-mouth resuscitation and thinks at first that he's doing harm because she has never seen it, although she lives with one of her district's most skilled healers.

During the Hunger Games Katniss uses her knowledge of plants, along with her hunting skills, although she does not have the gifts for tending the sick that her gentle mother and sister have. While she learns in her first trip to the Capitol that incredible medical cures are possible when the government chooses to provide medical care, we become increasingly aware of how dehumanizing that treatment can be and how brutal her society is for withholding care from all but the privileged few. The government has no remnants of our contemporary ideals about providing medical treatment for poor citizens, criminals, or victims of war. Katniss's mother treats Gale through a long, painful recovery in *Catching Fire* after he is physically punished for hunting illegally. In *Mockingjay,* Katniss's mother and sister, Prim, use whatever they can get in the woods to try healing the injured after District 12 is bombed. Then they work in a District 13 hospital during the war of rebellion. When Prim begins medical training, she says that she knows about medical care from her home experience although she still has much to learn. The idea of Prim's training to be a doctor gives Katniss hope that the rebellion can bring a brighter future, until she sees her sister, whom she has worked so hard to protect for years, die by fire while bringing medical aid to a crowd of children being bombed in front of the President's house, where they were gathered as a human shield.

After the war ends, their mother goes to start a hospital in District 4. In her period of isolation and recovery back in District 12 at the end of the trilogy, Katniss, who is named after an edible plant, saves her family's plant book. It gives her the idea to create a memory book with pictures and reminiscences of people they have lost. When Prim's bedraggled cat, Buttercup, shows up, Katniss nurses it back to health and releases her grief with the cat for company. Peeta brings primroses to plant in her sister's memory by her house. All these images of plants providing physical healing, emotional comfort, and food contribute to the trilogy's demonstration from beginning to end that living with nature is a basic human right and necessity. The Mockingjay, a manufactured celebrity persona for Katniss, is also based on a creature of nature and home. Artificial wilderness settings in the vast Hunger Games arenas are designed to cause injury and death, showing how sadistic humans can use technology to pervert nature, while the remnants of District 12's population who survive and choose to return home show that they can plow under the ashes and grow food. They will also build a factory to produce medicines. Without depicting folk medicine as harmful or maligned by accusations of superstition or witchery, these novels acknowledge that it is limited and needs to be combined in humane ways with modern medical practices. As in depressed areas around Appalachian coalfields today, health care also provides employment outside mines.

Another cultural tradition that helps to rescue Katniss's humanity centers on folk music — the ballads and "mountain airs" she had learned from her father and recalls during some of her most painful crises. When a younger ally, Rue, is dying in the first book, she asks Katniss to sing. Katniss recalls that her house was full of music when she sang along with her father's wonderful voice, but after he died she seldom sang except when her sister was sick. Then she remembers a very old lullaby from the hills that soothed fussy babies, with words promising that tomorrow would be better than today's dismal conditions. Mockingjay birds repeat the song "almost eerily" after Katniss sings for Rue (*HG* 235). The lyrics are repeated in the trilogy's epilogue as Katniss observes her children enjoying nature without knowing they play on the mass grave of district war victims. With limited knowledge of cruelty and suffering, they take for granted the comforting words of the old lullaby about love in the meadow.

Years earlier, during the wartime wedding of friends from District 4, traditions from different districts are blended. Katniss mentions kisses, cheers, and toasting with apple cider. The only fiddler from District 12 to survive with his instrument plays a tune that attracts the attention of everyone from the bombed-out district; they instinctively rise to dance and form a whirling circle around the bride and groom. Katniss and Prim dance well together since they had plenty of winter evenings to practice, and now they can escape into a rare interlude of carefree fun. When they teach District 13 guests how to dance and proudly demonstrate their footwork, Katniss could be referring to Appalachian clogging or flatfoot dancing, which mountain people of all ages continue to enjoy in formal and informal settings.

When Katniss is imprisoned after invading the Capitol and then demonstrating the complex layers of betrayal in this trilogy by assassinating the rebels' president, she considers suicide until she unexpectedly begins to sing day and night; she continues nonstop for weeks, hearing only her own voice. "Hour after hour of ballads, love songs, mountain airs" pour from her mouth (*M* 376). She is amazed that she knows the music and lyrics of her father's songs so well after years with little music in her life. Her voice improves as it warms up, and she imagines the mockingjays listening, wanting to sing with her. After the war ends, a rebel leader asks Katniss to appear on a new singing program he is planning, hoping she will perform something lively. But like many Appalachian people who live the oral traditions without pursuing fame or fortune, Katniss is not destined to become a singing star. In Virginia Hamilton's

M. C. Higgins, the Great, the protagonist hopes his mother's exceptional singing will make her famous and allow them to escape from the mountain where their home is threatened by strip mining and a slag heap, until a folk song collector who wanted to record her voice while it was so "unspoiled and beautiful" like the hills convinces M. C. that commercial success would change and spoil his mother (240). For Katniss, the rediscovery of music through experiences that are both public and deeply personal connects her with the people she loves.

During the war, Katniss sings the forbidden song "The Hanging Tree" for the first time in ten years (*M* 123), to wipe out more painful memories of her friends' deaths evoked by mockingjay birds imitating her old lullaby. She sings at this point in *Mockingjay* because she cannot turn down the request of her fellow rebel Pollux, a former slave who cannot sing himself because his tongue has been cut out by the Capitol. When the birds imitate this song after she sings four stanzas sweetly, as her father had done, she remembers a day when her mother had screamed at them to stop. Katniss was seven, innocently making rope necklaces like the ones in the song. This prohibition made Katniss remember the song perfectly, but she and her father never sang it again. She reinterpreted the lyrics gradually as she grew older. Hangings were real in District 12, and her mother hadn't wanted her to sing the song in public (or, when she was older, to speak out in other ways that could put her in danger). The child Katniss thought the dead murderer in the ballad "was the creepiest guy imaginable" (*M* 126), calling his lover to join him at the hanging tree. But after experiencing the horrors of the Hunger Games and war, in which her own benevolent and brutal actions have had complex motivations, she realizes there are multiple possible interpretations of the dead man's words in the ballad. She wonders whether he thought he left the woman in a place "really worse than death" when he called her to be free with him (*M* 126). Gale has a different perspective and compares himself to "The Hanging Tree" man, waiting for an answer since he loves Katniss and she does not return his love as he would wish.

When "The Hanging Tree" makes Pollux cry, Katniss fears she has revived some horrible memory of his, yet it sounds beautiful when the mockingjays repeat it. Then we are reminded that the song has been filmed for one of the rebellion's propaganda videos. Katniss is only effective in her role of symbolic spokesperson when she is being spontaneous, and one of the leaders says this video would not be believed if they had made it up, that she is "golden!" (*M* 127). This same leader observes at the wedding that the spontaneity of District 12 people is a benefit of having been neglected by the Capitol, since it shows well on TV. Appalachian folk traditions, including murder ballads, can seem wild and strange and spontaneous, but they are also exploited to promote both social justice and corporate interests. The CBS television network dropped plans for a reality show called *The Real Beverly Hillbillies* after the

United Mine Workers and many other advocacy groups protested in 2003 against ridiculing rural people by setting up a real Appalachian family in a Hollywood mansion. CBS's chairman commented that the network then planned an Amish reality show because they "don't have quite as good a lobbying effort" (Weinraub). Katniss's role as a showy figurehead in the spotlight deteriorates after Peeta's brainwashing turns him against her and she watches herself being shot on television. But folk music, which is absent through her adolescence and the first two books, is gradually reintegrated into her life as a personal part of her recovery.

The Hunger Games trilogy fulfills Collins's goal of depicting the horrors of war and totalitarian oppression for young adult readers (Dominus). Some readers are shocked at the extent to which — even after Katniss and Peeta survive two rounds of violent Hunger Games — the rebellion and their roles in it become complicated by corruption, betrayal, and further debilitating injuries rather than establishing a new era of peace and justice for Panem. Collins's dystopia does not offer solutions to the massive problems of the world, but like many earlier works of fiction, it does show through Katniss's return home that individuals and small groups of people can rebuild peaceful communities. Although Appalachians do not have a monopoly on the value of lifelong loyalty to home, they have an exceptionally strong tradition of devotion to home and returning home for those who are inspired or compelled to spend parts of their lives elsewhere. While the mines are closed after District 12 is firebombed, nearly everything else associated with Katniss's home district has been a positive influence throughout the trilogy, contributing to her self-sufficiency and her healing in the end. Many loved ones cannot return, yet Katniss has her father's hunting jacket, her sister's cat, and the plant book to represent her memories, along with her ability to rebuild personal relationships and renew skills that her family and friends taught her. Greasy Sae, the tough black-market dealer who returns in the role of benevolent grandmother and housekeeper during Katniss's recovery period, encourages her to go out and hunt. Katniss has inherited knowledge of folk medicine and the music and faith in nature's ability to renew the land. The traces of Appalachian history woven throughout the trilogy provide an appropriate framework for this story in which the heroes grow up in and return to a home that is labeled as backward and ravaged by war and oppression but is valued as home, as a place where people can reclaim the land, hunt and bake, revive their cultural traditions, seek healing, and raise children.

WORKS CITED

Collins, Suzanne. *Catching Fire*. New York: Scholastic, 2009. Print.
_____. *The Hunger Games*. New York: Scholastic, 2008. Print.
_____. *Mockingjay*. New York: Scholastic, 2010. Print.

Dominus, Susan. "'I Write About War. For Adolescents.'" *New York Times Magazine* 8 Apr. 2011: 30–33. Print.

Hamilton, Virginia. *M. C. Higgins, the Great.* New York: Aladdin, 1974. Print.

Hardy, Elizabeth Baird. "EBH: Don't Go down in the Hole — Coal Mining Life in District 12 and in Present-Day Appalachia." *Hogwarts Professor: Thoughts for Serious Readers.* John Granger Blog, 14 Apr. 2010. Web. 25 Apr. 2011.

Herrin, Roberta T. Preface. *Appalachian Children's Literature: An Annotated Bibliography.* Ed. Roberta T. Herrin and Sheila Quinn Oliver. Jefferson: McFarland, 2010. 3–11. Print.

Laskas, Gretchen Moran. *The Miner's Daughter.* New York: Simon & Schuster, 2007. Print.

Lyon, George Ella. *Gina. Jamie. Father. Bear.* New York: Atheneum, 2002. Print.

Matewan. Dir. John Sayles. Cinecom Entertainment Group. Lorimar Home Video. 1987. Videocassette.

Smith, Lee. *Fair and Tender Ladies.* New York: Ballantine, 1988. Print.

Still, James. *River of Earth.* 1940. Lexington: University Press of Kentucky, 1996. Print.

_____. *Sporty Creek.* 1977. Lexington: University Press of Kentucky, 1999. Print.

Vess, Charles. "Drawing on That Old Magic: Writing and Illustrating Fantasy." Children's Literature Assn. 38th Annual Conf. Hollins University, Roanoke, VA. 25 June 2011. Panel Discussion.

Weinraub, Bernard. "UPN Show Is Called Insensitive to Amish." *New York Times* 4 Mar. 2004, late ed.: E1. *Lexis Nexis.* Web. 16 Sept. 2011.

White, Ruth. *Way Down Deep.* New York: Farrar, 2007. Print.

6

The "Fine Reality of Hunger Satisfied"

Food as Cultural Metaphor in Panem

MAX DESPAIN

The destiny of nations depends on how they nourish themselves.—Jean Anthelme Brillat-Savarin, *The Physiology of Taste*

Suzanne Collins appeals to the most pervasive quality of culture when she centers the dissatisfaction of a dystopian future North America around the absence and abundance of food. Recognizing gastronomy as the essential descriptor of society and culture, she traces Katniss Everdeen from the most basic and uncultivated acts of hunting and gathering through her negotiation with the depraved political system in the sophisticated Capitol. Massimo Montanari, historian of food and culture, writes that food *is* culture and that food becomes one of "the most effective means of expressing and communicating that identity" (xi). Similarly, historian Donna R. Gabaccia insists that in order to "understand changing American identities, we must explore also the symbolic power of food to reflect cultural or social affinities in moments of change or transition" (9). I think that Collins concurs with these ideas when she maps out her characters' impulses for and against power as well as their yearning for justice and love through the alternately meager and opulent food portions they encounter. Collins consistently reveals her complex understanding of food as a metaphor for cultural, social, political, and personal longing when she produces a dystopian future where a brewing rebellion is best portrayed through hunger, and independence comes when that hunger and its metaphorical substitutes are finally satisfied.

The Hunger Games opens with the dysfunctional Panem society teetering in an imbalance of power portrayed by an imbalance of food. The Capitol reaps all of the benefits of the twelve districts' harvests and products while the districts themselves function at near starvation on substandard Capitol handouts. This unusual culture, rooted somehow out of contemporary America, reveals its complexities through social habits best portrayed in its use of food. Anthropologist E. N. Anderson describes culture as the rules, customs, and other shared plans and behaviors that result from interaction. He goes on to define culture as practice oriented, suggesting that "foodways" fall under the structure of class, gender, ethnic, and regional identities (6). Where Anderson's ideas dovetail into *The Hunger Games* trilogy is with his claim that "food is used in every society to communicate messages. Preeminent among these are messages of group solidarity" (6). Each outlying district in Panem forms an identity around not only the products the district is known for but also the ways in which its citizens cope with their lack of food.

The Capitol government has written the perfect recipe for revolution by producing an "us vs. them" mentality between itself and the districts. Although the Capitol practices important forms of isolation (including fencing out forbidden areas) to prevent the districts from developing group solidarity and joining forces, the people realize that the Capitol lives in luxury and leisure denied to the outliers. The Capitol further practices its tyranny over the districts by requiring tributes between the ages of twelve and eighteen to fight to the death as punishment for the last organized rebellion, of more than seventy years before. Collins claims the penalty was inspired by the Greek myth of Theseus and his defeat of the tribute-fed Minotaur ("Conversation"). The Hunger Games are televised, arena death matches between unlucky lottery-drawn children from the districts. Much the same as in the myth of Theseus when the hero lifted a rock to reveal the sword left to him by his father, Katniss counts on her father's foresight when she retrieves bows and arrows from hiding places in the woods outside the District 12 fence. She couples these weapons with important life lessons learned from her father in the wild to become the ultimate warrior against the manipulative Capitol. She begins the custom of group solidarity through her food practices outside the Capitol-determined boundaries of District 12 via the tradition built through her father's lessons.

Tapping into the complex contemporary guilt Americans feel about indulgence, abundance, and weight gain, Collins can count on her readers to find the Everdeen family's hand-to-mouth existence as unfamiliar as the hovercraft in her narrative. The future nation of Panem's evolutionary roots stem from present-day America, as evidenced by references to the Rocky Mountains and familiar regional food and manufactured goods production. Historian Harvey Levenstein writes that America's current culture has learned how to ensure an abundant food supply, but that ability gives us little satisfaction (256). We can recognize similar sentiments in the Capitol—but the outlying districts are starving. Collins seems to suggest that the bizarre structure of her future dystopia partially developed from the skewed, present-day perception Americans have about food. Levenstein notes from a cross-cultural study about many nations' attitudes toward food that "there is a sense among many Americans ... that food is as much a poison as it is a nutrient" (256). Collins clings to this theme of the poisonous quality of food throughout the novel as the connotation of foodstuff moves from daily sustenance to political power play, especially in Katniss's clever act of rebellion with the food-that-is-not-food: nightlock berries.

Katniss's defiant act finds fertile soil among the people in the district forced to watch the Hunger Games. More than crushing the districts with a long-standing debt of inferior food doled out as "tesserae," supplemental rations in exchange for extra entries in the reaping (*HG* 13), the Capitol actually forces independent thinking and action among its citizens by requiring the starving people to supplement their meager allotments by using ingenuity and illegal behavior. Food historian Reay Tannahill describes the shift from hunting and gathering to civilization as "tying [people] to the land they farmed and increasing their awareness of boundaries ... stimulat[ing] a sense of social unity and a recognition of communal need" (43). Still bound to District 12 at a community level, Katniss must slip out of the fence and seek further sustenance for her family to satisfy their need for nutrition, partly because her father dies before she is old enough to trade additional lottery entries for more provisions. As a hunter and gatherer, Katniss can operate independently and keep her family alive. Pairing with Gale is her first conscious experience with improving her chances of survival through social connections — the first step towards more society. They join District 12's underground social structure when they illegally trade their goods. Collins works with the origins of human social development (loose groups of hunters and gatherers), whisking Katniss through rapidly increasing levels of "civilization" until she arrives in the hyperbole of human society: the Capitol. As if proving what abundance and excess can lead to, the hyper-civilization in the Capitol is much more barbaric than the more "primitive" outlying districts.

Long before she becomes uprooted from the only community she has experienced, Katniss must be saved by human connections and mankind's ingenuity when Peeta rescues her from despair with burnt bread. While much of the food Katniss and Gale procure emphasizes their individuality and independence, Peeta becomes known, by the end of the first book, as the "boy with the bread" (*HG* 374), a symbol for cultivation and community. Montanari writes that "Bread does not exist in nature and only man knows how to make it" (6). Collins uses her Capitol to suggest that human society can be debauched and cruel when allowed undue control over other people, yet ultimately she uses Peeta's connection to bread as a symbol of the need for some form of community. When Katniss and her family surely would have died, the product that draws from nature's harvest but only becomes a digestible foodstuff through the processing of civilized humans is the key link that keeps Katniss going long enough for her to remember how to gather food, begin hunting, and become old enough to sign up for a tessera. This social quality of bread rises throughout the trilogy from saving Katniss and her family at their darkest, hungriest moment, to a community's thanks for Katniss's tender, elegiac lullaby at Rue's death, and finally to the representation of a rebel plan when the type and number of rolls signal the moment of rebellion in the Quarter Quell. Collins takes advantage of the uniquely civilized quality of bread versus the foodstuff that can be foraged to represent the way social groups exert more control over their food sources, a control that matches increasing sophistication in their political and cultural power.

As Katniss travels away from District 12 for the first time, food traditions continue to reveal the groundwork for revolution in *The Hunger Games.* From the opulent provisions on the high-speed train to meals available at the push of a button, Katniss's relationship with food immediately evolves from sustenance to social definition as she arrives at the Capitol. While food also held a social role in the Seam to celebrate special events, Katniss realizes that the abundance of food in the Capitol causes the people there to take their plenty for granted. Mentally calculating the days of hunting and gathering required to make a poor approximation of the first lavish meal with Cinna, her stylist, Katniss translates the meal before her into terms she understands. Then she agrees when Cinna offers the observation that she must find him and the other Capitol residents "despicable" (*HG* 65). And she does, but not before she has mentally run through questions about the amount of leisure time these people must have since they don't have to seek out food. This leisure alters the symbolism present in the provisions that largely functioned to keep her alive at home. Food is a political and cultural status symbol in the Capitol. By learning to read her meals as narratives about the antagonist sending her to fight for her life, Katniss is adding arrows to her quiver to defend herself against this greedy government.

The symbolic quality of food has a long lineage in Western history that Collins fully explores in her appalling Capitol. Because this community has nearly absolute control over the outlying districts, Panem has arrived at the point of present-day America: there is food in abundance, but that bounty is only available to a certain percentage of the population. Now that meals are no longer solely about sustenance, the food takes on the qualities of sumptuousness to symbolize prosperity. Similarly, near the turn of the twentieth century, French chefs focused on the appearance of food over flavor. The Capitol has both taste and appearance in favor of its extravagant banquets, but the galas remain largely about vulgar pretension. Reading about the relationship between food and affectation in the work of famous French chef

Marie-Antoine Carême, science journalist Jonah Lehrer writes that "fancy cooking was synonymous with ostentation. As long as dinner *looked* decadent, its actual taste was pretty irrelevant. Appearance was everything" (62). These lines about late-nineteenth-century French fare parallel the debauched society in Panem's Capitol, where the citizens' gluttony is common practice.

The ultimate example is the final banquet after the Victory Tour in *Catching Fire,* where lavishly outfitted people indulge in culinary delights beyond imagination. Alluding to the Roman practice of using emetics in order to be more excessive (Anthon 352), Katniss's prep team insists that regurgitating the delicacies is an important part of the experience because there is too much delicious and wonderful food to stop when they are full. Katniss notes that "here in the Capitol they're vomiting for the pleasure of filling their bellies again and again ... not from some illness ... [or] spoiled food" (*CF* 80). Remembering the emaciated children of District 12, Peeta and Katniss struggle with the affection they have for the prep teams they've come to know and the sharp contrast with their own life experiences. The immediate mental connection Katniss draws between the actual children's death match of the Hunger Games and the careless attitudes Capitol residents demonstrate towards the most precious of necessities from Katniss's home cements the direct correlation between the corrupt social food habits and the degenerate political practices in the Capitol.

Just as Katniss learns to interpret food differently after a short time in the Capitol, she also uses taste as another important function of eating, to discern the political nature of food and consumption in this unusual society. An important role of taste itself is learning to distinguish particular flavors from the entire grouping of food. Lehrer writes that when we "parse our sensations," we make choices about what we "think we are sensing," claiming that "this unconscious act of interpretation is largely driven by contextual clues" (67). Reading *The Hunger Games* trilogy from the perspective of hunger and eating helps us connect the neuroscience of taste to Katniss's increasingly mature understanding of the political foods around her, not in terms of actual flavor, but in the ideas the meals represent. When Lehrer notes that "what we taste is ultimately an *idea* and that our sensations are strongly influenced by their context" (68, emphasis added), we can read this description in the context of the trilogy and understand how the cuisine in the Capitol takes on social and political importance. Each step of Katniss's parsing must be tempered against her father's advice that if she can find herself, she'll "never starve" (*HG* 52). Literally, Katniss's father reveals the multilayered possibilities in food when he teases out the double meaning in Katniss's name: finding food for survival in the bluish tubers she's named after and finding confidence in herself as an individual to satisfy her metaphorical hungers. Complexly, then, finding herself is the key to literal and figurative survival. She tastes the world around her, not only through the food she eats but also through extending the weighted meaning behind her meals to the metaphorical qualities of love and justice that she hungers for. The emblematic hunger to find fairness in her government, paired with her own figurative quality as both a foodstuff and an individual person, turns Katniss into the social and political symbol representing the hunger for justice felt in some way by all the districts required to provide tributes to the Hunger Games.

A literal case of taste becoming complicated with ideas occurs when Katniss finds the Capitol's lamb stew with dried plums delicious. Fresh with thoughts of longing for Gale and excitement over her big eleven training score, she is halfway through the stew on a bed of wild rice before she recognizes that the silence around her means something. Learning that Peeta wants to be coached for the interview alone, her first feeling is betrayal. The dish of lamb stew now indicates moments when Katniss is out of control and at the mercy of the Capitol. Found completely lacking by Haymitch in her interview prep and floundering for an answer to the first question posed to her in the interview about what most impresses her in the Capitol, she manages to say it is the lamb stew. Based on her already critical appraisal of the lavish meal of chicken and oranges in a cream sauce with peas and pearl onions shared with Cinna, she knows that all the food in the Capitol symbolically taunts the impoverished need in the districts and flaunts the cavalier attitude of the rulers. Perhaps the earthy quality of stew appeals to the less sophisticated Katniss. Yet interviewer Caesar Flickerman takes control of the answer by not only designating *which* lamb stew she means by mentioning the dried plums, but also by replying that he eats it "by the bucketful" (*HG* 127). The power in the answer remains with Caesar, who subtly reminds his viewers of the opulent food choices he enjoys over Katniss's most special memory from the Capitol, and she remains the symbolic lamb, slaughtered for the stew.

More importantly, the stew's last appearance in the trilogy comes in the arena when Katniss and Peeta, trapped by bad, Gamemaker-made weather, experience severe hunger. Katniss has feelings for Peeta but works on convincing herself she's playing the Game. She knows just the words to say in order to receive a sponsor gift to alleviate their suffering, but she has to force out her private and, as such, reluctant sentiments. The prize is the lamb stew, symbolic of the power everyone outside the arena wields over her and Peeta's fate and the rewards she might reap if she will only conform to the Capitol's ideology. Collins's word choice, "[t]he very dish I told Caesar Flickerman was the most impressive thing the Capitol had to offer" (*HG* 302), suggests the way in which the stew denotes Capitol control over Katniss's destiny. The connection with the Capitol and its ruthless methods of subduing the districts causes the stew finally to become glue in her mouth, food she can't swallow when she learns Thresh is dead. Despite her literal hunger, the figurative ethical cost of enjoying the Capitol's provisions makes them unpalatable in the face of the government's wanton disregard for children's lives in its play to keep power over the subdued.

In contrast with the lamb stew, the berries Peeta gathers the next day become powerful only with Katniss's ability to interpret them, not through her pre–Hunger Games training but through the lens of the homegrown knowledge passed down by her father. Directly foreshadowing the ending of the first book, Katniss holds out a handful of the berries to Peeta when he asks how he could have killed Foxface. In the crucial moment when Katniss realizes that if both she and Peeta die, the Capitol won't have a victor, she holds out the berries again. In a distant nod to present-day Americans' attitudes that food is poison (Levenstein 256), Collins brings together a history of food that evolves into the Capitol's debauchery. Katniss defeats a powerful and corrupt government first by learning to analyze the unusual rhetoric of food in the Capitol and then by translating that knowledge into willingly ingesting a food-that-is-not-food to play off the Capitol's nuanced reading of eating. However, the narrative doesn't end with the first novel because the districts' hunger for justice isn't satisfied. District 12's rebellious act in the arena triggers a Panem-wide, grassroots uprising.

The plenty that Katniss experiences in the wake of her victory does not eliminate her need to scavenge for food. Even though she has earned individual comfort with enough food and money as a victor, her community of District 12 (particularly the Seam) sees almost no benefit from their tributes' coup. The implications of bread and civilization addressed earlier underscore bread's role as the secret code for the breakout from the arena in *Catching Fire*. And when the actual revolution takes hold, based out of the underground District 13, Collins still employs the social and cultural implications of food to describe the shifts in power. The strict rules about food motivate Katniss to claim that District 13 has methods that might be interpreted as more domineering than the Capitol. Initially, the newcomers to District 13 can scarcely consume the rations because of the unsavory and slimy quality of the food. However, a shift in the success of the revolution not only causes a shortage of fresh fruit in the Capitol but also, eventually, a boon of real food for the rebels provided by District 10. Collins describes the ineffable qualities that excellent food brings to a group when Katniss depicts "the rejuvenating effect" of tasty and well-prepared food, making the community's attitude invigorate under the delicious nutrition, noting that "it's better than any medicine" (*M* 241). The improved rations resulting from gaining revolutionary power encourage the diners to hope for a better future as a result of their rebellious actions.

Collins continues the layered meaning in food when she carries the symbolic nightlock forward in the name of District 13's cyanide-like purple-pills-that-are-not-berries — a poison provided so captured rebels can commit suicide rather than reveal secrets. While the rebels continue hungering for justice, Collins moves beyond recognizable food by playing with the multilayered meaning in the berries-that-are-not-food that began the insurgency. Nightlock continues as the symbol of revolt against the Capitol since the essential holographic map device for Katniss's final mission will explode with a five-yard destruction radius when anyone in the squadron repeats "nightlock" three times. Assigning this moniker to the destruction of rebels maintains the powerful political connection Katniss gave the term when she defeated the Capitol with the original berries. When Katniss finally has to employ the nightlock function with the map, the threat of nightlock first presented at the end of the Seventy-fourth Hunger Games becomes a reality when the explosion sprays the group with bits of mutt and human flesh, killing both the Capitol's abominations and Katniss's close-knit companions with its destructive quality. Nightlock as poisonous berries first became a rebellious political concept, then shifted into an intentional rhetorical twist that has become a literal weapon of war: politics by other means (Clausewitz).

District 13 and its President Coin conduct the war against the Capitol. As a symbol for the rebel cause formed through her radical acts as tribute and victor, Katniss has more need than ever to follow her father's advice to find herself. A prime example of the distance between her role as the rebellion's Mockingjay and her personal grievance with the Capitol occurs when the Capitol-trained rebel and media specialist, Fulvia, scripts propaganda for Katniss to act out. A person of action, Katniss has trouble delivering the canned line about people fighting to end their *"hunger for justice"* (*M* 72, emphasis in original). Although she feels the same passion, she can express her patriotic spirit only in genuine moments akin to the times she hunted for food to satiate her family's hunger. Knowing this distinction is part of finding herself according to her father's instructions. Her genuine passion for justice and the need to know herself come together when Peeta describes how killing people "costs everything you are" (*M* 23) and when Katniss meets with President Snow. Despite her resistance, Katniss understands that her archrival Snow is no longer the threat and that the new government under Coin also does not value human life, making it the new threat. When Katniss departs her meeting with Snow, the ethical rebel commander from District 8, Paylor, asks her if she found what she was looking for. Paylor's question highlights how Katniss has spent this entire trilogy searching for and coming to understand her identity in context of the corrupt government that has overseen her way of life. The moment brings the metaphorical quality of food in this trilogy full circle as Katniss finds herself, a girl quite literally named for the bluish tuber that is good to eat, and realizes that her purpose is ensuring that she and all of

Panem will never again starve — by ending the population's metaphorical hunger for justice. When she finds herself, she becomes the most elemental quality of food as a social and political metaphor by killing Coin and ending the people of Panem's communal hunger.

While Katniss's act sets a more humanistic government into motion under Paylor, she knows none of these facts when isolated in her old tribute room, presumably awaiting trial for assassinating Coin. Instead, she recognizes the cost Peeta described in killing people and rationalizes the choice to commit suicide by starving herself before she can be put to death for her act. In another rhetorical play on food, Katniss deprives the new government the pleasure of "consuming" her for her actions. With starvation as the only option, "the animal part of [her]" takes over and she eats on occasion (*M* 376), keeping herself alive. Katniss has found herself, has understood her role in the rebellion; now the most rudimentary part of her being will not let her starve, just as her father had promised. With her limited pardon to live out her days in the remains of District 12 comes the evidence of Panem's hunger satisfied. Justice is served, fairness takes a new root, and people begin their lives anew. With healing, Katniss will discover she has another hunger she needs to resolve: a desire for love.

Collins has undertaken the metaphorical complexity of food in the spirit of famous food writer M. F. K. Fisher when we can note that this trilogy is, as Fisher described her own writing to be, about "love and the hunger for it, and warmth and the love of it and the hunger for it ... and then the warmth and richness and fine reality of hunger satisfied" (13). When the larger cultural and social hungers of Panem are satisfied, all that is left is for Katniss to find a way forward. Her hunger to live finds its partner in Peeta, the boy with the bread, and with their hope for the future.

WORKS CITED

Anderson, E. N. *Everyone Eats: Understanding Food and Culture.* New York: New York University Press, 2005. Print.

Anthon, Charles. *A Dictionary of Greek and Roman Antiquities.* Ed. William Smith. New York: Harper, 1857. Hathi Digital Library. *hathitrust.org,* Web. 20 Aug. 2011.

Brillat-Savarin, Jean-Anthelme. *The Physiology of Taste.* 1825. Trans. M. F. K. Fisher. New York: Everyman's, 2009. Print.

Clausewitz, Carl von. *On War.* Book VIII, Ch. 6. *www.clausewitz.com/readings/OnWar1873,* Web. 19 Aug. 2011.

Collins, Suzanne. *Catching Fire.* 2009. New York: Scholastic, 2010. Print.

_____. "A Conversation." *Scholastic.com.* Scholastic, n.d., Web. 22 Aug. 2011.

_____. *The Hunger Games.* New York: Scholastic, 2008. Print.

_____. *Mockingjay.* New York: Scholastic, 2010. Print.

Fisher, M. F. K. *The Gastronomical Me.* 1943. Rpt. New York: North Point-Farrar. Print.

Gabaccia, Donna R. *We Are What We Eat: Ethnic Food and the Making of Americans.* Cambridge: Harvard University Press, 1998. Print.

Lehrer, Jonah. *Proust Was a Neuroscientist*. New York: Houghton, 2007. Print.
Levenstein, Harvey. *Paradox of Plenty: A Social History of Eating in Modern America*. Rev. ed. Berkeley: University of California Press, 2003. Print.
Montanari, Massimo. *Food Is Culture*. Trans. Albert Sonnenfeld. New York: Columbia University Press, 2004. Print.
Tannahill, Reay. *Food in History*. New York: Three Rivers, 1988. Print.

PART II.

Ethics, Aesthetics and Identity

Katniss Everdeen's Liminal Choices and the Foundations of Revolutionary Ethics

Guy Andre Risko

Despite the media-oriented focus on romanticizing at least some of the decisions Katniss Everdeen struggles with in *The Hunger Games* trilogy (witness the Facebook groups dividing into "Team Peeta" and "Team Gail"), the process by which Katniss makes decisions is as critical as the results of her decision making. For that process is deeply connected to the manner in which the possibility of ethics becomes activated within *The Hunger Games*. Focusing on moments informing Katniss's decision making can unearth the trilogy's central themes of agency and ethics. Such focus can also help the reader trace Katniss's actions through the political schema she finds herself thrown into. Here, by drawing on the work of political and cultural theorists, I wish to evaluate Katniss's behavior and the possibility of her agency within Panem's power structure, assembled and controlled by the Capitol. Engaging in such a reading ensures that both Katniss and Panem are viewed in relation to the dystopian politics and history constructed by the trilogy in close relation to our own world. Put succinctly, any reading that takes seriously Katniss's decisions as expressions of agency must also think through the historical and ethical complexities informing the world in which those decisions are made.

By viewing Katniss's ethical decisions through the lens of the differing political subjectivities offered to her by the Capitol's political constructions, *The Hunger Games* can be read not as a teleological young adult series yearning for a fulfilling, holistic ending; rather, *The Hunger Games* becomes unique within YA literature because of its focus on the process of emerging subjectivity. Within the specific confines of YA literature, it is important to pay close attention to the construction of subjects as they come under the eyes of the state and other societal structures. Katniss's relationship with the Capitol is not static; rather, as a young woman on the cusp of legal adulthood, her subject position is always already in flux. This forces critics of YA literature to pay attention to subjectivity as it forms around a slowly representable and slowly invented child (Zornado 28). In focusing on the processes of subjectivity, *The Hunger Games* opens up new spaces for the possibility of ethical representation and new possibilities for imagining agency. Only when Katniss emerges as a subject under the watchful eye of the Capital do the possibilities of ethics coalesce around her position.

April Spisak reads Katniss's "difficult to devastating" choices as the thrust of the narrative's starting point (112). Katniss finds herself being pulled from multiple angles, from the drive to "survive" and the desire to remain loyal. While these inner personal struggles are crucial to an understanding of Katniss's expression of choice, there is a prior series of power relations being fought in her political world. Even before Katniss steps in to replace her sister, there is a well-defined cultural/political structure controlling subjectivity that functions as the starting point for all of the later decisions. Within the power relations represented in *The Hunger Games,* the Capitol serves as the central point of power and population management. Its policies organize the bounds of subjectivity accessible to citizens of Panem. One of the important methods of organizing and separating people is the Hunger Games. Within the political discourses of the Capitol, the Hunger Games are articulated as a mechanism of remembering the history of rebellion, a necessary memorialization of ugly events. From the perspective of those in the districts, the Hunger Games are viewed as a control mechanism: each year the districts must offer up two of its youngest to get slaughtered for the enjoyment of the Capitol. The Games are presented as a reality show for those privileged enough to live in the luxury of the Capitol, distanced enough from the carnage to bet and gossip on the dying children, and as a horror show for those forced to live in the various districts. The mechanics of this political situation are critical to the schema upon which possible ethical actions will be inscribed.

Cultural theorist Giorgio Agamben's thinking on the state of exception is particularly helpful in this interrogation of Suzanne Collins's imagined future. Gaining increasing currency in American cultural thought since post-9/11 security policies, Agamben has theorized about the legalistic modes of thinking that led to the creation of such norms as indefinite detention of "nonenemy combatants" in places like Guantanamo Bay. According to Agamben, the state of exception is the condition where spaces are empty of juridical standing, where law is eliminated and no longer functions to protect that subject (*SE* 60). Governing bodies construct these spaces in order to control subjects without the necessity to treat them as "legal subjects," completely removing all norms of legal protection. Looking at the history of political power in Europe and the United States, Agamben worries that these spaces will become the norm, where "the state of exception ... has transgressed its spatiotemporal boundaries and now, overflowing outside them, is starting to coincide with the normal order" (*HS* 28). Agamben worries about a future where the normal functioning of law has become law without a figure, where the law ceases to apply to any subject.

This worry comes to its terminal point in the history of the post–United States imagined in *The Hunger Games*. In the post-revolution world of Panem, where a nuclear war has decimated North America and allowed a centralized totalitarian state to take control, the political organization has attempted to control every aspect of life. The yearly iteration of violence and the strict controls on movement allow us to see how Agamben's reading of exception applies to Panem. The districts are juridically empty spaces, especially from the position of those children who could potentially be chosen for the Hunger Games — and for their parents, friends, neighbors, and mere acquaintances. All subjects, especially young subjects thrown into the randomness of the Hunger Games, lack a fundamental aspect of their political being in that they lack recognition as citizens with political worth or import. In effect, they can be killed without being murdered, without juridical recognition of the act of killing. In order to function, Panem's political organization *demands* their death as symbols of national history.

An important moment within the ethical framing of the Hunger Games, especially from a point of view attuned to the state of exception, is the moment when a child is selected for the arena. At that moment, the child's relationship with both the Capitol and the local community fundamentally alters. Within Agamben's thought, the child is thrown into the state of exception, where the law no longer recognizes his or her being as juridically meaningful. Agamben understands this as a change to *Homo sacer*, a figure of law that is empty of political legitimacy (*HS* 48). The *Homo sacer* is a figure emerging from Roman law where the citizen has lost all legal value, can be killed but not murdered (the killer isn't held legally responsible) or sacrificed (*HS* 53). The change from recognized political subject to *Homo sacer* happens at the moment when the Capitol is *most enacting law*, exercising its ability to choose the exception (the tribute) from the norm (those living and suffering in the districts). As understood by Agamben, "If the exception is the structure of sovereignty, then sovereignty is ... the originary structure in which law refers to life and includes it in itself by suspending it" (*HS* 23).

From the perspective of Agamben, when legally forcing a community to sacrifice its youth and its future, the law at that moment is seen as already based on the power to decide the exception (*SE* 1). The imagined world of *The Hunger Games* does not depict some dystopian future where the law has been broken by problems of power, resources, or economic structures, enunciating some lawless state of nature; rather, *The Hunger Games* enunciates the legal logic of exception *as pure exception,* the liminal moments of a form of governance that we deal with every day. The sovereign power of the Capitol does not attempt to hide its nature through reworking and redescribing the foundations of the law in a manner akin to the memos that legally justified the torture at Guantanamo Bay. The Capitol uses a more transparent, yet eerily similar, version of the law that Agamben sees as "becoming the new nomos," or the new legal principle, of the Earth (*HS* 28). Far from being some dystopian future where nuclear holocaust fundamentally alters the logics ordering the post–United States/Panem, the future depicted by *The Hunger Games* is a proleptic vision of the future of American juridical power where juridical violence reaches its maximum threshold. Agamben describes this move in chilling language: "The proper characteristic of this violence is that it neither makes nor preserves law, but deposes it and thus inaugurates a new historical epoch" (*HS* 53). Panem, the "new historical epoch" in the trajectory of American law and politics, deploys the logic of the exception found in current law in order to justify deploying violent, destructive mechanisms of control.

What does this world mean in terms of Katniss Everdeen's potential agency and the possibility of her taking ethical actions? Agamben explains that the task of the current political moment, when the logics of exception have slowly morphed into the norms illustrated by the political organization of *The Hunger Games,* is to refuse the relationship between sovereign power, law, and the power of the exception. To understand how this process of emergent ethics works, one must first understand the process by which Katniss becomes a participant in the Games and how that process mimics the creation of *Homo sacer.* Within the world of *The Hunger Games,* tributes are chosen by an annual district lottery. At District 12's lottery for the Seventy-fourth Games, Katniss's sister, Prim, is chosen. Katniss saves Prim by stepping into the role of competitor — a choice offered every year to those who wish to "volunteer" to compete (*HG* 22). This moment of supposed choice enunciates Katniss's political position from which her agency emerges. Stepping into the role of competitor fundamentally transforms those in Katniss's position into a different type of subject. Prior to becoming a competitor, Katniss had attempted to avoid the Capitol's eye. Sneaking into restricted areas and hunting illegal game, she existed as a subject only affected by the constituting power of the Capitol. The bounds of her political choices were clearly visible. She was not allowed to go beyond the electric fence, but the economy allowed it. She stood as a nonexceptional figure of law who could clearly see its failures and limits. When Katniss volunteers to replace her sister, however, she suddenly becomes completely devoid of political and legal value. Katniss's only moment of "choice" recognizable by the Capitol is simultaneously her moment of becoming *Homo sacer.*

When reading ancient Roman law, Agamben sees the legal figure of *Homo sacer* as the primary example of what happens to the subject who experiences the complete loss of legal protection and acknowledgment, yet whose acknowledgment is simultaneously one of a legal basis:

> What defines the status of *Homo sacer* is ... both the particular character of the double exclusion into which he is taken and the violence to which he finds himself exposed. This violence — the unsanctionable killing that, in his case, anyone may commit — is classifiable neither as sacrifice nor as homicide, neither as the execution of a condemnation to death nor as sacrilege [*HS* 53].

The position of *Homo sacer* is that of complete juridical-political meaninglessness. The *Homo sacer*'s life has no imprint in either the legal or political world. A person can kill the *Homo sacer* without it being called murder; there is no subjectivity to speak of, no legal means of thinking of the *Homo sacer* as a subject of politics. Victimhood is removed from the possibility of the *Homo sacer*'s life.

To be sure, becoming *Homo sacer* is not some return to a formative state of anarchic nature where the concept of murder makes no sense, where the law, politics, and the sovereign have not yet be substantiated (Agamben, *SE* 51). The figure is excluded, *made different,* acted upon through the exclusion of the sovereign. Katniss does not *leave* the realm of political recognition, exiled to the arena; rather, Katniss is thrown into a legally determined emptiness. The violence of exclusion does not manifest itself only through the meaningless death of the *Homo sacer;* the attribution of such subjectivity is itself a violent act. Even if the subject never experiences the pain of physical violence/death, the complete loss of a legal/political being represents the terminal point of legal violence. The *Homo sacer* is no longer a subject recognized by the constituting forces that allow someone like an exile to exist. The *Homo sacer* literally *ceases to be political.* Katniss experiences a powerful force of law that constitutes her as *Homo sacer,* someone who can be killed but not murdered, at the moment of recognition: she is recognized as unable to be legally recognized. She has been reduced to "bare life," a body reduced to mere biopolitical control (Agamben, *HS* 11). The Capitol has not only decided whether she lives or dies; it has also written a blank check for her death as long as she finds herself within the state of exception encapsulated by the arena.

Given that the *Homo sacer* is a political position created through the ability granted by law to cease the functioning of law, it seems odd to think about the choice to fulfill that position outside the lens of the sovereign power that normally chooses the exception. Yet it is difficult to imagine any potentially revolutionary act coming out of that position absent the choice to fulfill it. In other words, the possibility of revolution from the figure of *Homo sacer* can come only when that position is taken rather than passively received. When thinking about Katniss's action in terms of Agamben's theories, it becomes more difficult to think through the question of ethics. At first glance, Katniss does not seem to "[think] ontology and politics beyond every figure of relation" (Agamben, *HS* 33); rather, she attempts to stand in for her sister, replace her sister for no articulated reason other than sisterhood. Katniss would not have thrown herself into the arena if some faceless person had been chosen. Her choice is not some Kantian maxim, nor some Levinasian infinite obligation. She protects her sister, no one else. From this perspective, Katniss's action seems less revolutionary and potentially less ethical. She does not act beyond those relations in order to fix the system, sneak into the Games in order to further her agenda, or even have the position of competitor thrust upon her; Katniss acts *based on relations,* those relations that Agamben finds potentially damaging. Despite this potential incongruity between the cause of her actions and Agamben's thinking about the exception, it is the choice to replace that allows Katniss's action to illustrate "thinking through" these relations, and to enunciate the question of ethics within the texts. At the moment she affirms the power of filiation, a relationship worrisome due to its arbitrary structure, she also allows for revolutionary ethics to emerge.

When thinking through both Agamben's vision of an emerging political system and Katniss's act of self-sacrifice, it is important to think about how that action is both received and intended to be received. It is in this space of reception that Katniss's act comes closest to Agamben's alternative ontological-ethical thinking. When Katniss acts to replace her sister, she is not the only subject in her world to replace another child chosen by lottery. In other districts, children prepare themselves for the possibility of the arena, choosing long before Katniss's moment of decision to replace whoever is chosen through the lottery. These youths, sardonically called "Careers" by the denizens of Katniss's district (*HG* 94), make their choice because they want to be part of the Games. They long for the arena, and although the person being replaced may find the action a favor of sorts, a Career's choice is never received as an ethical act from the position of the consuming audience. After the Careers step up to be chosen, the sovereign exception is not questioned but affirmed. In those moments of replacement, the exception is justified and recognized as politically meaningful: the Careers stand up to be recognized by the Capitol as willing participants in the Hunger Games. In contrast, no one regards Katniss's decision as that of a willing participant. Nor does Katniss intend for her decision to be read as anything other than an attempt to save her sister from the Arena. And so she understands when "[t]o the everlasting credit of the people of District 12, not one person claps" over her choice to replace her sister (*HG* 23). Katniss's action, unlike those of the Careers, illustrates the limits and slippages inherent in sovereign exception. Even if a narrative of "choice" circulates around the discourse of the exception, that supposed "choice" can illustrate how the exception acts coercively.

While Agamben sees moving through and past relationships and identities constituted through power as the political-ontological method of pushing past sovereign power, the question of how one pushes past those identities is unclear. How does one go about "undoing" those relationalities? Certainly, one cannot simply delete these relationships and identities that, despite their arbitrariness and creation out of the attempt to control, still construct us as subjects. One cannot simply stand up and say, "I am no longer an example" or "I no longer recognize these relationships as part of my being." Recognizing these relationships enunciates them, announces them as constitutive of the subject. The sovereign exception functions because these relationships are recognizable and malleable from the position of *sovereign power*. The position of *Homo sacer* is impossible unless someone can first be recognized as having a political-legal position thrust upon him or her prior to the removal of rights. Because of this construction, Katniss's action based on familial relations is not a death knell for her ethical action; rather, it opens up a way of thinking about Agamben's political alternative. When taken contextually with how the Capitol understands Katniss as a controlled subject, her decision appears as an ethical act that allows for the undoing of her relationship with the Capitol. We can begin understanding this act of replacement as ethical through its relationship with potentiality.

According to Agamben, we can understand ethics only through the question of the potentiality of action and effects demarcated by subjectivity and difference. Any other reading of ethics damns humanity to complete ethical determinism (where ethics emerges through pure infinite obligation or unchanging Kantian maxims) or to utter nihilism (the idea that the complete lack of connection between subjects prevents ethics from being possible). Agamben sees ethics as acting through one's own potential subjectivity and difference (*HS* 44). Only when one sees oneself as not stable can an ethical action take place. When Katniss decides to take her sister's place, she acknowledges the sphere of potentiality both subjects reside in. At the moment her sister is chosen, Katniss sees two different possibilities. For her sister, Prim, Katniss sees the potential for at least one more year of life before the next lottery. For herself, Katniss sees a lifetime — long or short — without her sister. Rather than acting as though the decision was made in finality, she replaces her sister — an act unthinkable without thinking ethically.

In and of itself, this act of replacement, despite its ethical value, may still do little to undo sovereign power; however, when understood within the realm of the Capitol's interpolation of subjects, Katniss's act can be understood as a subject acting *through* the bonds desired by the Capitol, transforming her into a subject of revolution. This subject of revolution opens up even more potential ethical imaginaries. Agamben understands the State (the Capitol in the world of *The Hunger Games*) as purely functional because of constructed identities:

> The State ... is not founded on a social bond, of which it would be the expression, but rather on the dissolution, the unbinding it prohibits. For the State, therefore, what is important is never the singularity as such, but only its inclusion in some identity, whatever identity.... A being radically devoid of any representable identity would be absolutely irrelevant to the State [*HS* 85].

While the act of replacement may not be an act of rebellion against the State as such, the moment of decision and replacement makes Katniss a unique subject in regards to the State, one taking up a role that no one else could take. All of the other competitors either choose themselves to go to the arena (the Careers) or are chosen by the Capitol. The Careers affirm the existence of *Homo sacer* as a legitimate, even celebrated, aspect of the Capitol's power. They give up their political being in order to affirm the Capitol's power. The others are cast into the arena, victims of the sovereign exception reduced to bare life, their subjectivity removed through the power of the State. In each case, despite the complete lack of political value inherent in their beings, they are still recognized as captured by the Capitol. The Capitol can still control them, put them through the motions of competition and death.

What the Capitol gets wrong, and what Agamben sees as the space for potential revolution within the logic of the State, is that Katniss does not embody the position of *Homo sacer* in the same ways that the other competitors do. Neither chance nor affirmation of power brings Katniss into the arena; Katniss's entrance comes out of a removal of her own political being. Katniss, by assenting to the Capitol's power on her own terms, removes from herself her own bonds, her own identity categories. By standing in for her sister, and accepting the horrible violence (both ontological and physical) that comes along with the identity of competitor, Katniss thinks past actuality and only of potentiality. She has chosen her own death, moved away from her own stability within the world, and given up on the possibility of existence. That Katniss strips herself from Agamben's "representable identity" (*HS* 85) allows her to take even more revolutionary political actions later in the narrative, each of which remains powerful only because of this act of agency that enunciates, on her own terms, an identity-less subject. Despite her being recognized by the Capitol as a *Homo sacer* in the same way it recognizes all participants in the Hunger Games, the conditions and enactment of Katniss's choice allow her to be radically devoid of any identity, even the identity prescribed.

The Hunger Games trilogy's deployment of ethical decision making illustrates how the question of agency brings new ways of thinking about the possibility of ethics to the literary theory table. *The Hunger Games* shows, through

Katniss's "choice" to work through the bounds of the state system that functions on the back of her own exclusion, the potential ways of imagining a revolutionary ethics. Unlike characters who are aware of their political options and the political import of their actions, Katniss acts from instinct, unaware of the secondary implications. As already noted, Katniss acts only *because her sister is chosen*. Whereas earlier it might appear as though this fact would hamstring the ability to read Katniss as a revolutionary figure, it now shows the extreme power of ethics in the determined political situation that Agamben describes and Katniss exists in.

An easy method of explaining this relationship comes from the adult revolutionaries in *The Hunger Games*. At the end of the trilogy's second novel, *Catching Fire,* the reader becomes aware of a massive plot to save Katniss during her second trip to the arena, and to use her image and skill set to aid in the revolt against the Capitol. Across the thirteen districts, Katniss's actions have come to ferment and kick-start revolution. These repercussions are unimaginable to Katniss, who acts only from the position of nonidentity. Choices and the exercise of agency may have further-reaching consequences than one might intend (or even imagine), but many times the position from which one acts trumps those large consequences. *The Hunger Games* reiterates this aspect of emerging subjectivity: despite the best attempts of hundreds of adults to make Katniss an emblem of the revolution, her power comes only out of her own actions from her space as identity-less. Every attempt to *make* Katniss something, to have her fulfill a larger identity category, fails. Katniss's political value can come only from a position absent identity. The power of Katniss comes from her ability to isolate agency to singular events. One's actions may always already be political, but one does not need to know that fact in order to be a political actor.

Works Cited

Agamben, Giorgio. *Homo Sacer: Sovereign Power and Bare Life*. Stanford: Stanford University Press, 1998. Print.

_____. *The State of Exception*. Chicago: University of Chicago Press, 2005. Print.

Collins, Suzanne. *Catching Fire*. New York: Scholastic, 2009. Print.

_____. *The Hunger Games*. New York: Scholastic, 2008. Print.

Spisak, April. Rev. of *The Hunger Games*. *Bulletin of the Center for Children's Books* 62.3 (2008): 112. Print.

Zornado, Joseph. *Inventing the Child: Culture, Ideology, and the Story of Childhood*. New York: Garland, 2001. Print.

8

Hungering for Righteousness
*Music, Spirituality and Katniss Everdeen**

Tammy L. Gant

In the world of Panem, it's easy to see traces of contemporary America. For example, our current obsession with reality TV, body art, and mass consumerism are all clearly extrapolated into this future society. Even our recurring and ongoing willingness to wage war and the growing emotional cost of that behavior are woven into the thread of this near-future remnant of America. Our nonchalance about such damaging conduct begs the question about the absence of other cultural norms in Panem. Most noticeably missing is religion. There is no reference in the trilogy to a sacred set of beliefs or practices. There's not even a reference to a higher power of any ilk beyond the oppressive government. Given that 80 percent of Americans profess belief in God, with no distinction given to a specific deity or faith group, the void seems noteworthy (Salmon). Nature, even human nature, abhors a vacuum, so that space has to be occupied by something. The ubiquitous presence of folk songs, lullabies, and songbirds suggests that Suzanne Collins uses music to fill the space meant for religion in Katniss's life.

Religion is undeniably a man-made system, but the work of that system is to develop and nurture the soul. Regardless of participation, the cultivation of religion is necessary because everyone who is a full and complete human being exists not just in the physical realm of the body but also in the spiritual world of the soul. The soul is the part of each of us that responds to beauty and morality and righteousness. Hope lives in the soul, as does our capacity for emotional growth and enlightenment. In "Music Education and Spirituality," musician and scholar Anthony Palmer writes, "[The] soul is integral to

*An earlier version of this essay was presented at the 46th Western Literature Association Conference (October 2011) in Missoula, Montana.

all life — genuine friend and experiences, great food and conversation that are memories forever. Soul is revealed in our relationships with others and with the community" (92). The soul holds the essence of who we are individually and collectively.

In the world of religion, the connection to a higher power nourishes the soul. Sacred spaces, rituals, texts, and, more often than not, music (along with rules for using all of these elements) guide that association in the religions of the world. In *The Sacred Canopy,* sociologist Peter Berger writes that "every human society is engaged in world building" and adds that religion is always a part of this enterprise (3). In other words, every human society has a means of soul building. But I maintain that religion, though important, is not the only means to nourish the soul. Panem has no religious structure. A large number of Americans profess no belief in God or believe in God but choose not to participate in religiosity. Drawing on the work of Carl Jung, Palmer creates a definition of spirituality that offers a helpful way of understanding the distinction: "Spirituality, especially by contrast to the doctrinal aspects of religion, is 'relating to, consisting of, or having the nature of spirit; not tangible or material.... Of, concerned with or affecting the soul'" (92). In other words, religion and spirituality are similar enterprises; they do the same work through different means. Palmer adds that "were organized religion to disappear by some quirk of social process, the human community still cannot and must not do without cultivating the spiritual" (92). Without the care and feeding of our souls, we are just bodies in meaningless motion on a physical plain.

In looking for that place of soul building in Panem, I turn once again to Anthony Palmer, who spent much of his academic career proclaiming the bond between music and spirituality. He writes that "each entry into the artistic realm is an attempt to define and identify our spiritual selves ... even when we are not conscious of [its] import.... The making of music ... validates being human" (100–01). Palmer also claims that music and art "cultivate those human attributes that will take us to a new level of human existence" (94). Walter Sargent's older essay, "One Contribution Which Art Makes to Religion," declares that art "reinforce[s] higher levels of consciousness" because of its ability to "quicken a highly complex type of emotional life and refine powers of sympathy" (363, 365). Through artistic expressions, Sargent and Palmer suggest, we grow in sympathy and compassion for more of the human family, thereby eventually evolving into a more enlightened society. Johannes Eurich, Professor of Practical Theology and Sociology at the University of Heidelberg, suggests a more concrete connection between Katniss's music and her spirituality. He identifies three key functions accomplished by traditional religious rituals: verification of identity, confirmation of rights and duties, and confirmations of social position (67). Music accomplishes each of these roles in Katniss's life, giving her the strength to live out her destiny.

At the opening of *The Hunger Games,* Katniss is not unaware of the moral failings of the Capitol; she just doesn't yet see the significance beyond her life. Her concerns are understandably pragmatic, physical, and immediate; she's consumed with feeding her family and keeping them safe. She thinks even discovering the truth about the Capitol's agenda is pointless since it doesn't feed the family. Barely keeping body and soul together, she doesn't have the luxury to nurture the essence of her spirit. Although Peeta tries to get her to see there's more to life than physical existence and to realize the importance of honoring their spiritual selves, she can't quite see the value of his belief. "[W]ho cares?" she asks him (*HG* 142). But a musical moment begins to change Katniss's beliefs. The lullaby she sings to Rue, which becomes the musical frame for the trilogy, helps her to see the moral failings of her culture more clearly and to begin to understand the limits of her worldview.

In the arena, Katniss forms a brief alliance with Rue, the smallest and youngest tribute. The alliance meets a violent end when one of the Career Tributes fatally spears Rue. Her dying request is for a song, and Katniss obliges even though she knows she's on screen in front of all of Panem. Katniss's song for Rue challenges the viewers with one question: how should we treat the young and the vulnerable? Just as spirituality helps to define our moral code, the lullaby has a similar purpose. Played out on the "altar" of TV in Panem's broadcast society, Katniss's eulogy for Rue imbues the scene with all the trappings of a religious ritual. The genre of the song evokes all the attendant connotations of childhood, including affection and protection during the most vulnerable phase of life. The lyrics further those implications with images of security and a promise of a bright, happy tomorrow where all dreams come true in an Edenic existence. But the ideal contradicts reality as Rue is in a world that fails to provide her those opportunities. She dies brutally in front of an audience that treats her death as entertainment. With the song, Katniss insists Panem see the tragedy as more. She makes Panem come face-to-face with its moral failings. In the double entendre of Rue's name, Collins implies the same intent: the Capitol should repent or regret this sin.

After the song, there's a pause or caesura. The whole world watches and seems to hold its breath. Then the mockingjays begin to sing. They repeat the song back to the viewers again and again, reiterating the message of the moment. Interestingly, this scene is one of the few places in the text — each connected to music — where Collins uses language that connotes the transcendent. *Eerie*— the word Katniss uses to describe the moment when the mockingjays begin to sing the lullaby (*HG* 235)— means "suggestive of the supernatural" (*OED*). *Eerie* can also mean frightening or dreadful, but even though she's in the arena, Katniss does not appear frightened at this moment, giving more weight to the supernatural definition. Later, in the final scene in the arena, Katniss describes the mockingjays' music as "unearthly" (*HG* 329), giving yet more credence to the metaphysical potential of music in her life. These words suggest Collins's understanding, no matter how tacit, of music's ability to transcend the physical world and lead practitioners and observers to a higher spiritual consciousness. As Rue's lullaby continues in mockingjay rounds, choral voice and echoes, holding all of Panem there in that spiritual space, the viewers have the opportunity to think about the significance of the moment they've just experienced. As does Katniss.

As she bears witness to Rue's death, Katniss's consciousness rises. She realizes the futility of Rue's death as well as the demise of her murderer (the nameless boy from District 1) and sees more clearly how vulnerable the tributes are in the face of the Capitol's power and injustice. Two words that come to her, "injustice" and "shame," keep the focus squarely on morality (*HG* 236). The Capitol is wrong, evil even, and in the face of that reality, Katniss is moved to an act of defiance. Determined to shame the Capitol, she creates an image that forces the watching world to acknowledge Rue's humanity. She covers Rue in flowers and salutes her with a gesture of thanks, love, and farewell unique to District 12. Katniss has no way of knowing for sure if her defiance will be broadcast, but she believes viewers will eventually see the flowers when Rue's body is removed from the arena. In *Catching Fire,* Katniss's conjecture is confirmed when the people of District 11 salute her with the same gesture. A few hours after Rue's figurative burial, the people of District 11 respond with a gift of bread for Katniss. The bread could be symbolic in so many ways, but the most important quality of the bequest is the precedent it sets. No district has sent a gift to a tribute from another district before. This gesture suggests the possibility for district solidarity against the Capitol. Further, it suggests a transcendence of self and a joining with a wider humanity; in this way, it foreshadows Katniss's spiritual growth.

As Rue's burial scene opens with music, so, too, does it close. In the ending of this scene, Collins exposes Katniss's greatest fear about the future and hints at her motivation for joining the rebellion. There is another musical pause as the hovercraft — the obtrusive arm of the Capitol — shushes the songbirds' singing and the solidarity and humanity it implies. Once the craft departs, the mockingjays sing again. Katniss focuses on a young bird singing just a few notes, reminding us of Rue's youth and her diminutive size. Youth also reminds us of the particularly vulnerable children of Panem who most need the better tomorrow promised in the lullaby. Poignantly, the young bird cannot yet sing the lullaby Katniss used to mesmerize the nation and eulogize Rue; however, it can manage Rue's own small song, notes that celebrate the end of the workday, the time to go home. In that word *home* are all the associations of the meadow in the song — safety, comfort, and belonging. Since Rue had earlier assured her ally that this song is a sign that all is well and that Katniss shouldn't worry, Katniss takes this sudden serenade to mean that Rue is still safe. Her statement that Rue is "[g]ood and safe" tells us more than that the young tribute is beyond harm (*HG* 238). She is in that good place of beauty and peace and hope promised in the lullaby. Her life is now indeed good and finally safe. The safety of the meadow where Rue now figuratively resides becomes the metaphoric goal of the rebellion for Katniss in due course. That refuge is what she eventually fights to create for all of Panem's children.

In the next musical interlude, Collins packs many of the spiritual benefits of religion into a short composition. As Rue sings to Katniss in a dream, the music brings Katniss peace and restoration, insight into her identity and purpose, and greater awareness of her spiritual duty. Many religious traditions have the experience of the dream or vision of a significant figure to deliver an important message. This dream vision of Rue does the same for Katniss. Following Rue's death, Katniss — despite her brave words around the mockingjays — soon sinks into despair. Rue had become like family to her, and Katniss's defining feature is the need to feed and protect her family. In fact, in recognizing Rue's vulnerability, she knows protecting her was more important even than protecting her sister, Prim. In the face of her failure to save Rue, Katniss slips into an almost suicidal lethargy. Collins uses music to revive her spirit. Bathed in beauty, the Rue in Katniss's dreams retains the flower shroud Katniss created for her. She is uninjured and happy and laughing. In her appearance is the verification of Katniss's claim: Rue is in a better place. This scene holds the hint of an afterlife as Rue sings all new songs and she sings on and on and on, suggesting eternal happiness. The peaceful dream comforts Katniss for a brief time. The peace doesn't last long after the dream, but it's enough to urge Katniss on to the next step and then the next.

In addition to comfort, in the dream Rue gives Katniss a hint about her identity when she tries to teach Katniss to talk to the mockingjays. Knowing Katniss's future, the reader can look back at this moment as Rue revealing Katniss's future role in the revolution. But the most important example of spiritual development happens in the coda that follows this musical interlude. As Katniss comes out of her grief one step at a time, she realizes a new and more meaningful motivation for her victory. Just as the gift from District 11 showed her a wider capacity for caring for others, Katniss now expands her own circle of concern. She has always wanted to win for Prim, but her deepening awareness shows her the more important victory is actually for Rue. Her victory, she realizes, will make Rue's life go on and make her life and death matter. The victory will also make the Capitol remember what they literally did to one little girl and symbolically did to thousands of little girls. Katniss realizes it's not enough to win food to feed the body; she has to challenge the moral stance of the Capitol and hold its people accountable. That victory will be food for the soul.

For many who describe themselves as either religious or spiritual, faith helps them to discover their life's identity and purpose. Music provides the same for Katniss. Collins makes the link between music and identity most clearly in the choice of a songbird as Katniss's token and namesake. Recalling Palmer's claim that music validates our humanity, one can see the brilliance in choosing a songbird as the symbol and figurehead of the rebellion. Since the Capitol maintains power by denying the essential humanity of all citizens, any music undermines that authority. In choosing a songbird, Collins also evokes such metaphors as finding one's voice and singing a new tune. There's even the canary in the mine analogy that is both literally and figuratively significant to Katniss and explicitly discussed in *Catching Fire*. As Katniss explains to the other tributes how the canary stops singing and then dies when the air in the mine becomes dangerous, she thinks of the long line of dying songbirds connected to her life: her father, Rue, Maysilee Donner (the original owner of the mockingjay pin), and the songbird Maysilee left behind (*CF* 330–31). The symbolic imagery is clear. If the songbirds are dying, the world is obviously a poisonous place. Additionally, in choosing the mockingjay as the specific songbird, Collins reveals yet more insight into to Katniss's character. Madge asks, "They're just songbirds. Right?" (*CF* 92). But they are so much more. These genetically modified animals defied the Capitol's expectation and continued to live when the Capitol wanted them to die. They also created a whole new species that can adapt and make beautiful music and is only dangerous when its nest is threatened. These traits are also integral to Katniss's personality. She is stubbornly adaptive, a gifted singer, and fiercely protective of her family. Katniss is the mockingjay in more than just visual imagery; like that bird, she is a survivor, and she asserts that fact with every song she sings.

In addition to defining her identity, music leads Katniss to her purpose in life. Katniss's second dream about Rue also carries a spiritual message. Rue has already become a martyr for the cause, giving her presence and voice in Katniss's dream more spiritual weight. The dream occurs in *Catching Fire* on the last night of the Victory Tour, after Snow has told Katniss she wasn't successful in convincing him of her true feelings for Peeta, leading her to think she has no real hope of keeping her family and friends alive. When she should feel her most devastated, she has this dream. Rue comes to her as a mockingjay and sings as she leads Katniss to an unknown destination. The dream makes Katniss inexplicably happy. Although she doesn't fully understand or take on her role as the Mockingjay yet, it's in the music of the moment that she gets her calling. The voice of the martyr sings out to her and shows her a new path. The path isn't clear, the end is unknowable, but the journey is necessary and empowering.

But like most spiritual journeys, the way becomes less clear and more difficult as the path continues. Several religious traditions speak of a phase of spiritual development marked by loneliness and despair. Commonly called the "dark night of the soul," this is a time when the pains and doubts and disappointments of life threaten to raze spiritual growth. There is no doubt Katniss's soul is in this bleak place at the end of the revolution. Prim is dead — despite all Katniss's efforts to keep her safe — and Gale may have been the instrument of the young girl's death; the rebellion hasn't brought the promised improvement, and the potential for change seems dim. Katniss loses all hope and surrenders to death. Spiritual practitioners insist that the only way out of spiritual darkness is through it by means of spiritual disciplines such as solitude, prayer, chants, austere living, or fasting. Collins seems to be aware of these traditions as she takes Katniss through several of them. The ruined representative of the rebellion is alone in her bare training room, refusing to eat, when suddenly she begins to sing. Once again, music is central to Katniss's spiritual growth, becoming both the soundtrack of and the metaphor for her journey. As she sings the songs of her past, her voice becomes truer and more confident and finally "splendid" (*M* 376). Without the discord of other voices, she learns to trust her own voice above any other. As she passes through this dark night of the soul, she discovers the strength and beauty of her own voice. As she sings to herself, Katniss achieves her final spiritual enlightenment. She rejects the models given to her by both the Capitol and District 13. She rejects the immorality of a world where children are sacrificed in violent power struggles. Though she has no idea what's going on outside her monastic room, she knows she will never again join the endless cycle of revenge and oppression. Katniss does not yet have the vision to create the world embodied in the song she sang to Rue because her emotional healing is not complete, but in refusing the models offered to her by the Capitol and the rebels, she sets the stage to construct her own more humanistic worldview. Before she can do that, however, she needs emotional healing — and once again music is the instrument.

By this point in the trilogy, Katniss has suffered extreme emotional trauma. The list of events she has lived through creates a near-perfect match of the list of the leading causes of posttraumatic stress disorder (PTSD). She has endured combat and violent assault; she's suffered through man-made "natural" disasters in the arena and lived with the knowledge of Peeta's capture and torture; worst of all, she has watched family, friends, and strangers suffer brutal deaths, and she has killed several people herself. It is no wonder then that her behavior includes textbook symptoms of PTSD. Katniss suffers from recurring nightmares, difficulty sleeping, social avoidance, and self-loathing. When Katniss returns to District 12 at the end of *Mockingjay,* it doesn't look as if she can ever be whole again. Music may have preserved her soul, but she is clearly a damaged person as she sits in the same spot day after day, unkempt and uncaring. Psychologists are increasingly investigating the role of spirituality in healing, particularly emotional healing. These investigations suggest that spirituality is an essential component in recovering from PTSD, an important connection in my reading of Collins's trilogy. A 2001 literature review published in *Current Directions in Psychological Science* provides a snapshot of several studies researching that connection, citing fifteen major studies conducted over the space of ten years (Seybold and Hill 24). Early research suggests that resilience is one of the most important factors for determining both the severity and the duration of PTSD in a trauma victim.

In a 2007 article titled "Spirituality and Resilience in Trauma Victims," Julio Peres, collaborating with researchers from the University of São Paulo and Duke University, proposes an explanation for the connection: "When people become traumatized they often look for a new sense of meaning and purpose in their life.... Religious beliefs and practices may reduce the loss of control and helplessness, provide a cognitive framework that can decrease suffering and strengthen one's purpose and meaning in the face of trauma. Religion can also provide ... hope and motivation" (346–48). For Katniss, music is the key to resiliency again and again. Rue's lullaby, Rue's four-note melody, the songs Rue sings in Katniss's dreams, the memories of her father's songs, and even the emotionally uncomfortable "Hanging Tree" (*M* 123–24) each give Katniss a sense of comfort or purpose or a means to deepen her understanding of the world. But it's the last song she sings that most explicitly announces her healing and the return of hope. The music she makes in the Training Center as she traverses the depths of her spiritual darkness seems to hold enough of her soul together to allow emotional healing. But when she wails with the long lost Buttercup in a sound she describes as "part crying, part singing" (*M* 386), she finally embraces her despair — so that she can eventually relinquish it. Their duet is more than just vocal: they are both injured and scarred and missing the one person they each loved most. And they are both survivors. They adapt to "previously unthinkable acts" (*M* 386) and find new meaning in life.

After this last song, Katniss eventually "comes back to life" (*M* 387), and she gradually finds meaning in bearing witness, honoring the dead, and validating those whose lives were stolen by the depravity of the Capitol. Early in *The Hunger Games,* Katniss claims that music ranks "somewhere between hair ribbons and rainbows in terms of usefulness" (*HG* 211), but she and the reader soon see otherwise. In music she finds the courage to face the Capitol's atrocities, the strength to forge her own path, and the healing to survive the trauma that has been her life story. In the finale of the score of her life, music takes center stage in restoring her soul.

Rebirth, renewal, resurrection, new life — many world religions incorporate these beliefs either literally or figuratively. Collins uses the music of Katniss's world to create a leitmotif of these ideas. In the beginning of the trilogy, Katniss Everdeen has shut music out of her heart and life. She thinks little beyond her daily bread and has no faith in the future of humanity. The spiritual journey that begins with the musical tribute to Rue's life and death eventually allows Katniss to sacrifice herself to secure a better future for all of Panem. In the epilogue, the final refrain of Rue's lullaby indicates the depth of Katniss's spiritual growth. Because of her sacrifices, the meadow described in the song has finally become a reality. The Meadow grows on a literal and figurative graveyard, but it grows. Perhaps this new world really is the "evolution of the human race" mentioned by Panem's new Secretary of Communications (*M* 379). The closing image of Katniss's children playing in the Meadow suggests she finally believes in a future where that advancement is possible. Sending life forward into the unknowable future is a supreme act of faith in the potential for humanity to transcend its violent instincts and nurture its spiritual essence. After a lifetime rejecting this risk, Katniss embraces hope with a song.

WORKS CITED

Berger, Peter L. *The Sacred Canopy: Elements of a Sociological Theory of Religion*. New York: Anchor, 1990. Print.

Collins, Suzanne. *Catching Fire*. New York: Scholastic, 2009. Print.

_____. *The Hunger Games*. New York: Scholastic, 2008. Print.

_____. *Mockingjay*. New York: Scholastic, 2010. Print.

"Eerie." *OED*. Oxford English Dictionary, 2011. Web. 11 Sept. 2011.

Eurich, Johannes. "Sociological Aspects and Ritual Similarities in the Relationship between Pop Music and Religion." *International Review of the Aesthetics and Sociology of Music* 34.1 (2003): 57–70. *JSTOR*. Web. 6 June 2011.

Palmer, Anthony J. "Music Education and Spirituality: A Philosophical Exploration." *Philosophy of Music Education Review* 3.2 (1995): 91–106. *JSTOR*. Web. 11 Aug. 2011.

Peres, Julio F. P., Alexander Moreira-Almeida, Antonia Gladys Nasello, and Harold G. Koenig. "Spirituality and Resilience in Trauma Victims." *Journal of Religion and Health* 46.3 (2007): 343–50. *JSTOR*. Web. 11 Aug. 2011.

Salmon, Jacqueline L. "Most Americans Believe in Higher Power, Poll Finds." *Washington Post.com*. *Washington Post*, 24 June 2008. Web. 19 Sept. 2011.

Sargent, Walter. "One Contribution Which Art Makes to Religion." *The Biblical World* 41.6 (1913): 359–65. *JSTOR*. Web. 6 June 2011.

Seybold, Kevin S., and Peter C. Hill. "The Role of Religion and Spirituality in Mental and Physical Health." *Current Directions in Psychological Science* 10.1 (2001): 21–24. *JSTOR*. Web. 11 Aug. 2011.

9

Revolutionary Art in the Age of Reality TV

KATHERYN WRIGHT

Written more than a decade before the golden age of television in America, Walter Benjamin's seminal essay, "The Work of Art in the Age of Its Technological Reproducibility" (1936), examines how the meaning of art has changed under the new conditions of production in the modern era. Benjamin argues that technological and cultural values shape aesthetic experience, where aesthetics is defined as "the sensory experience of perception" (Buck-Morss 6). In the early twentieth century, the loss of the "aura" in an artwork resulting from its sense of authenticity gave way to the technical reproducibility of creative forms such as the cinema, where an entire population could experience the exact same movie simultaneously (Benjamin 103). Thus, the "cult value" of an original artwork has been replaced by the "exhibition value" of the reproducibility of mass media and popular culture (Benjamin 106). A viewer transforms into an audience member, while the audience transforms into a collective mass in front of the projection screen. Like Benjamin, Suzanne Collins explores the way technology and popular culture shape the meaning of contemporary aesthetics. Instead of film, however, she examines the changing nature of mass communication technologies, specifically television, and the way television shapes human perception. In *The Hunger Games* trilogy, where television plays a key role in the narrative, the very definition of art seems to be at stake. What role do art and aesthetics play in the dystopian world Suzanne Collins creates and, more broadly, in the American cultural context within which the trilogy has been produced, distributed, and consumed?

At the center of the trilogy is the annual event known as the Hunger Games, a competition that is televised live across the twelve districts of Panem. Everyone watches the Games. They represent a media event much like the Olympics — but combined with the horrific spectacle of a tragedy like 9/11.

Brian Massumi argues that contemporary television, in all its forms, is no longer the primary information source in a networked society connected through the Internet; instead, television is now a "social event-medium" (33). Positioning television as an event medium extends the "Work of Art" argument about the power of the cinema as a common ground through which mass audiences gain political relevance (Benjamin 119). Examining the role of television in the public response to 9/11, Massumi notes, "The collapse of the World Trade Center towers had glued the populace to the TV screen with an intensity not seen since the assassination of President Kennedy in the medium's early days.... In a time of crisis, television was once again providing a perceptual focal point for the spontaneous mass coordination of affect" (33). Massumi's primary example is the terror alert system developed by the U.S. Department of Homeland Security in the wake of 9/11, where a color like orange indicates a particular level of anxiety an American citizen should feel in anticipation of a potential terrorist threat (31). Disparate audiences converge through the shared experience of watching a media event unfold on the television screen. The television coverage of the event, in turn, determines how people feel about what is happening onscreen. Depending on how the content is constructed, television has the capacity to evoke a particular emotional response or, for Massumi, coordinate affect. Contemporary television functions as a space through which emotional responses of segmented audiences and niche markets can be regulated and repurposed (Lotz 181).

In *The Hunger Games* trilogy, the Games themselves structure the affective capacities of the citizens of Panem. Similar to Massumi's discussion of the terror alert system, the goal of the Hunger Games as they play out in the first two novels is to cultivate a public that is emotionally invested in the power of the Capitol. Before each reaping, the story of the failed rebellion and creation of the Games acts as both a warning for everyone forced to participate and an unyielding demonstration of the Capitol's dominance over the entire population. Watching yourself and your loved ones on television being killed in the name of the Capitol's overarching power is what counts for entertainment. Because the Games encourage audiences to cheer for the success or failure of certain tributes, the Gamemakers affect how people feel by structuring the narrative of the media event to evoke whatever collective emotional response the Capitol desires. As an event medium, television is a primary technological apparatus through which the dispersed districts of Panem come together as a living, breathing public — a public that is subsequently the primary subject of the Capitol's exploitation.

Establishing an aesthetic connection between the politics of a media event like the Hunger Games and the formation of an audience echoes Benjamin's assertion about the fusion of art and politics. At the conclusion of the "Work of Art" essay, Benjamin turns to his own historical context to consider how aesthetics shapes political regimes. For Benjamin, fascism seeks to organize the masses culled together through the exhibition value of film and to give them "expression" by aestheticizing political life (121). In the futuristic world of Panem, aesthetics and politics fuse together through the media event. The reactions of the audience to what's happening onscreen shape how the Games evolve: e.g., when the audience seems bored, the Gamemakers throw in a wall of fire. Much to the Capitol's dismay, however, the viewing public in the Hunger Games isn't a collective mass of people who come to think and act in the same way (like fascists). Perception of the Games depends upon the viewers' relative position in relation to the institution of power that controls them. Citizens of the Capitol view the Games as just entertainment (their perceptions desensitized to the inhumanity of their logic until iconoclasts such as Cinna step forward). Those in the Capitol-dependent districts see the Games as sport while members of the 12 districts see them as certain death. The television show in *The Hunger Games* doesn't cultivate a mass audience so much as unite a diverse population pushed to the edge of their own humanity.

The Hunger Games and Catching Fire are novels about the live broadcast of a television show, but aesthetically, the novels reference both the characters viewing the Games and the real-life readers experiencing the narrative. Unlike the multiplicity of participants and scenarios that make up a media event like the Olympics or 9/11, knowledge of the Games comes through first-person narrator and protagonist Katniss Everdeen. When she volunteers to take her sister's place in the Games, her personal decision connects Katniss's story to the television viewers watching this act of selflessness both in person and on television within the narrative framework. The affective connection between Katniss and her viewing audience begins when she stands on the podium after she volunteers for the Games and the crowd falls silent. Then, members of District 12 begin to touch three fingers to their lips as a gesture of admiration, saying goodbye to a loved one. This salute from the crowd is a silent reminder of the oppression the Hunger Games represents; it's an acknowledgment that the Capitol's cruelty has immediate and visible consequences for the children taking part. In this unplanned and spontaneous made-for-television moment, viewers put their trust in Katniss as their representative. This trust continues as Cinna uses his genius to make over Katniss into the "girl who was on fire" with her dramatic costume of flames (*HG* 70). Both the audience within the novel and the reader follow Katniss as she transforms into the "mockingjay" symbol (*HG* 42). Both viewers and readers want to know what happens next. The narrative focus on Katniss erases the possibility of aesthetic distance, a distance that audiences in the Capitol enjoy, and implicates the reader in her success or failure. Both the media event for the citizens of Panem and the novel's events for the reader signify a personal journey as much as they do a political struggle. The emotional content of this journey and struggle turns into the primary material for personal expression.

The media event in *The Hunger Games* trilogy becomes a site of aesthetic engagement. More than a series of happenings or a raw feed of unedited footage, the live broadcast is highly constructed in order to evoke particular responses from the public. Stephanie Marriott makes the following assertion about the temporal and spatial implications of live television: "To view an event is in any case to watch something that has been mediated through the sense-making activities of television. We can never access the world through the broadcast; we can only access the world of the broadcast" (73). There are many choices producers of a live television broadcast make, beginning with what to show and what to leave out. Decisions about camera movements and editing choices like cross-cutting one image with a game statistic or adding a brief clip from a past interview to flesh out the narrative do more than shape the experience of the event for the television audience; they also *constitute* the event as it unfolds in real time. Similarly, interspersed within the live broadcast in the Hunger Games are features such as instant replays and summaries of the day's events. Camera feeds cut from player to player depending on whose narrative is most entertaining or aesthetically engaging. If action wanes, the Gamemakers mix things up by making a surprise announcement: e.g., the news that two tributes can win or the creation of a puzzle that tributes must solve in order to survive.

The live television broadcast at the center of *The Hunger Games* trilogy uses the formal elements of reality television to structure the plot of the Games in the first two novels. Although it is wildly popular in the Millennial era, the reality television genre seems as far from art as one can possibly get: it includes a broad range of programming from talk and game shows to documentaries, makeover shows, and talent competitions (Hill 2). Reality TV also uses the Internet to expand its audience base by featuring additional programming, outtakes, commentary, discussion forums, and interactive gameplay that all contribute to the larger narrative "world" of the reality TV show (Jenkins 113). Even though reality TV is filmed or taped and not typically live, the television broadcast in *The Hunger Games* combines several conventions from the reality genre that mediate the live event, beginning with its talented interviewer, Caesar Flickerman, a Hunger Games celebrity host with outlandish costumes and an eerie smile. Too, Seneca Crane and, after Crane's execution, Plutarch Heavensbee serve as producers who design the unfolding Games. After the viewing audience in *The Hunger Games* first meets Katniss when she dramatically steps in to volunteer as tribute in place of her sister, she's whisked away to the Capitol to undergo a makeover into a spectacle, warrior, survivor, and then victor. Each transformation is accompanied with a new look, a new outfit, and a new aesthetic. Katniss's on-air romantic relationship with Peeta, which helps her to survive throughout the course of the series, echoes the overtly dramatic romantic tensions at the center of so many reality shows, ranging from *The Real World* to *The Bachelor.* Viewers form opinions on who should or shouldn't be together. And, as with *American Idol,* audience members support their favorite tributes throughout the Games. By using the conventions of this genre, *The Hunger Games* asserts that the Games are "just entertainment" for the Capitol, an assumption often made about television and, more generally, about all popular culture (Gray 6).

When a reality-show competition is over, all of the contestants from the show (although in the case of the Hunger Games, it's just the one who survives) return in an after-special or reunion where they talk about their experiences and future plans. Citizens of Panem have the opportunity to see the victors in real life throughout the tour that occurs in the first part of *Catching Fire,* much like the *American Idol* tour or special appearances by *Top Chef* "cheftestants" at a store near you ("*Top Chef: Texas*"). These generic conventions heighten the entertainment value of the Hunger Games by transforming tributes into characters in a narrative and connecting viewers with their personal stories. They also make the Games familiar for the intended audience of the trilogy, young adults who presumably recognize the codes and conventions of reality television. The primary difference between the plethora of reality shows that inform the contemporary popular cultural context and the trilogy is the explicit political objective that underlies the formation of the Hunger Games. When each tribute dies, his or her story dramatically and unapologetically ends. Their children's fates collectively demonstrate the power of the Capitol over its people. The Games are reality television, for real.

Katniss interrupts the television reality of the Hunger Games. More than a player involved in an on-screen love triangle or makeover episode, she understands how the Games are constructed for a viewing audience because she has been part of that audience. Put another way, she recognizes the aesthetic value of the Hunger Games. Because the event occurs every year with the same basic structure, Katniss manipulates the Games in order to survive, incorporating the prior knowledge of the Games into her strategy as a tribute. She plays the Game with the knowledge of not only how others have played it, but also how audiences perceive the contestants' actions. Even with her knowledge, however, Katniss still requires a learning phase. During the initial interview stage, Haymitch gets fed up with her inability to act in front of the camera. Peeta's admission of love for Katniss is what saves her during the early phases of the televised portion of the competition, but she soon becomes more adept at manipulating the situation. She recognizes how certain rewards she receives from Haymitch during the Games come from her actions, like kissing Peeta to play up the love angle. Katniss critically evaluates her televised reality as an art form and, in doing so, she actively participates in the media-making process.

Katniss's subjectivity within the Hunger Games reflects the changing nature of media production and consumption in contemporary culture. Unlike the cinema, where audiences watch an already completed film, consumers play an active role in the media-making process: "rather than talking about media producers and consumers as occupying separate roles, we might now see them as participants who interact with each other according to a new set of rules that none of us fully understands" (Jenkins 3). Reality television, where real-life people are stars of the show, allegorizes this new form of participation. In the Hunger Games, Katniss acts as both producer and consumer. Prior to the first book, she is part of the television audience that has watched the Hunger Games each year. Then she actually participates in the Games; she is part of the televised broadcast and made over into a proper tribute for the competition. The tributes' choices in the arena affect how the story for that particular year unfolds. This form of participation by the fan as "empowered consumer" is at the core of the reality-show experience (Jenkins 169). The significance of the active participation in the formation of televisual narratives creates a new type of critical engagement where artistic expression and aesthetic interpretation intersect with each other; Katniss's survival depends on this intersection.

More than evaluating the content of the Games, however, Katniss begins to create meaning through them with the event as her primary medium. She becomes, for better or worse, a performance artist who composes what can only be considered art by using the seemingly crass and debased realism of reality television as a starting point. When Rue becomes Katniss's ally during the course of the Games, Rue develops into an integral part of Katniss's narrative arc as it plays out for the television audience, especially considering that Rue's murder marks the end of the second part of the first book. Katniss's dramatic dispatching of Rue's killer is a turning point as sharp as any formal section designation. Even more significant is her comforting Rue as she dies. Katniss salutes her dead ally with flowers, sending Rue off with the same gesture District 12 uses at the reaping. All the while she knows, "They'll have to show it" (*HG* 237). In this made-for-television moment, the tragedy of Rue's death (even though Katniss later finds out the scene is never broadcast in the way she intended) is made into something, well, beautiful. Katniss uses her knowledge of how the Games work to make a statement about their cruelty that is as aesthetically pleasing as it is politically relevant.

The burial scene illustrates another means of artistic expression. After Rue's death, Katniss makes Rue into an art object for the viewing and reading public. Ironically, the Capitol already objectifies the bodies of Rue and Katniss (along with all of the other tributes) by placing them at the center of a reality television show. But Katniss appropriates Rue's body and changes what both she and Rue signify as tributes. Rather than representing the power of the

Capitol, Rue's body symbolizes its brutality. As Katniss buries Rue in flowers, she learns how to express her hatred for the government by using the materials the Capitol provides.

Recognizing the aesthetic potential of the Hunger Games inscribes Katniss with a new type of agency. Her position in front of the camera throughout the Games affords her both privileged access to the Capitol and visibility to a broader public. While some "real life" participants-turned-television stars use their celebrity to advance their careers or popularity (Jenkins 204), Katniss does something else entirely. She, alongside her supporters, appropriates the meaning of the Games from the Capitol. Rather than representing the Capitol's unquestioned dominance, the Games come to symbolize the political potential of a population ready for change. The potential is affective, meaning it is rooted in the emotional content of the Games themselves. This content knits groups of people together through a shared sense of loss and through the collective anxiety underpinning their everyday existence.

Katniss's growing awareness of herself as an artist marks her evolution as a character in the trilogy. During her victory speech at District 11 (Rue's district) in *Catching Fire,* Katniss extemporizes by telling the audience about the role Rue played in helping her win the Games. In return, they sing Rue's mockingjay tune and hold their hands up as a salute, the same gesture Katniss's district gave to her and that Katniss gave to Rue when she died. This gesture honors Katniss not necessarily as a victor of the Hunger Games, but as an artist who has painted a picture of an atrocity. This gesture is almost like the audience giving Katniss permission, even if it is after the fact, to try and use Rue's body to expose the Capitol in the way that she did. Katniss's artwork has celebrated Rue's humanity rather than erasing it. Katniss uses her position to take what is entertainment for the Capitol — the reality show in the novel — and make it into something really meaningful for both her and her audience. Her exposure to the mechanisms of control that underlie the political system that created the Hunger Games allows her to more readily expose those same mechanisms to the general public. When she returns to the backstage area, Katniss sees a Peacekeeper kill the man who began the salute. She learns that making a statement comes at a price.

This demonstration of Katniss's ability to inspire the citizens of Panem, an ability cultivated through her star status as victor of the Hunger Games, initiates yet another transformation. More than an artist, Katniss changes into a symbol of the revolution. In the same way she uses Rue to make a statement about the Hunger Games, others use the character Katniss cultivated during the Games to represent the political struggle against the Capitol. Katniss's celebrity status in the Seventy-fourth Hunger Games culminates with her refusal to kill Peeta. When the rules change again and there can be only one victor, Katniss tells Peeta he can't kill himself to save her. Her rationale is one of self-preservation, as his death would always leave her alone in the arena no matter where she went or how long she lived. When she realizes that if the Games don't have a victor, "the whole thing would blow up in the Gamemakers' faces" (*HG* 344), Katniss manages to blackmail the Capitol by having both remaining tributes attempt suicide by poisonous berries. The trumpets sound, the Game ends, and two victors are allowed. Katniss's actions in the arena transform it into a public site of aesthetic engagement for those who participate and those who watch. Recognizing the aesthetic potential of the Hunger Games for the tributes allows the revolution to form from within.

While everything up to this time and place in the Games and everything after is freighted with the politics of the Capitol, this made-for-television moment between Katniss and Peeta with the poisonous berries is authentic. Benjamin asserts, "*[A]s soon as the criterion of authenticity ceases to be applied to artistic production, the whole social function of art is revolutionized. Instead of being founded on ritual, it is based on a different practice: politics*" (106, emphasis in original). Although authenticity is lost through the process of reproduction, in *The Hunger Games* trilogy it exists in the time and place of aesthetic connection. Perhaps "authenticity" is the wrong word: in this moment there is something real that is being felt by the characters, television audience, and readers. Katniss's struggle to survive transcends the televised reality of the media event. There is something real that cannot be contained by the narrative of the Hunger Games, the cameras watching Katniss's every move, or by the book as it unfolds for the reader in real time. Unbeknownst to her, this act of defiance cements her symbolic position at the center of a political revolution. In the first part of *Catching Fire,* President Snow warns Katniss about the "spark" she ignited with her little stunt; he also warns her to resist the urge to ignite the proverbial fire (*CF* 2). Katniss challenges the Capitol in order to survive in the Game that is, from its outset, rigged against her. This survival instinct manifests in her ability to create her own artistic response to the Hunger Games whose meaning exceeds the framework of the televised broadcast.

Television coverage of the couple beyond the arena, from the fashion shoot and marriage proposal to the surprise announcement about the Quarter Quell, represents an attempt to take back the meaning of the Hunger Games. But, as *Mockingjay* illustrates, it is too late. Meaning has been made, and nobody, not even Katniss, has control over how it spreads. President Snow's effort to control meaning fails miserably, as does the power of Katniss as the ironic symbol of both the oppression by and rebellion against the Capitol. This meaning is wrapped into a bigger cause, one in which Katniss struggles to come to terms with herself as a symbol of the revolution. Her proximity to the rebellion and participation in it both in front of the camera and behind the scenes expose her completely to the reality of her sacrifice. As the embodiment of the Mockingjay, Katniss represents an unstable reality that leads to another realization, another lie, and another murder. Echoing the Capitol's inability to control the aesthetic potential of the Hunger Games, Katniss cannot control the production and consumption of her own persona by the public. She is a star. The struggle to view tributes as actual people rather than celebrities during the Hunger Games mirrors Katniss's own struggle to preserve her humanity and reach her aesthetic potential as a revolutionary symbol.

Collins's trilogy explores the aesthetic dimensions of popular culture by creating the dystopian world of Panem, in which television is the population's primary means of communication. Katniss volunteering in place of her sister, Rue's death, and the suicide threat with the poisonous berries come to symbolize both the beauty and brutality of the Hunger Games for those watching (and reading about) the arena. These scenes affect every character's perception of the world and their place in it, with diverse perspectives reverberating throughout the larger narrative frameworks of *Catching Fire* and *Mockingjay*. The polysemy of each dramatic made-for-television moment in the first novel shapes public perception and ignites yet another media event — the revolution — that grows uncontrollably beyond the delimited boundaries of the Hunger Games themselves. This revolution is aesthetic as much as it is political. As Katniss, Peeta, and the rest of her group move into the Capitol during the third book, the narrative conventions of the reality genre that mediate the live events in the first two novels give way to a new form of popular entertainment. When they work through the rubble with the main objective of assassinating President Snow, the story resembles more of a video game narrative than a reality television episode. In this scenario, Katniss as the Mockingjay stands in as the playable character of this game rather than the gamer who controls the action onscreen. Just as when she was a tribute, her subjectivity within this video game represents a negotiation between her aesthetic potential and entertainment value coupled with the political interests of those in (or those who want to rise to) power. Ultimately, the ambivalent symbolism of the Mockingjay crafted through Katniss's celebrity status in a time of war represents what revolutionary art in the age of reality TV has become.

Works Cited

Benjamin, Walter. "The Work of Art in the Age of Its Technological Reproducibility (Second Version)." *Selected Writings, Volume 3: 1935–1938.* Cambridge: Belknap-Harvard University Press, 2006. 101–33. Print.

Buck-Morss, Susan. "Aesthetics and Anaesthetics: Walter Benjamin's Artwork Essay Reconsidered." *October* 62 (1992): 3–41. Print.

Collins, Suzanne. *Catching Fire.* New York: Scholastic, 2009. Print.

_____. *The Hunger Games.* 2008. Rpt. New York: Scholastic, 2010. Print.

_____. *Mockingjay.* New York: Scholastic, 2010. Print.

Gray, Jonathan. *Television Entertainment.* New York: Routledge, 2008. Print.

Hill, Annette. *Reality TV: Audiences and Popular Factual Television.* New York: Routledge, 2005. Print.

Jenkins, Henry. *Convergence Culture: Where Old and New Media Collide.* New York: New York University Press, 2006. Print.

Lotz, Amanda. *The Television Will Be Revolutionized.* New York: New York University Press, 2007. Print.

Marriott, Stephanie. *Live Television: Time, Space and the Broadcast Event.* London: Sage, 2007. Print.

Massumi, Brian. "Fear (The Spectrum Said)." *Positions* 13.1 (2005): 31–48. Print.

"*Top Chef: Texas.*" *Bravotv.com.* BravoMedia-NBC Universal, 2011. Web. 2 Dec. 2011.

10

(Im)Mutable Natures

Animal, Human and Hybrid Horror*

Sharon D. King

I am still a beast at bay. — Rainsford to General Zaroff— Richard Connell, *The Most Dangerous Game*

What is the measure of humanity? What is, or should be, humankind's relationship to the other creatures that share our world? The often-troubled connection between humans and animals, symbolized by animal-rights protests as well as the by the recent pop trend of Spirit Hoods (Alimurung 32), remains a dominant theme in Western culture. Scientific inquiry and speculative fiction alike teem with narratives debating whether the essence of humanity stems from socialization or from biology, probing the ethical implications of cloning and deliberate genetic mutations, questioning the long-standing but increasingly arbitrary moral separation between humans and animals. These issues form the backdrop against which Suzanne Collins plumbs the depths of human depravity in the world of *The Hunger Games*. The human fascination with the monstrous, as incarnated by the numerous hybrid creatures that are omnipresent in Panem, is but one aspect. Another is the terrifyingly porous nature of predator and prey that charges the heroes' many forced competitions with a sense of irony as well as horror. Hunting is both a profound metaphor for, and method of, exploring the boundaries of the difference — or the lack thereof— between humans and the other creatures in their world. The heroes also seek — but do not find — certainty in their own identity: the main characters are truly players on a stage, endlessly construing their identity as they must, depending on their audience and co-per-

*An earlier version of this essay was presented at the 33rd International Conference on the Fantastic in the Arts (March 2012) in Orlando, Florida.

formers. And although the two main characters do survive, the land of confusion and despair described by their trajectory through the trilogy suggests a permanent state of liminality, a society frozen in crisis mode, so far from reintegration that little long-term hope remains for any of its creatures.

Science has long emphasized the fundamental connection between animal and human, categorizing the latter as "a biological species ... among many" (Wilson, *On Human Nature* xiv). Such deep ties between man and beast are inherent to the fictional universe of *The Hunger Games*. There are simple names that make the connection explicit: Castor (beaver), Woof and Mags (magpies). Temperaments also show the link: Foxface demonstrates surprising cunning in the Games. Electrical expert Beetee is, like the bees his name reflects, actively and consciously social and tireless in his work, including the invention of the wire Katniss uses to destroy the force field surrounding the Quell Games arena. In the final novel, Tigris, owner of a Capitol fur shop, shelters and provisions Katniss and her crew in their hunt for President Snow. Her name recalls not only the great feline predator that she affects through surgical transmogrification and makeup (as well as her habit of eating only raw meat), but also an archetypical Western river of life. The name of Head Gamemaker Seneca Crane evokes the highly vocal bird currently under threat of extinction. Crane is executed for allowing Katniss to devise a way to victory; later, she hangs his image in effigy as a warning to other Gamemakers.

The parallels go beyond names and temperaments to dress, habits, personality: Octavia, who keeps pet mice and once used a mouse motif to ornament her hair, is herself tiny, furry, and shrill. Intrepid rebels Castor and Pollux are dressed in armor that reminds Katniss of hard-shelled bugs. Beetee's partner Wiress is heralded as the coal-mine canary whose intuition helps the others determine the clockwork precision of their Game-world terrors in *Catching Fire*. Katniss's dissipated mentor Haymitch is often as inebriated as a skunk. The despot Snow is likened to a serpent; he has even had frequent recourse to poison, the human equivalent of a snake's venom, in his ascent to power.

Even more inextricably linked to animals, as well as other sources of food, are the names and characters of protagonists Katniss and Peeta. Katniss is the huntress/provider whose name evokes both predator — the carnivorous feline that toys with its prey — and food itself, the word *katniss* designating an edible tuber. Even before the Games, her identity has merged with the consumable: she recalls her father saying that she would never starve if she could find herself. Peeta Mellark (the surname possibly short for "meadowlark") is a savior-figure. When they were both children, Peeta saw Katniss desperate for food, rummaging like a hungry dog. The son of a baker, Peeta contrived to offer the Everdeen family a ration of bread — bread that was said to be only fit for pigs — which spared their lives and got him punished. The pronunciation of Peeta's name, moreover, unswervingly points to the global organization of ardent creature protectors, the group that stresses the ultimate equality of all living beings: People for the Ethical Treatment of Animals. Peeta and Katniss complement each other. Although a defender of her friends, Katniss will unflinchingly kill creatures for her own survival and, at the end of the first Games, feels herself a feral creature, untamed and fierce. In contrast, Peeta does not actively hunt, is poor at it, and is, until brainwashed, essentially humane and compassionate.

In the background, real animals serve both as parallels and counterpoints to the knife-edge status quo of Katniss's world. For the most part, these creatures are functional and useful, provisioning or otherwise servicing the human populace. Little Prim's pet goat Lady goes far beyond a companion animal, providing milk for cheese to supplement the family's meager food supply. In District 12, feral dogs are taken and used for consumption, passing as domesticated meat. In the Capitol, show carts are pulled by horses trained so well that they have no need for reins. Wild geese are shot and plucked, the task of preparing their bodies providing space for an intimate conversation between Gale and Katniss. The heroine's family cat, ironically named Buttercup, conjures up the image of dainty flowers or even the delicate character of *The Princess Bride,* yet the animal is worm-ridden, scarred, and sickly. Still, he is a survivor, persisting to the end of the trilogy's main narrative. From the start, readers may divine something of Katniss's destiny in the raw guts she occasionally offers the cat as food, food he accepts without a hiss but also without affection — a rapprochement said to be all the love Katniss will ever get from this creature.

In Katniss's world, hunting is necessarily the default mode for existence: she and her companion Gale must hunt in tandem to obtain sufficient food for the good of all in her district. Their actions of putting aside competitiveness and teaming up in a difficult environment in order to obtain the most from scarce resources is biologically driven (Wilson, *Sociobiology* 330); it is the way animals evolved into pair bonding. Yet the novels never cease to stress that predator and prey are often interchangeable. In the forest, where Katniss and Gale hunt, the natural predators (wild dogs, cougars, bears, venomous snakes) are flesh eaters that are kept out of the human living space and that become food if the humans have courage and skill. Katniss recalls the young buck deer she shot while out hunting with Gale. For a moment she felt guilty for killing something so "fresh and innocent" (*HG* 269), yet in the next moment she anticipated the taste of the deer's savory flesh. Much later, Katniss and Gale laugh about former encounters with the wild creatures they have hunted, encounters that will of necessity inform their future assaults for freedom. In training for the final conflict, Katniss acknowledges that shooting at clay pigeons is amusing, like "hunting a moving creature" (*CF* 232). This need to secure food for existence permeates both Katniss's and Gale's natures. Like the aloof, chaste huntress/goddess Diana, Katniss also chases away suitors as often as she hunts with her bow and arrows, and slays the lynx who follows her around in the forest like a pet because it drives away the game she needs to survive. Inevitably, Katniss likens Gale's voice, as he gives her the sad news that her district has been destroyed, to the one he uses "to approach wounded animals before he delivers a deathblow" (*CF* 391).

Yet animals are hardly the sole focus of hunting in the world of the Hunger Games. The horror of humans hunting their own kind for sport has long been a trope of speculative literature and film, from depictions of alternate-history gladiatorial combat, to variations of *The Most Dangerous Game* (even a parodic episode of *The Simpsons*), to the Japanese *Battle Royale*. So it is in the trilogy: those sent to the Games are forced, if not specifically to be predators, at least to defend themselves against competitors. By the Capitol's rules, only one tribute can survive. In the Hunger Games, competitors are on equal terms with the arena's animals for food and shelter, one with them in fleeing from fires and other deliberately created terrors — at least until the humans can fashion or find weapons. Nothing separates predator and prey except their relative success. In the Quell Games, Katniss's foe Enobaria is overtly beast-like, using her teeth to tear out the throat of an opponent during her first combat. Katniss herself demonstrates her ability to set snares that will leave enemies hanging, as she has done in the past with animals. In *Mockingjay,* Katniss equates the rebels with fish and birds, too easily caught and snared. When her prep team is kidnapped and tortured, Katniss thinks of the too-trusting animals Gale and she once hunted. Even the viciously pursued rebel squad members taking refuge in Tigris's abode in the Capitol wrap themselves in thick pelts from her shop before sleeping, further obscuring the distinction between man and beast, hunter and hunted.

After predation, of course, comes preparation: as Frans de Waal observes in his study of animal ethics, "Meat differs from fruits and vegetables in that it *moved* before it was put in the cooking pot" (139, emphasis in original). Numerous references in the trilogy make clear how perilously slippery the slope is between consumer and consumed. During Katniss's grooming for the Games, she compares herself to a plucked and dressed fowl, or an oven-ready roast; later, she fears she will be broiled alive by her costume being set afire. Her stylists are compared to strangely colored birds, and Katniss fears that Peeta's kindness will make her easily preyed upon. In the Quell Games, other tributes are dressed as cows, as if inviting themselves to be barbequed like steaks. On the eve of the Quell, Katniss's own mockingjay costume invites jokes about cooking birds. The fight to overtake the tyrannical regime is characterized by Gale as a matter of chasing out a den of feral dogs, whose meat was passed off as commoners' beef in their district. Lethal mutant birds kill

Maysilee Donner, ironic not just because of her surname but because she is the aunt of the girl who will one day give Katniss her mockingjay pin. And though cannibalism per se is rejected by the Gamemakers, the rejection stems not from its lack of ethics but from its lack of popularity with the TV audience. The trilogy's ultimate metaphorical use of sustenance may be the lamb stew that Katniss favors so much while she's in the Capitol. The image of the sacrificial lamb, whose blood and flesh are given for others, is inextricably linked to Katniss herself, by the self-abnegating devotion she shows towards Prim, Peeta, Rue, and others. Similar comparisons are as inescapable, if less grisly: in the humid jungle of the Quell Games, Katniss notes, "We're all just one big, warm stew" (CF 362).

Indeed, the Games are only the most extreme manifestation of existence in the autocratic dystopia of Panem, in which the concept of human civilization is a cruel joke. Throughout the trilogy, Katniss's narration of the manipulated ebb and flow of sustenance reminds us that food is not just a necessity but a blessing: it makes people feel better, is in fact a potent reason to continue to live. Yet within her world's über–Social Darwinist society, irony reigns alongside tyranny: in Panem (the word consciously evoking the staff of life), the single greatest challenge for inhabitants is obtaining their daily bread. The people of Katniss's home sector, District 12, are in a constant struggle to overcome starvation, while the well-to-do in the Capitol constantly overindulge, to the point of debauchery. Before the Quarter Quell, future combatants revel in banquets while they watch their imminent opponents, as well as past losers, in recorded assaults. Food is even seen as a means of getting the attention of those in power: an enraged Katniss sends an arrow flying into the Gamemakers' roasted pig at their banquet, flaunting their decorum in a daring bid to make them aware of her presence. The Games provide a final means of stripping human beings down to their most primal nature, further highlighting the general suffering of those outside the Capitol: the competitors are left with their basic need for food constantly in question. They must actively find it, steal it, hunt and kill for it; it may be taken from them, abandoned, or ruined. The Cornucopia, where the combatants seize whatever supplies they can, is yet another instance of Panem's ironical manipulation: it pours forth its wealth of food, clothes, and tools to help fighters survive long enough to kill one another.

The linking of food to entertainment throughout the trilogy — most specifically to the Roman practice of "Bread and Circuses" (M 223) — is singularly important: the people of Panem are, literally and metaphorically, "eating up" the combatants' performance in the Games. Tellingly, however, the more-sought-after images, and often the best rewarded, are at least sometimes the actions that are most humane. Selling herself more times into the lottery of the Games via the "tesserae" both protects her sister and earns Katniss's household more bread (*HG* 13). Her loyalty to Peeta — and its interpretation as a budding romance — plays well to sponsors and is ultimately a game changer: near the end of the first novel, Katniss's pandering to the audience's voyeuristic need to glimpse her intimacy with Peeta earns the starving pair a feast. Still, the media adage "If it bleeds, it leads" applies equally to Panem: the suffering of the tribute Cato, once her foe and then merely a "hunk of meat" (*HG* 340–41), provides a great show for audiences. The novels illuminate the profound divide between oppressed humans forced to perform this intensified struggle for survival and the elites who consume such extreme public spectacles as entertainment.

The trilogy equally thrusts into the forefront questions of the monstrous stemming from hybridity — the combination of several elements from two or more bodies, animal or human (Burke 25). Studies of monstrosity note that these chimeric entities generate terror by creating confusion: "In the jumbled limbs and motley order of its body, the monster threatens to destabilize all order, to break down all hierarchies. Monsters stink ... of that space outside the law" (Hanofi 2–3). The horror of hybrid creatures infuses Western cultural consciousness, from myths of Greek centaurs and Egyptian sphinxes, to medieval tales of werewolves, to H. G. Wells's *The Island of Dr. Moreau* and its tortured entities, to recent films such as *Spiderman* (Cox 18). In Collins's trilogy, the novels present manifold ways in which the monstrous hybrid appears, the creatures resulting from calculated manipulations of human and animal and providing a new twist to the gruesome sport faced by the combatants.

During the trilogy's pitiless competitions and war, competitors face death in a hundred guises: artificial drought or downpours, horrendous fires, acid fog, blood rain, even machines that reduce human fighters to matter fit for sausage casings. Most terrifying of all, however, are the weaponized hybrid creatures that are effective killing machines: tracker jackers with the venom that maddens humans before it dispatches them, wolf-like mutants formed in the image of the competitors who had once been defeated by Katniss and Peeta, heartbreakingly recognizable: "The green eyes glowering at me are unlike ... any canine I've ever seen. They are unmistakably human" (*HG* 333). Jabberjays designed to be spies also scream in the tortured voices of humans' loved ones. There are flesh-eating rats as well as genetically modified monkeys that turn on humans in a vicious mass assault. Hissing four-legged lizard-human creatures in *Mockingjay* are specifically programmed to seek out Katniss's destruction.

Even the less violent mutations have dark overtones. The mockingjays' projected utility has been eclipsed by Nature, which caused their evolution from the jabberjays, yet the birds use their ability to mimic song to take up hauntingly sad refrains. The genetically heightened scent of the roses President

Snow sends Katniss blends inextricably with the smell of his vanquished enemies' blood. The monstrosity of the hybrid creatures goes beyond even their carnate forms: tracker-jacker venom is used to help brainwash Peeta, ironically making him think that Katniss has lost her own humanity.

The deliberate commingling of hybrid and human in Panem's media creates another kind of monster, albeit one with a pretty face. In the first novel, Katniss receives the iconic gold mockingjay pin as a gift and wears it first innocently, then as a deliberate challenge during the Games. In *Catching Fire* she is calculatedly dressed by designer Cinna as the mockingjay, the hybrid creature that changed and adapted far beyond its creators' designs. Her further transformation occurs behind the scenes: the revolutionary Mockingjay is carefully crafted, through propaganda, as a symbol of another kind of evolutionary defiance, an emblem of the rebellion against tyranny. By then the mockingjay emblem has become a popular trend, even being baked into bread like a secular version of the sacred host. Panem is now stamped indelibly with its own treachery turned back on itself. The apotheosis of Katniss's fusion with the rebellious hybrid creature comes when, near the end of the trilogy, she is burned during the final assault, the tongues of fire likened to feathers of charred black and ash white. The inferno that sets her ablaze also recalls her elaborately designed outfits during the first Games, when she was safely set aflame to the astonished appreciation of the masses, and later clad in a gown that shimmered. Nearly dead from the conflagration, Katniss yet rises like a phoenix from the ashes to live on.

But the narrative of the trilogy describes another, more pernicious chimeric tendency, one that destabilizes the entire society: both Katniss and Peeta ultimately construe their view of themselves through impermanence. There is no set definition of self, no real integrity of identity in this precarious locus between life and death called survival. Throughout the novels they constantly redefine their relationship to their rivals in the Games, to their various audiences, and to each other as they see the need or sense the expectation. Katniss's first night in the Games makes her acutely aware that her struggle is now a matter of role reversal: will she be a source of food for the animals or their competition in the hunt for food? Near the first book's conclusion, Katniss reflects that her identity as hunter/predator defines her — as much as she can be defined — and she wonders who she could be without it. Throughout the Games, too, Katniss recognizes that her foes, such as the innocent Rue who saves her from the tracker jackers, may be temporarily useful as allies; yet she also recognizes that the Games require allies to become enemies again as a matter of individual survival.

Above all, her relationship with Peeta is endlessly fraught with pandering to viewers and sponsors as a means of survival. Their contrived romance, so compelling to spectators, creates the ultimate adolescent confusion: Katniss cannot sort out her own feelings, cannot parse whether she is truly in love or just playacting. Pretending to love someone is the most dangerous game of all. For his own part, Peeta's declaration of love for Katniss is seen by her mentor Haymitch as just "for show" (*HG* 135); what matters is the people's perception of Peeta's love, not its reality. In the first arena, Peeta confesses his terror at the thought of losing his own identity to the whims of the Gamemakers. His fear is only too justified: it foreshadows his capture and brainwashing by Snow's forces. Peeta becomes what the Capitol perceives as the ultimate weapon against Katniss. In the final novel, as Katniss confronts the extent of the torture and manipulation Peeta is undergoing, her identity seems to her to merge with that of the distracted, near-broken cat Buttercup: she is inconsolable, fearful, frustrated in her inability to discover how to help her friend. Ironically, it's not Peeta's near ruin but Prim's violent death that completes the torture. Believing the rebels guilty of the bombing that killed Prim, Katniss assassinates Coin. By then, any clear distinction between the human monsters such as the cold-blooded Snow and the deceptively cool Coin and the humane characters such as Peeta or even Katniss has evaporated. If monstrosity is defined by hybridity, by the blurring of boundaries between self and other, Peeta and Katniss are indeed monsters.

And if the characters are mutable, their world is also one of constant inconstancy. As Victor Turner has described it, liminality, the threshold state, is reflected through social dramas that involve phases of breach, crisis, redressive action, and finally reintegration; not incidentally, they are intimately inflected with animal symbolism (35–43, 253). Other scholars such as Arpad Szakolczai see the terrifying potential for fixed liminality, including stages with the society either frozen in place, trapped within countless fixed rituals or games (220), or in an endless downward spiral of stirring up rivalries, redressing past grievances, and cycling through terrors (223). This seems only too descriptive of Panem. The world of the first two novels reflects the first possibility: the rigid divide between rulers and ruled — the court society of the Capitol versus the districts — and the harsh ritual writ large across the populace in the guise of the stylized, media-driven ceremonies and rules of the Games. The individual tributes trapped there, in their different roles, costumes, and masks, repeat their required mode of play until, as Szakolczai describes, play becomes "deadly serious" (222).

Szakolczai's second possibility — in which the court society breaks down and the promise of reintegration ironically seems imminent — would appear to describe the fragmented country of Panem in the trilogy's final novel, both prior to the war against the rebels and after the regime change has been effected. As *Mockingjay* begins, Katniss blames herself for her home district's total destruction, her image having been used to foment the rebellion. Despite being the symbol of the new society, she comes to recognize that it has been organized in ways possibly even more monstrous, more manipulative than Panem's former oppressiveness; that in this new world order, people are prized not just as survivors but as reproductive matter to help renew humankind. During the battle to take the Capitol, Katniss confronts hideous truths about herself and her compatriots: that the rebel president Coin wants her dead, sensing a threat to her own power; that Gale is willing to destroy an entire group of noncombatants — the District 2 citizens employed in the Nut — to defeat the enemy; that the hazards of war include casual, unintended death as well as intentional, as evidenced by the aqua-robed woman calling for help whom Katniss slays without thinking.

Later in the novel, Katniss confronts her many losses: Peeta's questionable trustworthiness, Prim's shocking death, and Gale's divided allegiances. Peeta's truth-guessing game, where he must reconstruct his past little by little, is yet another manifestation of the society's brokenness, where reality itself is — and must be — challenged at every turn. After the war, the Panem we see is hardly reintegrating; instead, it is reestablishing its own endless loop of recrimination, distrust, and hopelessness: the new government excoriating the cruelty of former president Snow for using children as pawns despite the rebels having exploited Katniss with abandon until her utility plays out. If, indeed, ethics stem from social order, if "conscious community concern is at the heart of human morality" (de Waal 208), then the society of the Hunger Games would seem to be in an end state, a "freak show" (*CF* 211) in which the monstrous reigns supreme. Near *Mockingjay*'s end, Katniss faces execution for Coin's assassination, Coin, the new president who had wanted to continue the Games as a means of revenge and thus reintroduce terror. Katniss attempts suicide, considering it a final rebellion: "It benefits no one to live in a world where these things happen" (*M* 377). She rejects her human identity, no longer wishing to see the stain of human inhumanity replicated, no longer willing that the "monsters called human beings" continue (*M* 377).

Yet Katniss does ultimately live and perpetuate her kind, her final actions seemingly stemming more from resignation than from hope. And once more, the return of the stubborn, disfigured cat Buttercup parallels Katniss's own tenacity, her will to survive; it also foregrounds her decision to live with Peeta and reproduce in spite of her despair. Katniss's final acquiescence, in the epilogue, is evoked by her language, couched in a passive voice that contrasts with the words of the active, direct young woman who had blurted out truth even through her terror. Then, too, the reconstructed society, barely sketched out in a page and a half, remains on the fringes of integrity and stability. Reintegration is envisioned, yet hardly achieved: though "the arenas have been destroyed" (*M* 389), Katniss will forever be marked by the Games that she knows, one day, she will have to reveal to her children. And the new Panem she describes, where children play games, all unknowing, on graveyards, evokes the horror that these people may never escape their past, and that, for human and animal alike, another siren song of tyranny might beckon in their future.

WORKS CITED

Alimurung, Gendy. "The Weirdest Startup Ever: Four Fashion Neophytes Create the Spirit Hood Rage." *L. A. Weekly* 29 July–4 Aug. 2011. Print.

Burke, Peter. "Frontiers of the Monstrous: Perceiving National Characters in Early Modern Europe." *Monstrous Bodies/Political Monstrosities in Early Modern Europe.* Eds. Laura L. Knoppers and Joan B. Landis. Ithaca: Cornell University Press, 2004. 25–39. Print.

Collins, Suzanne. *Catching Fire.* New York: Scholastic, 2009. Print.

_____. *The Hunger Games.* New York: Scholastic, 2008. Print.

_____. *Mockingjay.* New York: Scholastic, 2010. Print.

Connell, Richard. *The Most Dangerous Game.* 1924. Rockville: Arc Manor, 2008. Print.

Cox, Christoph. "Of Humans, Animals, and Monsters." *Becoming Animal: Contemporary Art in the Animal Kingdom.* Ed. Nato Thompson. Cambridge: MIT Press, 2005. 18–25. Print.

de Waal, Frans. *Good Natured.* Cambridge: Harvard University Press, 1996. Print.

Hanofi, Zakiya. *Monster in the Machine: Magic, Medicine and the Marvelous in the Time of the Scientific Revolution.* Durham: Duke University Press, 2000. Print.

Szakolczai, Arpad. *Reflexive Historical Sociology.* London: Routledge, 2000. Print.

Turner, Victor. *Dramas, Fields, and Metaphors: Symbolic Action in Human Society.* 1974. Ithaca: Cornell University Press, 1987. Print.

Wilson, Edward O. *On Human Nature.* Cambridge: Harvard University Press, 2004. Print.

_____. *Sociobiology: The New Synthesis.* Cambridge: Belknap-Harvard University Press, 1975. Print.

"Killer" Katniss and "Lover Boy" Peeta

Suzanne Collins's Defiance of Gender-Genred Reading

ELLYN LEM *and* HOLLY HASSEL

Few would deny the influence of rigid, gender-segregated visual and material culture on its child consumers. From advertisements that place girls in domestic spheres and boys in outside settings to Happy Meal "Tonkas" for boys and "My Little Pony" for girls, children early on are taught that male and female spheres are separate, with scripted roles and expectations. Elizabeth Segel has examined the way youth literature is similarly segregated as separate "boy" and "girl" book genres, a binary that emerged over a century ago and that persists. Defying these highly marketable categories is Suzanne Collins's *The Hunger Games,* a publishing phenomenon that has challenged this gender stratification. Two key features of Collins's novel demonstrate her bridging of these spheres. First, we contend that Katniss Everdeen is a female character who balances traditionally masculine qualities such as athleticism, independence, self-sufficiency, and a penchant for violence with traditionally feminine qualities such as idealized physical female beauty and vulnerability. As a "male-identified" female character, Katniss capitalizes on patriarchal values that privilege traditionally masculine characteristics while leveraging other, gender-appropriate qualities in ways that appeal to all readers. Second, the book complicates gender binaries of masculine and feminine in its portrayal of war and romance, fiction genres traditionally targeting gendered readerships even when those readers are adolescent consumers. Collins posits the romantic story line as a delicate balance between farce and spectacle, strategy and inevitability; by setting it alongside a story for survival in a hostile environment, Collins's narrative draws from these two generic traditions (war stories and heterosexual romance) in ways that appeal beyond gender lines.

Queer theory, as well as much feminist theory, has argued against reductive binaries surrounding gender identity and sex; in this essay, we use these binary terms to reflect reading audiences that have been both constructed by the publishing industry and echoed by scholars of reception theory who have addressed the phenomenon of gendering and YA literature. Given the rigid gender segregation of contemporary childhood, it is a small miracle boys and girls share any mutual space, especially as sources of pleasure and entertainment. The toy industry, for example, has a notorious reputation for exaggerating gender difference and scripting roles that delineate male and female spheres of experience. Susan Kahlenberg and Michelle Hein comment on this phenomenon in their study on toy commercials, noting that "girls-only" toy commercials have generally been set "in the home" and have emphasized family and domestic affairs while many "boys-only" toy commercials take place "outdoors," where there are "more opportunities" (844). While not everyone believes that play objects influence children's socialization, others like Stephen Kline convincingly point out that the "sex-typing of toys" does, in fact, lead to a separation in the "cognitive, emotional and social skills that children acquire" (qtd. in Inness 79). Girls, then, too often are being steered away from risk taking and adventure-filled paths, just as boys' more violent toys do not provide encouragement to explore creative talents in the kitchen or other domestic places. Iron Chef Bobby Flay, for example, recalled his disappointment in asking for an Easy-Bake Oven when he was a child and receiving a G.I. Joe instead from his father (Newman 9).

Since television shows for young people are often ancillaries of the toy industry (e.g., *Hot Wheels Battle Force 5*), much of the programming also seems to cater to one gender or the other as a way to reach a defined market — an argument used by toy companies as well to justify their regressive gender stereotyping (e.g., the absence of boys in doll advertisements and cooking toys' packaging). In recent years, however, television has broken new ground in creating shows that are not gender specific. Nickelodeon, for example, has prided itself in creating independent, strong female leads for programs intended to appeal to gender-diverse audiences. In the past, many producers believed that boys would not watch shows that prominently featured girls. But a perfect example of a successful television show that transcends gender is *iCarly,* the number-one television series for all demographics of children and tweens in August 2011 (Seidman). The series follows the viral video antics of a Web show put on by Carly and her best friend, Sam. Given that television, Nickelodeon in particular, has found a way to appeal to mixed-gendered audiences, Suzanne Collins's background as a writer on children's programs makes sense. Not everyone will see *Clifford's Puppy Days* as a logical precursor to her

Hunger Games trilogy, with its brutal depiction of deprivation, murder, and war; but Collins has proved in both narrative forms that to write against the grain of gender expectations is not only possible but also necessary.

The *Hunger Games*'s story line engages both male and female readers, who have been conditioned from the bassinet to think in terms of blue and pink. And while there have been a few influential predecessors who helped to pave the way by creating literary works that also defy traditional gender roles, the tradition of classifying books as "girls' books" or "boys' books" has a much longer legacy. Elizabeth Segel provides a useful overview of how children's literature has a history of gender polarization. Girls' books were traditionally intended "to keep females pure and their imaginations unsullied — by restricting their world, even within the home" (170). Segel quotes an 1886 essay by Edward Salmon titled "What Girls Read," which refers to girls' books as "mental food for the future wives and mothers," emphasizing the necessity that girls learned from their reading how to maintain the status quo of females as the primary caregivers (171). Several scholarly works point to *Adventures of Huckleberry Finn* (1884) as the archetypal boys' book, with its focus on "an escape from domesticity" and the "female domination of the domestic world" (Segel 171). Boys' books tend to have exotic locales fraught with danger, surprise, and adventure, sending boys messages that reinforce their agency and remind them of their self-sufficiency. Nina Baym, in "Melodramas of Beset Manhood," argues that not only are gendered literary texts separate, but they are also stratified wherein male-coded texts are privileged and female-coded texts viewed as limited, subordinate, or inferior (for example, the privileging of canonical books such as *Huck Finn* over contemporaneous "sentimental" women's novels, such as *Heidi* (1880) and *Little Women* (1868–69).

Besides the contrasting settings, which reify social roles in girls' and boys' books, another obvious difference can be seen in character development. Whereas boys were often encouraged to rebel and challenge authority, female characters were given fewer opportunities for rebellion in girls' books and often "settled down" to a conforming complacency. Jo March, for example, in *Little Women* has been regarded as losing some of her willfulness and individuality as she weds and becomes a matriarch. Scholars have noted the need for more characters like the earlier Jo, characters who are, according to Judy Simons, "literary tomboys" (152). Simons explains that characters such as these, who display "gender dissidence," are necessary to provide an "alternative means of fulfillment for girls" that traditional "gender propriety" curtails (157). This can be contrasted with the strong emphasis in YA literary traditions that focus on heterosexual romance in stories targeted at female readers, traditions dating long before *Romeo and Juliet* and up through today's immensely popular *Twilight* series.

Over the years, the categories of clearly delineated girls' and boys' books have eased with the greater presence of "literary tomboys" contributing to this less-defined schema. *Harriet the Spy* (1964) and *A Wrinkle in Time* (1962) are often singled out as books that deviate from traditional gender dynamics and invite a cross-gendered audience. Despite these groundbreaking works, however, social and material forces still impose gender segregation on young readers in ways that foreclose a fuller understanding of experience from another perspective. Since publishers seem to believe that boys are less apt to read a girl-centered work than vice versa, writers have been asked to change their central female protagonists to male (e.g., Scott O'Dell's *Island of the Blue Dolphins*). Educational publications also have advised teachers to select books geared toward male audiences for fear of alienating boys, who already may not enjoy literature as much as girls (Segel 180). Even government officials have sought to reinvigorate the notion of literature for boys versus literature for girls. Alan Johnson, the British Secretary of State for Education, gave a 2007 speech in which he recommended Anthony Horowitz's Alex Rider series as good for boys since males are shown in the novels as "powerful ... sporting, spying or fighting heroes" (qtd. in Simons 154). The commercially and critically successful Harry Potter series epitomizes this cultural tendency to be overly concerned with boys at the expense of girls. Children's literature critic Seth Lerner observes that despite Hermione being a powerful female presence in the Potter series, the books "remain a story about men and boys and their searches for fathers" (228). Similarly, Rowling was asked by her agent, the Christopher Little Agency, to "adopt more gender-neutral initials" for the book cover precisely because of concerns about discouraging male readers if a woman author's name appeared on the cover — despite the book's male protagonist (Adney and Hassel 11).

Amid this backdrop of gender segregation and industry catering to male readers, Collins has produced a literary work with a female protagonist who appeals to males *and* females with equal ardor. Female writers such as Stephenie Meyer offer praise on the book's cover, and publishing heavyweight Stephen King has embraced the series publicly for its "addictive" qualities (qtd. in Lewit). Collins appears to have succeeded in the seemingly impossible task of creating "the most important female character in recent pop culture history" (Lewit), a character who defies gender segregation in her story and among her readers.

One of the ways that *The Hunger Games* bridges the divide between boys' and girls' culture is Collins's portrayal of a heroine who embodies traditionally masculine characteristics — in her role within her family, in her behavior, and in her adherence to patriarchal expectations regarding masculinity. Sociologist Allan Johnson writes in his book *The Gender Knot* that a society is patriarchal to the extent that it "promotes male privilege by being *male-dominated, male-identified, and male-centered*" (5, emphasis in original). In the case of *The Hunger Games,* Johnson's argument is most relevant when he discusses the culture characteristic of "male identification" or the way that particular qualities (usually those associated with higher cultural status) become gendered as "masculine" or "feminine." These qualities are to some degree disconnected with the physiological realities of sex. Johnson argues that in patriarchal cultures, the "cultural description of masculinity and the ideal man" comes from "the core values of society as a whole" (7). Male-identified qualities such as "control, strength, competitiveness, toughness, coolness under pressure, logic, forcefulness, decisiveness, rationality, autonomy, self-sufficiency, and control over any emotion that interferes with other core values (such as invulnerability)" are viewed as valuable, worthy of achievement and emulation, and are culturally rewarded (7). Johnson contrasts these qualities with those traditionally associated with femininity: "cooperation, mutuality, sharing, compassion, caring, vulnerability, a readiness to negotiate and compromise, emotional expressiveness, and intuitive and other nonlinear ways of thinking" (7). Johnson's definitions provide a useful lens through which to examine the character of Katniss Everdeen, who adheres in complex ways to both masculine and feminine qualities. This hybridity or androgyny, we argue, partly explains the series' popularity with both male and female readers, as indicated by its long-term status as a national best seller.

From the first novel's opening, Katniss's prowess in traditional male realms is emphasized: she uses a bow and arrow, does an army crawl under the fence that encloses District 12, and confesses the illegality of these actions — highlighting her daring and subversiveness in the face of an oppressive dictatorship (a subversiveness that will ultimately become a critical part of the plotline across the trilogy). As readers learn more about Katniss's role as the family provider following her father's death, they also see multiple examples of her adherence to the qualities Johnson outlines in his book: she is unemotional (as when she confesses that she initially preferred to drown the family cat rather than provide for him), and she remains emotionally detached throughout much of the narrative, sometimes exerting emotional control at critical junctures in the plot. For example, when Prim cries out after her older sister volunteers to take her place in the Hunger Games, Katniss rejects her little sister's hysterical embrace. She also refuses to cry with Prim since tears would just make Katniss another "easy target" (*HG* 23) when televised across Panem. Throughout the Games, she steadfastly tries not to show weakness — coded as emotional vulnerability.

When Katniss does have emotional lapses, a number of these are manifested as anger, not sadness — whether lashing out at the Gamemakers for their failure to pay attention to her display of talent by shooting the arrow into their dinner, or shoving Peeta after his declaration of love on camera, concerned that she appeared "weak" (*HG* 135), the ultimate transgression in a patriarchal culture that values invulnerability over emotional capitulation. Collins continues to emphasize Katniss's ability to refrain from emotional expressions of pain, sadness, or loneliness throughout the novel. For example, at the end of the first day, her reaction to Peeta's possible death is detached. She thinks it might be "better if he's gone already," not because she wants him to be done suffering but because it will mean she will not face the "unpleasant task" of being the one who kills him (*HG* 153). After her leg is burned by the wall of fire, she decides to camouflage her pain in hopes that her stalwartness will win sponsors. Always strategizing, Katniss uses her ability to maintain emotional control as a key component of her victory.

Other female characters serve as foils to Katniss due to their stereotypical femininity, which almost always highlights her male-identified strength against their feminine weaknesses: Katniss's sister, the innocent and naive Prim; their emotionally fragile mother, whose inability to care for the girls after their father's death earns Katniss's contempt; Effie Trinket, shallow, vain, and twittering. This use of feminine foils gives Collins an opportunity to stress Katniss's survival instinct, which fulfills traditional narrative expectations for a heroic protagonist. She steps into the void left by her father, the former provider, her protective instinct manifesting itself both as protection of others (Prim, Rue) and preservation of the self. Early in the novel, when she describes stepping into her father's provider role, Katniss explains that her willingness to take up hunting was essential for the family's survival. The reverse side of this independence and autonomy is her resentment at having to accept help. When Peeta saves Katniss after she endangers her life for a bow and arrow, she is shocked by and vaguely resentful of his behavior. Yet Collins's narrative also blends elements of traditionally masculine- or feminine-coded behaviors in Katniss's occasional willingness to acknowledge weakness — if only to herself. For example, although she feels like a fierce protector when she takes on Rue as an ally, Katniss also feels the force of her own loneliness, even as she contemplates ways of disarming the Careers while sharing a sleeping bag with her new ally. Katniss is simultaneously connected, emotionally available, even while she plots her offense.

In this way, Collins challenges our traditional understanding of the heroic modernist narrative by making Katniss the one with physical prowess, with the skills to defeat opponents, with the self-preservation instinct. When she almost leaves Peeta behind as they are being chased up the Cornucopia, she has to remind herself that she is, indeed, part of a team. Katniss's skill and fortitude — both in self-preservation and in mercy — drive the narrative. Readers see this again when the rule change is revoked, and Katniss immediately returns to her survival instinct, raising her bow to Peeta's heart. She feels shame when she sees that he is dropping his weapons, illustrating his purpose as the book's moral center: he's the one constantly holding Katniss accountable to the higher moral purpose behind their actions, the right course. Yet Katniss's ingenuity, cleverness, quick and strategic thinking ultimately save their lives (qualities that Haymitch recognizes and uses).

Interestingly, a critical part of making Katniss into a compliant participant in the Capitol's oppressive enterprise is remaking Katniss into a feminine character both physically and behaviorally; these are simultaneously the moments when she is made the most vulnerable. On the one hand, these feminine moments may invite girl readers to identify with her anxieties, vulnerability, and, sometimes, her pleasure at embracing the trappings of physical beauty; on the other hand, they seem to reinforce the idea that Katniss is most powerful when she embraces masculine ways. Collins further complicates this narrative maneuver by allowing Katniss alternating feelings of rejection of the artificial beauty expectations imposed by the Capitol and acceptance of them.

When Katniss is first brought to the center where she is remade physically, her attendants feminize her by eliminating body hair; they also emphasize how her utilitarian and unadorned appearance is insufficient by the Capitol's vain standards. When Cinna remakes both Katniss and Peeta into visually stunning spectacles, Katniss feels powerful and hopeful, largely because their fiery appearance earns admiration but not necessarily objectification. In contrast, the makeover scene prior to the critical interview with Caesar Flickerman poses a genuine challenge because it requires her to subsume her actual emotions — anger, disgust — and portray herself as enchanting, beguiling, and feminine. Under Cinna's guidance, she becomes otherworldly: she assesses her appearance as not simply pretty or beautiful, but "radiant" (*HG* 121). In these scenes, Katniss seems alternately pleased by the transformation and disgusted by the artificiality of the "beauty" that is required by Capitol audiences, and so she frequently comments on the over-produced, superficial — and often bizarre — beauty adornments of Capitol residents. Perhaps readers — girl readers, in particular — connect with the beauty artifice the heroine is subjected to, recognizing in it their own familiarity with cultural expectations. Such artifice can arouse public sentiment (much like the Mockingjay image that Katniss emblematizes) but is without substance.

It's clear, then, that traditional femininity — while a critical part of the story and her character development — must simultaneously be made artificial for Katniss if she is to maintain believability as a character and as a hero. Collins manages this twist by allowing readers access to Katniss's self-consciousness and her conflicted feelings about her romance with Peeta — heterosexual romance being framed as yet another survival strategy. Always playing to the cameras, once the regulatory revision allows for two victors, Katniss quickly adopts the persona of the "beloved," a strategic attitude. She refers to the "star-crossed lover routine" (*HG* 281), essentially an angle to win the Games, but Collins avoids making her heroine unlikable by allowing for some margin of verisimilitude in the story line — that Katniss may have actual feelings for Peeta, but circumstances prevent her from realizing them.

Trying to put *The Hunger Games* into a specific genre is not an easy task. Even its category as a young adult book does not fit precisely since the book has a tremendous adult following as well. Perhaps it can best be described using U. C. Knoepflmacher's term "hybrid" (159) since it is both "trans-generational" and "trans-gendered" (Simons 157). Part of how the novel achieves its "trans-gendered" quality is by being "trans-genred," using elements from two highly familiar genres in ways that resonate with readers regardless of age: war narratives and romance fiction.

In the interviews that Collins has given to the media, she has discussed how her father's military career as a Vietnam veteran influenced her creation of this series. Collins's agent recalls the author describing the eventual death of Prim as proof that her series' narrative "is not a fairy tale; it's a war, and in war, there are tragic losses that must be mourned" (qtd. in Dominus 31). One of the devices in the first book of *The Hunger Games* that emphasizes its warlike affinity is the importance of weaponry. Collins admits to having watched *Rambo* clips in order to get a better understanding of specific weapons (Dominus 32). The plot also employs the use of booby traps in Katniss's raid on the Cornucopia, not unlike the dangerous land mines faced by soldiers in modern wars, including the tension of not knowing who will fall prey to the traps. The arena in which the Games are played is constructed to present a warlike atmosphere, sometimes full of "flame and smoke" (*HG* 172), a hell where random killing inevitably happens with little time for remorse. For many male readers, who have been drawn to literary war classics like Ernest Hemingway's vivid portraits of foreign battles, to video games like *Call of Duty*, and to science fiction/fantasy narratives from *Star Wars* to *Lord of the Rings* that feature war and battles as a central focus of the story line, *The Hunger Games* offers gritty verisimilitude as it depicts fighting for survival. However, like Hemingway, Collins does not glamorize war; in fact, she critiques and challenges it through the human relationships that take central stage.

Relationships are the lifeblood of this novel. From the outset, there are the familial bonds that first bring Katniss to the arena. Rather than send Prim into the Games to kill or be killed, Katniss volunteers to take her place, showing family loyalty in her action rather than in emotional language, smooth rhetoric not being her style. Besides blood relations, the novel also centers on surrogate families, whose members display loyalty and selfless love even at great personal risk. Haymitch, the man with no wife or children of his own, acts in this capacity and becomes integral to Katniss's survival just as Katniss takes care of Rue, both by sharing food and shelter and by honoring her death with flowers and song. When he was himself a child, Peeta once risked physical violence to give bread to a starving eleven-year-old Katniss. By including these powerful interactions between characters' families and even virtual strangers, Collins touches on values that are not inscribed with gender ideology. Like the Greek myths that served as part of Collins's inspiration, *The Hunger Games* emphasizes primal connections between people who exist outside social influence. As a result, the novel and its sequels reach a wide and diverse audience both in terms of gender and generation.

It is difficult to determine how Collins's use of the conventions of the romance genre influences readers, since Collins both employs tropes of classic romance and challenges them simultaneously. At the novel's center appears to be the tragic lovers plot à la *Romeo and Juliet*. This play is often taught in high schools and kept fresh in people's minds with Taylor Swift's popular ballad, Clare Danes's film version, and every *West Side Story* production. To begin with, Peeta and Katniss are from different parts of town, from families that don't associate with each other. The teenagers' inability to play out their relationship according to their own desires due to powers outside their control duplicates some of the plot structure of Shakespeare's play, which also uses poison in the end to bring out a dramatic climax. That there is also an alternative possible suitor in Gale, Katniss's friend and hunting partner, further elevates romantic tension.

Despite these familiar romance-story patterns, the novel defies allegiance to this genre, alluded to cynically when Katniss references the "romance thing" (*HG* 264). First, readers are given a female character who broadcasts early on that she will not have kids, a position that does not change by the end of the first book, when she reaffirms her commitment never to marry or have children. Katniss's character also challenges the *Romeo and Juliet* motif when she tells Haymitch that Peeta and she are "not star-crossed lovers!" (*HG* 135), even as readers, like Panem's TV audience, are increasingly encouraged to see them that way. Clearly, Katniss's feelings for Peeta do grow over time. However, the forced nature of their relationship, a ploy to win sympathy, creates an artificiality in much of their interaction; this state of unknowing confuses the characters and the readers as to which emotions are real. By stripping away some of the conventions of traditional romance, Collins invites readers of both genders and trans-genders, who might not be apt to favor love stories, to mine the novel for clues about what the characters really feel, as opposed to what they must demonstrate for onlookers. This process almost turns *The Hunger Games* into a detective story, as readers try to figure out who genuinely feels what — an altogether different genre.

By blending genres, blending gendered characteristics, and crossing gendered divisions, Collins's *The Hunger Games* becomes a hybridized entry into the canon of adolescent literature. The novel is able to bridge the gaps between the binary boy and girl cultures through Collins's innovative blending of traditional narrative genres. Boldly centering a war novel on the experience of a female character makes *The Hunger Games* compelling, but it is Suzanne Collins's infusion of the war story with a narrative thread of romance that not only puts her characters at cross-purposes with their initial objectives but that also makes the book — and its sequels — complex. While other writers may seek comfort in the well-paved separatist paths of boys' and girls' books, Collins blurs those boundaries in *The Hunger Games* series and charts a new course.

WORKS CITED

Adney, Karley, and Holly Hassel. *Critical Companion to J. K. Rowling: A Literary Reference to Her Life and Work.* New York: Facts on File, 2010. Print.

Baym, Nina. "Melodramas of Beset Manhood: How Theories of American Fiction Exclude Women Authors." *American Quarterly* 33.2 (1981): 123–39. Print.

Collins, Suzanne. *The Hunger Games.* New York: Scholastic, 2008. Print.

Dominus, Susan. "'I Write about War. For Adolescents.'" *New York Times Magazine* 10 Apr. 2011: 31–33. Print.

Grenby, M. O., and Andrea Immel, eds. *The Cambridge Companion to Children's Literature.* Cambridge: Cambridge University Press, 2009. Print.

Inness, Sherrie. "'It's a Girl Thing': Tough Female Action Figures in the Toy Store." *Action Chicks.* Ed. Sherrie Inness. New York: Palgrave, 2004. 75–94. Print.

Johnson, Allan G. *The Gender Knot: Unraveling Our Patriarchal Legacy.* Philadelphia: Temple University Press, 1997. Print.

Kahlenberg, Susan, and Michelle Hein. "Progression on Nickelodeon? Gender-Role Stereotypes in Toy Commercials." *Sex Roles* 62.11/12 (2010): 830–47. Print.

Knoepflmacher, U.C. "Children's Texts and the Grown-up Reader." Grenby and Immel 159–73.

Lerner, Seth. *Children's Literature: A Reader's History from Aesop to Harry Potter.* Chicago: University of Chicago Press, 2008. Print.

Lewit, Meghan. "Casting 'The Hunger Games': In Praise of Katniss Everdeen." *atlantic.com. The Atlantic,* 9 Mar. 2011. Web. 20 Aug. 2011.

Newman, Andrew. "Half Baked." *Adweek* 15 Mar. 2010: 8–10. Print.

Segel, Elizabeth. "'As the Twig Is Bent ...': Gender and Childhood Reading." *Gender and Reading: Essays on Readers, Texts and Contexts.* Ed. Elizabeth Flynn and Patrocinio Schweickart. Baltimore: John Hopkins University Press, 1986. 165–86. Print.

Seidman, Robert. "Nick Nabs Basic Cable's TV Spot." *TV by the Numbers.* Zap2it, 16 Aug. 2011. Web. 20 Aug. 2011.

Simons, Judy. "Gender Roles in Children's Fiction." Grenby and Immel 143–58.

Of Queer Necessity

Panem's Hunger Games as Gender Games

JENNIFER MITCHELL

Katniss Everdeen is the most active character within *The Hunger Games* series, as the positions that she occupies throughout the trilogy span the broadest spectrum of possibilities and encompass such seemingly disparate roles as sister, love interest, killer, and political symbol. That mobility is contingent upon her constantly shifting gender identity and, thus, is itself a gesture of queerness. As the first novel progresses, Katniss is torn between two competing impulses — to cultivate the girly romance that has been cast upon her and to rely upon the masculine survival instinct that has so often defined and saved her. While Katniss strives to survive the Games, cultivate sponsors, and understand her own desires, she makes conscious and circumstantial choices to adopt various gender roles that suit her situational needs.

Of course, there may seem to be a sense of innate femaleness in the earliest versions of Katniss; her gesture of taking Prim's place in the Games can be ascribed to her undying notion of maternal protection. That femininity, though, is undercut by early presentations of Katniss as channeling her father's masculine lineage when it comes to hunting, bartering, and surviving. Yet as the preparations for Katniss's entry into the Games progress, Cinna, his team, and the collective audience at large seek to highlight the femininity that can be located in, or — importantly — placed on Katniss. During her pre–Games beautification, Katniss is exposed to the ways in which gender deviation is a part of the Capitol's economically privileged position. In fact, although Katniss conceives of herself as constantly violating Capitol philosophy and protocol, the Games actually embrace the same type of gender transitioning that Katniss embodies; thus, it is the Capitol's approach to gender that, in many ways, allows Katniss to flourish within the Games. Katniss's ability to negotiate, try on, and experiment with various gender roles is a testament to the lack of stable substance underneath them.

Eve Sedgwick has stated that typical cultural binary oppositions "actually subsist in a more unsettled and dynamic tacit relation"; therefore, "the question of priority between the supposed central and the supposed marginal category of each dyad is irresolvably unstable" (10). That is, Sedgwick's primary concern — the hetero/homo dyad — is filled with complexities suggesting that both parts of the binary rely upon each other for meaning, even though one part of the binary is always presumed to be marginalized and subordinated to the other part. For the purposes of this analysis, the binary in question is the foundational male/female opposition. When Sedgwick considers this opposition, she deems gender "a far more elaborated, more fully and rigidly dichotomized social production and reproduction of male and female identities and behaviors.... [T]he meaning of gender is seen as culturally mutable and variable, highly relational ... and inextricable from a history of power differentials between genders" (27–28). *The Hunger Games* centers on questions of power: how one accesses, uses, and abuses it. Importantly, for Katniss, the most useful form of power at her disposal is her ability to perform — both consciously and unconsciously — various genders. Tellingly named after the unisexual Sagittaria plant, Katniss becomes the prime site of constantly shifting gender variance throughout the series. Indeed, the hermaphroditic nature of the plant itself speaks directly to the configuration of Katniss as a character who blurs, erases, transcends, and challenges traditional representations of gender in the series.

Her ability to transition from one gender to the other speaks directly to the arbitrariness of its presentation as oppositional; rather, for Katniss, "male" and "female" or "masculine" and "feminine" become circumstantial parts that she plays, distinctly parallel to the roles forced upon her in District 12 and in the Games: "survivor" and "killer." The Hunger Games forces its participants to assess their situations and adapt themselves accordingly. Katniss, who virtually becomes the mascot of the Games, also becomes the site at which a variety of gender roles converge. Ultimately, then, Katniss's necessary movement from gender to gender, along with her often unconscious blurring of the categories of "male" and "female," is a testament to the way in which such genders exist on a malleable spectrum — a spectrum built into the infrastructure of the Games themselves.

The Katniss who greets readers on the earliest pages of *The Hunger Games* in District 12 is immediately gender-anomalous. Despite allusions to her long, dark braid — a seemingly feminine trait — Katniss's other gendered markers are primarily masculine. Her hunting boots, hidden bow and arrow, and personal relationship with the woods draw a significantly manlier portrait of Katniss. Indeed, all aspects of Katniss's life involve a blurring of gender boundaries. As a hunter, Katniss is a predator in the woods, following in her father's footsteps and adopting the traditionally masculine approach to the hunt. In fact, the earliest descriptions of Katniss reference her father and his legacy countless times, drawing herself into a male lineage. Using the lessons that her father taught her — and rejecting what she perceives as incompetence in her mother — Katniss is able to provide for and maintain her family. Even though Katniss uses the distinctly dire circumstances of District 12 as a means of explaining her predatory habits, Katniss's success in and enjoyment of the woods defy conventional associations between women and the hearth. Instead of cooking the food, Katniss stalks it, traps it, and kills it; ultimately, she thrives in the woods, and subsequently in the arena, as a result of this power and prowess.

The expression of power built into a successful hunt is obviously in direct contrast to the subjection and subservience built into the formulation of District 12. For Katniss, a rewarding trip to the woods is an act of rebellion; not only are the woods outside the accessible areas within the district, but Katniss's momentary, circumstantial contentment crossing the fence flies in the face of the Capitol's merciless regulations. Additionally, her time in the woods is, perhaps, the most overt gender equalizer in the earliest section of the text. While the insinuation of possible sexual attraction between Katniss and Gale may serve to reinforce notions of our heroine as a heterosexual girl, she is an equal partner to Gale in virtually every way, a deliberate erasure of gender differentiation. A match for him in adventurousness and skill, Katniss approaches Gale in a way that foreshadows the barter system at play in the rest of the district. Additionally, Katniss brings up the possibility of having romantic feelings for Gale only in order to dismiss them. A simultaneous acknowledgment of and refusal to acknowledge presents Katniss in a most ambiguous way; her overt denial of sexual attraction toward Gale can be viewed as a facade (an attempt to prevent herself from turning into her love-struck and subsequently heartbroken mother) or as authentic (the reaction of someone without romantic or sexual inclinations). Either way, Katniss is marked by an unsettled and undefined sexual presence by virtue of this gesture.

Rather than Gale, it is the woods to which Katniss is primarily attracted. She explains her attachment to the woods in a variety of ways: it provides her with solace and freedom, links her to her family, and gives her a sense of purpose and productivity. All of these explanations can be traced back to the role that Katniss has carved out for herself relative to her mother and Prim. Katniss explicitly rejects virtually all aspects of her mother's femininity, manifested primarily in her art of healing and in her melancholy and weak temperament. Aggressively resentful of her mother's depression, which Katniss implicitly reads as a luxurious overreaction to the death of her husband, Katniss becomes the primary caretaker of her sister. Filling the void left by her father's death and her mother's disengagement with life, Katniss becomes both mother and father to Prim. Justifying her all-encompassing position relative to Prim with her mother's parental incompetence, Katniss feels compelled to actively distance herself from all things overtly female.

Doting on Prim like a good parent, Katniss gives Lady, the goat, to her sister as a present, but also as a testament to her recognition of Prim's compassionate nature. Accordingly, Prim is the single most powerful motivating force in Katniss's life. While it is in her father's memory that Katniss patrols the woods, it is for the sake of her sister's health, well-being, and safety that Katniss becomes an active participant in the District 12 black market. Confident that no one could take responsibility for Prim as effectively as she can, Katniss must believe in her mother's emotional and pragmatic inadequacy. Consequently and perhaps unrealistically, Katniss idolizes her father, seeking to emulate what she assumes would be his role in the family, yet Katniss unconsciously embraces a maternal position as well, attempting to be Prim's entire world. Katniss is immediately willing to take her sister's place in the Games when Prim's name is pulled at the reaping. In what may be the quintessential maternal gesture, Katniss's instinct is to sacrifice herself for the sake of "her" child.

Katniss feels tremendous comfort in a parental position that blurs traditional boundaries between mothers and fathers. That comfort, perhaps unpredictably, resurfaces in the Hunger Games. Indeed, Katniss is most at ease during the Games when she finds Rue, an obvious surrogate for Prim. Rue's youth, small stature, and physical appearance all remind Katniss of Prim, and readers are wary of the inevitable opposition that the Gamemakers set up between tributes. That Katniss could kill anyone who reminds her of her own sister is, in fact, an impossibility. While Rue is immediately presented as a potential Achilles heel for Katniss, the alliance forged by the two enables Katniss to reposition herself in a far more familiar role — that of parent. When Katniss asks Rue to be an ally, she presumes that Rue needs protection; such conjecture betrays Katniss's need to be a protector and is, in its own way, a nostalgic gesture. In fact, her assumption that Haymitch will bemoan her alliance with the "wispy child" (*HG* 201) suggests that she views Rue and Prim as virtually interchangeable, projecting what Katniss and readers alike recognize as Prim's inability to survive the Games onto Rue. The ease of their interactions, the honesty of their giggles, and the repetitive reminders that Rue is a whole lot like the Everdeen clan allow the two to establish a quick familial intimacy.

Eventually shocked by Rue's resourcefulness and independence, Katniss realizes that she is not the only one with a set of remarkable skills in this partnership; even with that awareness, however, Katniss continues to approach

Rue as her ward. The same instinct of self-sacrifice and protection that fuels Katniss's volunteering at the reaping resurfaces when Rue is killed. Katniss's first deliberate kill in the Games is enacting revenge as she avenges the death of her ally/sister/daughter. At various moments related to her mother, father, Prim, and Rue, Katniss is able to unconsciously adopt multiple gender roles. Such transitioning without awareness reveals that Katniss's undefined and unstable gender is, in fact, natural and intrinsic to her.

Long before she enters the arena as the "girl on fire" (*HG* 354), Katniss is conscious of her gender performance and the confines of traditional gender roles. By occupying both male and female positions in her household and the district at large, Katniss is able to transition immediately and seamlessly between genders whenever necessary. Yet it is during some of the most intense moments in the Games that Katniss's awareness of her audience leads her intentionally to perform very specific genders. Katniss's consciousness of her performance never hinders her transition from one gender to another. Consequently, the ease with which Katniss navigates Panem's gendered matrix speaks directly to Judith Butler's theories about the arbitrariness of gender traits. In *Gender Trouble,* Butler argues:

> If it is possible to speak of a "man" with a masculine attribute and to understand that attribute as a happy but accidental feature of that man, then it is also possible to speak of a "man" with a feminine attribute, whatever that is, but still to maintain the integrity of the gender. But once we dispense with the priority of "man" and "woman" as abiding substances, then it is no longer possible to subordinate dissonant gendered features as so many secondary and accidental characteristics of a gender ontology that is fundamentally intact [32].

Butler is calling the authenticity of gender into question. By highlighting the flimsiness of the relationship between gender traits and the sex that they supposedly reflect, Butler purports that "there is no gender identity behind the expressions of gender" (33). That is, gender expressions bear no necessary relationship to any gender "truth" underneath them. Throughout the part of *The Hunger Games* that takes place in District 12, Katniss consistently reminds readers that her reality is one of survival; to ponder questions of gender identity is to waste time and energy that would be better spent on sustenance. Yet there are moments in the Games themselves — moments that primarily involve Peeta — that force Katniss to be conscious of the presentation of her gender identity. Thus, readers and Katniss soon realize that questions of gender play a vital role in Katniss's means of survival and her approach to Peeta Mellark.

It may take readers the entire first book, or even the entire series, to realize that from his earliest descriptions, Peeta is an equally complicated match for Katniss. Just as Katniss's masculinity is expressed in her status as hunter, so Peeta's femininity is expressed in his role as baker. Even Peeta's shrew of a mother undercuts his masculinity by suggesting that Katniss might actually win this year, a sharp testament to his perceived feminized weakness. Prior to the Games, both tributes spend their day-to-day lives doing things that undercut conventional gender delineations. Of course, it is by virtue of their pairing that both tributes begin to play by traditional rules that define and govern social gendered behaviors. From the moment that Peeta articulates his feelings for her during his interview with Caesar, Katniss and the audience become hyperaware of her status as "girl." The revelation of Peeta's crush does far more to identify Katniss's gender than even the beautiful dresses that Cinna designs, as Haymitch claims that Peeta's declaration makes Katniss appear "desirable" (*HG* 135). Peeta's public acknowledgment of Katniss's girlhood bolsters Cinna's presentation of Katniss as identifiably female — and Peeta's own presentation of himself as identifiably male. This moment suggests that District 12 has, indeed, sent in a now easily identifiable and distinctive male tribute and female tribute.

Katniss's interpretation of her own public reaction to Peeta's revelation is the reader's first glimpse into Katniss actively playing with her gender presentation. At home, Katniss could be male, female, any combination of or between the two without actually thinking about gender performance. At this moment, Katniss begins to become aware that she can consciously perform a gender identity, as the audience deafeningly responds to her girly blush. When Katniss and Peeta reunite during the Games, Katniss pays careful attention to the way in which she presents her gender to viewers. With a heightened awareness of the cameras, Katniss begins her role as tragic female lover by smiling at the audience — made up of familiar viewers at home and strangers in the Capitol, alike — and later equating kisses with gifts from sponsors. In the cave while Peeta lies gravely wounded, Katniss mixes her conscious gender performance with her unconscious gender discourses; even though she is often intensely aware that all of Panem is watching and vicariously participating in the Games, Katniss cannot help but be her protective, parental self at some points and her exaggerated, love-struck girly self at others. Then the roles change, and Peeta becomes the caretaker of a wounded and exhausted Katniss. The fluidity with which the pair changes positions relative to each other reflects the ease with which genders can be adopted and expressed, and the way that the exigencies of the Games demand such easy transitions.

Although Katniss's performance becomes slightly convoluted in the cave when she actively dismisses the presence of the cameras and kisses Peeta, elsewhere Katniss continues conscious deployment of traditional gender traits. The most overt suggestion of her heterosexuality, Katniss's time in the cave with Peeta, also reinforces her ability to decode Haymitch's plan. By rewarding Katniss for her explicit presentation of herself as feminine and heterosexual, Haymitch reflects the sentiments of audience members across Panem. In *Homos,* Leo Bersani writes that many of those concerned with issues of sexual identity believe "sexual behavior is never only a question of sex, that it is embedded in all the other, nonsexual ways in which we are socially and culturally positioned" (3). Katniss's social and cultural position is, without a doubt, complicated by her need to survive. As Katniss plays the game within the Games and, accordingly, plays *the girl,* her success is contingent upon her ability to read, assess, and reframe her gender according to situational needs.

Katniss's personal affinity for switching gender roles is distinctly parallel to the Capitol's prioritization of gender malleability. From the moment that Katniss Everdeen gets to the Capitol, she gets a glimpse into the spectacle of physical and gender primping that goes on behind the scenes of the Hunger Games. While on the surface this acts as the oft-used "makeover" process in film, television, and texts alike, Katniss's physical transformation reflects the surprising truth that the Capitol's approach to gender in many ways mirrors Katniss's approach to her own gender. The Katniss of District 12, with her long braid and hunting boots, is suddenly faced with an unsettling, corporeally altered crew of beauticians and stylists; Venia, marked by her blue hair and gold facial tattoos, tackles Katniss's physical imperfections, focusing primarily on hair removal. This process is undoubtedly meant to feminize Katniss and to remind readers of the luxury of caring about appearance that Katniss and most of Panem's districts have never experienced. The team's space, the Remake Center, is a testament to the Capitol's power, position, and primacy. In the Center, Katniss will be broken down, beaten up, and physically transformed so that she can be refashioned as more palatable and appealing. Indeed, Katniss explains the process as initially superficial while she is scrubbed, manicured, waxed; that superficiality, however, is compromised as Katniss explains that the process itself makes her feel exceptionally vulnerable. Clearly the Remake Center, with its meticulous attention to detail, has gotten under Katniss's skin — literally. The process of superficial feminization that Katniss undergoes obviously affects her exterior, but also magnifies her unsettled internal sense of self.

While Katniss is disturbed by the comprehensiveness of the process, Venia and Octavia are clearly enamored by the transformation that they are able to catalyze. Both stylists actively participate in the Capitol's prioritization of bodily transmogrification; Venia's tattooed eyebrows and Octavia's dyed body speak to the evolution of fashion trends into body trends. Katniss calls these changes "decorations" (*HG* 65), but they are far more invasive than the embellishments that such a term calls to mind. The prime example is Caesar Flickerman, the host of the tribute interviews. Katniss notes that his appearance has remained eerily similar after more than forty years in this position, referencing the Capitol's use of surgical procedures to hold on to the illusion of youth. Indeed, with light blue hair and lips tinted to match, Caesar is the quintessential representation of the Capitol's ideal of style and popularity, and the necessary bodily alterations therein.

The embodiment of trendiness for the Capitol is, indeed, a comment on bodies themselves. Nikki Sullivan highlights the ways in which a variety of bodily transformations have been appropriated by critical theorists as embodiments of "transgender body modification(s)":

> Perhaps at bottom, what procedures as diverse as mastectomies, penectomies, hormone treatments, tattooing, breast enhancement, implants, corsetry, rhinoplasty, scarification, branding, and so on, have in common, is that they all function, in varying ways and to varying degrees, to explicitly transform bodily being — they are all, in one sense at least, "trans" practices [552].

The people Katniss reads as artificially and superficially altered become models for a particular type of "trans-ness," which reveals the Capitol's fluid approach to gender. While the self-presentation of characters like Venia and Octavia may initially exist as an extreme projection of contemporary feminized makeup application, the far more gender-inclusive transformations of the Capitol blur previous gender distinctions. It is not simply that women have a more exaggerated sense of altered self-presentation, but that men in the Capitol play by exactly the same rules and use the same gendered markers. The artifice inherent in their treatment and presentation of their bodies is suggestive of an approach to gender that equates bodily reality only with surface appearance.

In a similar theoretical vein, Butler highlights her approach to the body as a social construction, as "a passive medium on which cultural meanings are inscribed ... only externally related" (12). For Butler, bodies do not presuppose gender; they do not exist prior to the ascription and application of socialized gender roles and, thus, are equally subject to social rules and regulations. Rather, the body is the means by which certain gender traits and identities are conveyed to and interpreted by the outside world. In the Capitol, the most privileged individuals actively distance their bodies from traditional markers of gender as they exist within our world; instead, they embrace a culture that celebrates the malleability of body and self, using corporeal transformation as a means of espousing identity. By removing the typically gendered connotations associated with activities such as makeup application and plastic surgery, the Capitol has severed the tie between body and gender.

Accordingly, although Katniss is forced to play by Venia and Octavia's rules — and the rules of the Capitol, by proxy — her experience is notably different than that of the wealthy. While Venia and Octavia pride themselves on their appearance, and the choices they make to modify that appearance, the beautification process is placed upon Katniss from without, yet another exercise in the Capitol's control over the tributes *but* also a reminder of the Capitol's ties to the rest of Panem. While the Capitol's aesthetic sensibilities decry traditional gendered traits, Venia, Octavia, and Cinna are all working to turn Katniss into superficially recognizable girl. That is, in order for Katniss to be recognizable throughout the districts, the stylists still adhere to a set of gendered norms that unite physical appearance with gender identity. For Katniss, the efforts at making her appear as a more readily identifiable female are completely foreign. The stylists themselves may be working to uncover some raw, feminine material underneath Katniss's rough-hewn appearance, but Katniss's description of the process itself suggests that this girlhood is merely a disguise that she puts on at the behest of her styling team. Because she never previously paused to consider her own physicality beyond imminent starvation, Katniss is overwhelmingly critical of all that Venia and Octavia do to her to make her appear more overtly feminine. For Katniss, it is not her "real self" that is being molded to be presented to audiences; it is an entirely different artificial self in question.

Furthermore, Katniss's rejection of the falseness inherent in each stage of the remake process is perfectly in accordance with her adamant rejection of the excesses of the Capitol. When Katniss compares herself, all primped and prepped, to a "plucked bird" (*HG* 61), she channels the premise of the Games themselves and the position of the tributes therein. Yet Katniss ultimately gives her assertive approval over the transformation when she sees the final touches, the costumes that Cinna designs. While audience members and readers might approach them simply as articles of clothing, the outfits are a vehicle through which Katniss can become a different person; they are, above all, costumes that reveal alternative Katnisses. Prior to the Games, the most traditionally feminine of these outfits is the dress made from gemstones, inspiring Katniss to suggest that, far from being pretty or beautiful, she is "as radiant as the sun" (*HG* 121). While the description of the dress's details evokes an aura of femininity, Katniss transcends gender boundaries yet again by comparing herself to the sun. The Capitol's approach to Katniss suggests an adherence to traditional markers of gender: makeup, dresses, long hair; because the Capitol itself has seemed to move beyond such archaic markers, those elements are meant for the sake of the districts, by making Katniss (and the other tributes) legible.

The question of legibility is one that sustains the entire narrative, even the whole series. When Katniss returns from the Games, she is far too thin and angular to be palatable to audiences. Her previously small stature has become grotesquely asexual, so the Gamemakers attempt to surgically alter Katniss with breast implants. Because Haymitch argues against them, the compromise they reach is to "add padding" to the dress she dons for her (theoretically) final interview (*HG* 354). Perhaps the most important of Katniss's wardrobe changes, this dress is a reminder of all that Katniss has lost. Readers are reminded that the charade of femininity is for the benefit of the audience; it's a necessary element of Katniss's continuous popularity. But Katniss's eerie description of herself as "wearing candlelight" actually suggests that she becomes a vigil for herself (*HG* 355). She stands before audiences as a girl who never was and never could be; the artificiality of her body at that moment is a testament to her impossibility.

WORKS CITED

Bersani, Leo. *Homos.* Cambridge: Harvard University Press, 1996. Print.
Butler, Judith. *Gender Trouble: Feminism and the Subversion of Identity.* New York: Routledge, 1989. Print.
Collins, Suzanne. *The Hunger Games.* New York: Scholastic, 2008. Print.
Sedgwick, Eve Kosofsky. *Epistemology of the Closet.* Berkeley: University of California Press, 1991. Print.
Sullivan, Nikki. "Transmogrification: (Un)Becoming Other(s)." *The Transgender Studies Reader.* Ed. Susan Stryker and Stephen Whittle. New York: Routledge, 2006. 552–64. Print.

PART III.

Resistance, Surveillance and Simulacra

13

Costuming the Resistance
The Female Spectacle of Rebellion

Amy L. Montz

The Hunger Games is a novel obsessed with the stylized presentation of girls. From the beginning of the novel, when Katniss is dressed by her mother for the reaping, to the end, when Cinna once again dresses her in fire — a soft candlelit hue of fabric — the novel understands the purposeful exhibition of the female form. Part of the success of the spectacle is due to the Capitol's obsession with outrageous fashions and physical display. As a statement on the postmodern obsession with reality television or the dystopian future rooted in mythological sources, *The Hunger Games* knows the power of a good performance. But as the trilogy progresses and Katniss's role develops from the fiery image of a memorable tribute to the symbolic image of the districts' revolution, her life becomes simultaneously more secure and more precarious. The spectacle she becomes is itself a rebellious demonstration of the power of costuming, fashion, and femininity.

Katniss Everdeen, District 12's female tribute, meets the Capitol for the first time with the help of her stylist, Cinna. Her costume is a simple black unitard that is accented by reddish hues on the cape and headpiece — and the synthetic fuel Cinna uses to ignite it. When Cinna comments that Katniss will forever be known as "the girl who was on fire" (*HG* 67), he argues for the duality of its meaning: Katniss will quite literally be remembered as the tribute lit ablaze in the opening ceremonies, but she will also be marked by this visual representation throughout her life. Her stylized outfits make her socially and politically "on fire" as well. As Cinna predicts, the public remembers Katniss as the fiery girl who was the innocent tribute at the Seventy-fourth Hunger Games, *and* the Mockingjay, the symbolic rebel of the districts. The spectacle of fire and darkness is achieved through the careful costuming of Katniss, costuming that solidifies the Resistance (here defined as the core of the rebellion) behind a common image. As a stylist and designer, Cinna understands what many resistance groups have known: physical presentation and public spectacle are the two most important components of protest, particularly when placed on the bodies of women.

The followers of the Mockingjay use Katniss's female body as the visual and public site of resistance through consistent, stylized use of spectacle. And that spectacle is, almost always, rooted in the fashionable. Katniss is groomed to be the Mockingjay both figuratively and literally; all three novels pay particular attention to the details of dress and the preparations made to present a composite image of Katniss to the public. Katniss's fashions become visual representations of the Resistance that are, ultimately, more important than her actions. Ironically, *The Hunger Games* trilogy also judges the use of female spectacle in rebellion by questioning the distribution of Katniss's likeness and her loss of agency. By the time of the events of *Mockingjay,* Katniss is told that she herself is no longer vital to the cause; the Resistance has her image, and it is the image alone that matters. Yet the final events of *Mockingjay* ultimately reclaim female agency for Katniss because she *becomes* the Mockingjay; the spectacle of Katniss, crafted by others to incite rebellion, is determined by Katniss herself.

To establish how Collins integrates the fashionable into her trilogy's themes — and to fully appreciate the delicacy with which she does so — it is necessary to understand how spectacle, fashion, and femininity are traditionally understood and manipulated. Because the spectacle of the Games is designed with a voyeuristic agenda, it becomes easy to place Katniss and the other tributes into positions of passivity. Whether male or female, all of the tributes would then become the objects and passive recipients of a dominant, aggressive gaze. Looking at *The Hunger Games* with the lens provided by Laura Mulvey allows us to see the tributes as having objective rather than subjective status, what Mulvey connotes as "*to-be-looked-at-ness*" (2088). And, of course, this is true, as the tributes seem to have no control over their roles within the Games, or over their stylizing in the opening ceremonies. But Peeta succeeds in not letting the Games change him, and Katniss actually changes the outcome for everyone by stepping in for her sister. Thus, tributes do have a modicum of control, if not over their lives, then at least over some of their actions.

Partly, of course, the dystopian future presented by *The Hunger Games* trilogy accounts for the severe limitations on control felt by the tributes, but also, and perhaps more importantly, the constant assault of spectacle that is the Games complicates our traditional understandings of power dynamics and the gaze. The novels are in part responding to the reality-television craze of the twenty-first century; Collins herself notes the connection, stating that the idea for the first novel came to her when she "happened upon a reality program, recorded live, that pitted young people against each other for money" (qtd. in Blasingame 727). Because the Games are constantly recorded, the tributes understand them as public spectacle. We must then ask whether the fact that everyone now has the power of the gaze means that everyone possessing the gaze now has power. More importantly, we must question whether those who are the visual spectacles have no power of the gaze at all. Knowledge of participation in a public spectacle does not, of course, grant one power over the gaze, but knowledge and manipulation of the spectacle precisely to control what the viewers see and comprehend, in no small way, do. There is a power dynamic existent in the Games (the culling of tributes from the districts has been a death sentence for almost all of them for the past seventy-three years), but it is not rooted in spectacle. In fact, spectacle may be the only small amount of power any of these tributes have. For Katniss, her manipulation of spectacle begins and ends on two fronts: that of "girl" and that of "fashion."

Fashion and dress are the most common visual representations thought to embody individual expression, social conformity, economic status, and national recognition, as well as other, even more complicated factors specific to women, such as morality and sexual availability or invitation. It is no accident, then, that fashion and feminism have had a troublesome and complicated relationship through all three historic waves of feminism. First-wave feminists chose their clothing carefully as they knew their Votes for Women cause would garner suspicion from English and American middle-class audiences who opposed suffrage for women. American second-wave feminists rejected traditional standards of femininity in elaborate, highly publicized protests, the most famous of which was the "freedom trashcan" at the 1968 Miss America Pageant, into which feminists threw trappings of femininity (Groeneveld 181). Third-wave feminists complicate women's political and personal relationships with fashion and dress even further, as they understand fashion to be a personal choice with global ramifications, investing in what Elizabeth Groeneveld calls "the reclamation of feminism as stylish and sexy and the representation of feminist politics as a set of lifestyle choices" (187). Groeneveld's use of the word "representation" is particularly key here, in that she discusses feminism as something that can be "stylish and sexy" as well as political. Fashion is understood as a language that can be used to write, read, and interpret all manners of messages, including political agendas — especially on the bodies of women.

Resistance groups use costuming and dress in order to present an organized and visual spectacle. The constant use of specific, purposeful clothing maintained on the bodies of young, attractive women helps give causes the constant public exposure they need to rally support. Sometimes, wearing specific costuming and dress becomes an act of rebellion in and of itself. In January 2011, a Toronto police officer publicly suggested that women should be careful of what they wear if they wish to avoid becoming the victims of sexual assault. The result was a protest called SlutWalk, which organized over a thousand women to dress as demurely or as "slutty" as they wanted. Laura Stampler of *The Huffington Post* understands SlutWalk's goal to be "to shift the paradigm of mainstream rape culture, which [the protesters] believe focuses on analyzing the behavior of the victim rather than that of the perpetrator." By calling overt attention to their bodies and making a spectacle of themselves, the SlutWalk protesters ultimately turn their viewers' attention to the ridiculousness of the proclamation that a victim of rape could be "asking for it" by the way she was dressed.

To prove this, the SlutWalk protesters gather in a wide variety of costumes, everyday dress, and outrageous fashions. Joanne Laucius reports that, among the protesters she observed, "[o]ne wore a bridal gown, another wore fishnet stockings. Some wore far less" (J1). When asked, "What to wear to SlutWalk?" Laucius suggests, "Something slutty. But only if you like. Polly Esther wore a plunging neckline and knee-high platform boots. But you can wear a burka, if you'd rather. Or a grey cardigan and sensible shoes" (J1). In the end, the specific clothing chosen is not important; what matters is the gathering of hundreds and even thousands of women dressed with purpose, to exhibit a specific goal, all for the benefit of the twenty-first-century's ever-present media eye. Tanya Gold of *The Guardian* explains exactly why SlutWalk is a popular and ultimately effective form of protest: the appeal of public spectacle. She cites a moment when a protester and a Christian preacher begin to argue with each other, and the protester "turns to the crowd, which is growing bigger and more interested with the promise of violence. They watch it, like TV. They take pictures and they should. *This is a very photogenic movement.* Bras and sluts everywhere" (emphasis added). And it is a "very photogenic movement," as all good movements should be, and as its sister first-wave feminist protests were as well. The British and American Suffragists of the late-nineteenth and early-twentieth centuries sponsored large-scale public spectacles to promote their cause and attracted attention through visual display, taking full advantage of the new media documentation of photography, newspapers, radio, and even cinema. The rebellion in the world of Collins's *Hunger Games* trilogy understands the benefit of "photogenic" stagings that use the bodies of women to speak to a literate viewing audience. As the residents of the Capitol — and beyond, the people of the districts — understand the language of dress and costume, using it to subtly manipulate the audience's opinion of tributes such as Peeta and Katniss becomes an integral part of establishing the rebellion and garnering support for it throughout Panem. It helps that Katniss is a young, seemingly innocent-looking girl.

The grassroots protest SlutWalk has gained international fame because of its controversial and highly visual nature. Clem Bastow, an organizer of

SlutWalk Melbourne, argues that while some feminists see SlutWalk as "little more than a dress-up party in which 'girls' will tart up and celebrate their sexual proclivities," it is, in fact, what the article defines as a "rally to protest against rape culture and its sinister byproduct, victim-blaming" (11). Bastow's use of the word "girls" and the quotation marks included around the words are particularly important. The term "girl" becomes problematic when used to refer to a woman, as it implies someone who is not in charge of her own political body and, therefore, cannot be in charge of her own physical body. The addition of the phrase "dress-up party" offers further judgment on how some feminists see protests like SlutWalk as damaging to the feminist movement. But Bastow understands how powerful the dichotomy of that image truly is: that of the girl playing dress up and that of the sexualized tart. In a culture in which girls — those younger than sixteen — are over-sexualized, the shock of young women protesting in a variety of costumes will draw attention, both positive and negative. Of course, for a generation in which the media are so pervasive, any attention is positive attention.

However, because Katniss and, to no small extent, Peeta are costumed to present a very specific spectacle to the audience, the traditional understanding of the feminized, passive spectacle and the masculine, aggressive gaze becomes problematized. Like SlutWalk participants' fashion agenda, Cinna's costumes for Katniss and Peeta, as well as Haymitch's coaching, manipulate the expectations of the audience for the political agenda the burgeoning Resistance movement is trying to put forth. Katniss's first experiences of the Hunger Games and physical spectacle come both as a "girl" and as a stylized figure of rebellion. When she has her personal interview with the host of the Hunger Games, Katniss wears another one of Cinna's creations. Her dress is covered in jewels that, when put into motion with a twirl of skirts, emulate the fire she was engulfed in just the night before. Katniss compares her on-stage antics to the solemnity of her competitors and finds herself "A silly girl spinning in a sparkling dress" (*HG* 136). However, what Katniss forgets in this self-deprecating moment is that she is trying to appeal to the Capitol, full of its own collection of silly, sparkling people; her persona in the televised interview, with its girlish laughter and its twirling in a pretty dress, speaks to the very audience from whom she needs to garner support. As Katniss becomes a Capitol favorite in the Games, she does so as the District 12 girl who saved her sister and as Peeta's conflicted lover; most importantly, she does so as the silly, sparkling girl aligned with fire. With the Machiavellian planning of her stylist and her handlers, she gives the audience exactly what it wants and thus exactly what she needs to survive the Games: what Haymitch calls "'[j]ust the perfect touch of rebellion'" (*HG* 79). The "perfect touch of rebellion" in this moment refers to the hand-holding of Peeta and Katniss in the arena, but throughout the trilogy variants of that touch become vital to the fiery girl and the Mockingjay, each played out in Katniss's costuming and through her willing participation in her stylized staging.

Full participation in rebellion and willing engagement with political resistance have not, of course, always been the province of women. More often than not, women have been used as passive symbols of rather than active participants in political agendas: e.g., Britannia, Lady Liberty, or Rosie the Riveter. In *The Hunger Games,* Katniss's fiery moniker helps keep her alive. Feminine agency is often a survival instinct, and while Katniss is never in charge of her styling, she concedes authority over her body to Cinna's superior fashion knowledge. When she wins the Games, however, she must assume a new persona for exactly the same reason: self-preservation. This persona is dependent on her connection to Peeta, yet even her wedding dress is chosen by the adoring Capitol, without her input. Her stylization as the Tribute Bride is done by outside forces, including those voting in the Capitol and the ever-present Cinna.

Even more important than child Tribute Bride is the role of the Mockingjay. Katniss finds herself being turned into the Mockingjay emblem throughout the trilogy, most often without her consent, her approval, or even her desire. While hunting in the wild, she runs into Resistance fighters from District 8 and, as a sign of their good intent, is given a cracker imprinted with a mockingjay. Katniss's last words in Part I of *Catching Fire* are of ownership; she acknowledges and even declares the image as hers. Katniss understands that the Mockingjay has become her token. However, she begins Part II by once again declaring ownership of the image of the bird, seeing it as emblematic of herself but also noticing that its meaning has changed from the original tokens of remembrance. When Katniss states that "this is definitely not a fashion statement" (*CF* 139), she acknowledges the image's shift from representation of her body to literal embodiment of the Resistance.

Problematic for Katniss, of course, is the fact that she has not scripted her own entrance into the rebellion. Her likeness is being used to promote the rebels' agenda: she has become the literal "face of the hoped-for rebellion" (*CF* 150). While she seems quite capable and willing to *participate* in the rebellion, at no point is she eager to *lead* it. Nor, it seems, is Katniss willing to be its poster child. In *The Fashioned Body,* Joanna Entwistle argues that "dress, the body, and the self— are not perceived separately but simultaneously, as a totality" (10). Once she becomes the girl the public aligns with fire, Katniss can no longer be separated from that public performance of rebellion. She has been marked by difference, and at each stage, clothing has been an integral part of her process: Prim's untucked shirt pulls Katniss out of her shock at the reaping, and Cinna's flame-dresses call attention to Katniss's body at the opening ceremonies. But it is not until *Catching Fire* that Katniss truly loses control of her image; despite the publicity of the Seventy-fourth Hunger

Games and despite the constant recording of the horrors, she still remains unaware of how her performances will be interpreted in the Capitol and beyond.

Once she becomes Peeta's Bride for the benefit of the Capitol and, more importantly, becomes the Mockingjay, Katniss loses agency over the presentation of her own body and the reality in which it exists. When the Games of the Quarter Quell are declared, the fantasy — however scripted — of Katniss's marriage to Peeta is consumed by the reality of the Quell. Katniss is once again presented to the Capitol, forced by President Snow to wear what would have been her wedding dress. Because this is an action Cinna considers to be "barbaric" (*CF* 248), Katniss's stylist does something Katniss understands as "fantastic and reckless" (*CF* 262), thus enacting his own revenge against Snow. Given the Capitol's and the districts' appreciation of the power of spectacle and a good show, Cinna stages a true fantasy as he turns Katniss's wedding dress into the fashionable and quite literal embodiment of the Mockingjay. She is already becoming the physical image, the "face," associated with the rebellion, but here, Katniss is transformed into the physical embodiment of the Resistance entirely through Cinna's styling. In her second interview with Caesar, Katniss repeats her childish twirl with entirely different effects. Instead of representing fire through jewels, Katniss's wedding dress is literally consumed by flames, leaving her in an exact replica that is also an entirely new version of her wedding dress. Changing from white to black, from pearls to feathers, the dress has another specific element that completes Katniss's physical transformation: wings for sleeves.

In this moment, as Katniss embodies someone else's definition of the Mockingjay, she shifts from ownership of the persona to a more passive recipient of the designation. She notes that "Cinna *has turned me* into a mockingjay" (*CF* 253, emphasis added), a designation that is now essential rather than simply suggestive. It is a highly successful transformation, which even Caesar Flickerman notes as "spectacular" (*CF* 253), but because it is Cinna's "fantastic and reckless" act and not Katniss's, it strips her agency and usurps her place within the rebellion. She remains its symbol rather than its leader; she is sent to incite the crowds and rally them to the cause rather than to fight for the cause itself. Often declared too valuable to be allowed to come into danger, Katniss, so much the protector of others in the first novel, spends the majority of the second and third novels struggling against those who would protect her rather than be protected by her, not because she is Katniss but because, as the face of the hoped-for rebellion, she is entirely too valuable to come to harm.

Throughout the events of *Catching Fire* and *Mockingjay,* Katniss understands that she must perform as the Mockingjay. The rebellion *is* necessary, after all, given how easily the Capitol sacrifices its districts' children. But Katniss's involvement with the Resistance is initially mostly symbolic. Her image, as well as the emblem of the Mockingjay, is printed and distributed, and video of her is manipulated and transformed without her approval. Even though in the third novel Katniss declares, "I'm going to be the Mockingjay" (*M* 31), her soldier suit is made from designs Cinna left behind. Katniss notes, without irony, that "[i]n his hands, I am again a mockingjay" (*M* 43). When she realizes that she has been turned into "a" mockingjay, she states, "I was *their* Mockingjay long before I accepted the role" (*M* 90, emphasis added). The Resistance's proprietary relationship with Katniss is proven when she realizes that the rebels need only her image and not her body. It is not until the rebellion is over and the revolution won that Katniss, instead of embodying the Mockingjay, truly *becomes* the Mockingjay. And it is only in that moment that Katniss regains the agency stripped away from her throughout the revolution she unwittingly started.

When the Resistance first scripts propaganda with Katniss's image, the rebels discover that she is most successful at inciting revolution in those moments when she is at her most "'[u]nscripted'" (*M* 75). Later, when she realizes that Coin was probably responsible for Prim's death, Katniss murders President Coin in a televised spectacle that was meant to showcase Snow's execution. She is subsequently arrested, and her Mockingjay suit — the fashionable symbol of the Resistance — is taken from her. The new political regime understands that Katniss as spectacle is also Katniss as political insurgent. Katniss, as the "face" of the revolution, is a constant reminder of the defiance of government and authority, and the new regime still believes that Katniss's power lies in the *spectacle* and not in herself. They are proven wrong, however, when a captive Katniss begins to sing, becoming a songbird that even the real mockingjays might envy. In this moment, she no longer embodies the Mockingjay. She is not its stylized representation, and she is not the "face" of the Resistance. She *is* the Resistance. She *is* the revolution. For these reasons, she is far more dangerous to the political regime dead than alive. Unable to allow her to become a martyr for the people and unwilling to escalate the disarray into which the government of Panem is thrown, the new administration exonerates Katniss. She is released from prison to live her life in District 12 because, as she notes, the face of the rebellion is quite useless once the rebellion is done.

But she was useful, and she was important, and it is through Katniss that the Games are brought to an abrupt end and Panem is rebuilt from the ground up. She is the physical embodiment of political insurrection, begun quite accidentally when she holds Peeta's hands as they both are lit on fire, continued when she stumbles into the role of the Mockingjay, and cemented when she takes the revolution into her own hands and destroys the one person who would turn the Resistance into a new tyranny. Katniss, who begins her revolution as "the girl who was on fire," continues as the Mockingjay, that fashionable, televised spectacle of the districts' revolution. But Katniss ends her journey as herself. By visually becoming the Mockingjay, she manipulates the spectacle of the Capitol so that her spectacle of hope stops the spectacle that destroys. Katniss ends the trilogy as she truly begins it: as an intelligent woman who understands the inequality of hunger and deprivation, the weight of sacrifice, and the importance of never underestimating the power of a girl spectacularized by fashion, costume, and a good performance.

WORKS CITED

Bastow, Clem. "Hey Girls, We're All Sluts Now." *The Age* [Melbourne] 24 May 2011: 11. *LexisNexis.* Web. 9 June 2011.

Blasingame, James. "An Interview with Suzanne Collins." *Journal of Adolescent and Adult Literacy* 52.8 (May 2009): 726–27. *Academic Search Premier.* Web. 17 Sept. 2011.

Collins, Suzanne. *Catching Fire.* New York: Scholastic, 2009. Print.

_____. *The Hunger Games.* New York: Scholastic, 2008. Print.

_____. *Mockingjay.* New York: Scholastic. 2010. Print.

Entwistle, Joanne. *The Fashioned Body: Fashion, Dress and Modern Social Theory.* Cambridge: Polity, 2000. Print.

Gold, Tanya. "Marching with the SlutWalkers." *The Guardian.* Guardian News Ltd., 7 June 2011. Web. 9 June 2011.

Groeneveld, Elizabeth. "'Be a Feminist or Just Dress Like One.'" *Journal of Gender Studies* 18.2 (June 2009): 179–90. *Academic Search Premier.* Web. 31 Aug. 2010.

Laucius, Joanne. "Sensible Shoes and a Gray Cardigan at SlutWalk." *Ottawa Citizen* 9 Apr. 2011: J1. *LexisNexis.* Web. 9 June 2011.

Mulvey, Laura. "Visual Pleasure and Narrative Cinema." 1975. *Norton Anthology of Theory and Criticism.* 2nd ed. Ed. Vincent B. Leitch et al. New York: Norton, 2010. 2084–95. Print.

Stampler, Laura. "SlutWalks Sweep the Nation." *Huffpost Impact. huffingtonpost.com.* Huffington Post.com, Inc., 20 Apr. 2011. Web. 9 June 2011.

14

"Perhaps I Am Watching You Now"

Panem's Panopticons

KELLEY WEZNER

In the dark days after her extraction from the Quarter Quell, Katniss Everdeen returns to the burned remains of District 12, obliterated by Capitol hoverplanes in response to her escape. There she finds a perfect white rose, left for her by President Snow. The rose's implied message for Katniss is clear: "Perhaps I am watching you now" (*M* 15). In an earlier and unexpected visit with Katniss, Snow had appeared in her house right before she left for the required Victory Tour, a traveling show designed to remind Panem of the brutality and the inevitability of the Capitol's control. During that interview, Snow justified the Capitol's methods by intimating that Panem would self-destruct without the government's control. Snow's frank discussion with Katniss revealed their mutual awareness of incendiary devices. But Snow also threatened Katniss by revealing the extent of his surveillance: he saw through her fabrications regarding her romance with Peeta, and he knew of her continuing relationship with Gale. His demand was that she maintain the fiction of her relationship with Peeta on the Victory Tour, with the lives of her family and friends tied to the quality of her performance. And now, he has isolated her even more by leaving her a rose.

The tableau of the white rose and its message illustrates the disciplinary network at work as well as Katniss's interpretation of the network's control through surveillance and spectacle. In fact, her eventual understanding of how the Capitol and District 13 function as panopticons, disciplinary structures that use surveillance and spectacle for control and punishment, allows her to manipulate and exploit those very mechanisms. Accordingly, Katniss's transformations, many constructed for public consumption, must be read within the context of the use of confinement, surveillance, and spectacle, embodied in and mediated by Panem's panopticons.

Jeremy Bentham's panopticon (1791) is a prison in which a centrally located, unseen guard observes all the cells simultaneously, while prisoners are uncertain whether they are currently being watched. This inequity in gaze creates a "sentiment of invisible omniscience," causing prisoners to modify their behavior as if they are always being watched and, eventually, to internalize that surveillance (Bentham 2). Michel Foucault elaborates on Bentham's concept in his work *Discipline and Punish,* suggesting that the panoptic structure elucidates how something real, such as the panopticon, depends on something fictional — the omnipresent idea of punishment. Punishment, then, becomes a spectacle staged more for the watchers than for the condemned, for the principal object of punishment becomes the deterrent of others rather than the rehabilitation of the prisoner.

The physical structure of Bentham's panopticon appears throughout Collins's trilogy. The Capitol is located in the Rockies, with the mountains shielding the city from districts to the east. The Capitol's location elevates it over the districts that it controls, mirroring the warden's raised watchtower that allows him to survey, unseen, all the prison's inhabitants. Arguably, the thirteen districts may even ring the Capitol, yet are separated from each other. District residents are forbidden to venture past their fences, which are often electrified and rimmed with barbed wire; real dangers threaten them beyond the fences, like tracker jackers, wasps bioengineered into deadly attackers. The districts' isolation reduces the possibility of sharing information or joining forces in rebellion. So commonplace are the Capitol's efforts to separate the districts that Katniss wonders whether her innocuous discussion about their districts with Rue, a tribute from District 11, will be edited out of the Games' broadcast. The Capitol ensures compliance with constant surveillance by informers and Peacekeepers, but also with frequent theatrical reminders of the districts' powerlessness and the potential punishments for disobedience.

The most potent reminder of the Capitol's control and the possible punishment is the Hunger Games, created by a "Treaty of Treason" (*HG* 18), which initiated laws and customs to suppress future rebellion. The arenas themselves are panoptic structures: enclosed, controlled spaces observed by both the Gamemakers, who mete out dramatic punishments, and the people of Panem, who must watch mandatory broadcasts. Implanted tracking devices allow the Gamemakers to locate tributes anywhere in the arena; the tracking devices and/or cameras must also monitor the health of the tributes, as the Gamemakers seem to know exactly when to fire the cannon and send a hovercraft to collect dead tributes. The Quarter Quell arena, designed to be especially spectacular and dangerous, emphasizes the connection to Bentham's panopticon with its clocklike construction of twelve spokes of land extending outward from the central Cornucopia, surrounded by water and a force field, with threats — poisonous fog, bioengineered monkeys, tidal wave, rain of blood, jabberjays, insects — that occur in a chronological sequence. Thus, the arena mirrors the panopticon prison as it symbolizes the Capitol's control over the twelve tribute-sending districts.

The deadly competition among tributes maintains the districts' segregation while it serves a surveillance function for the Capitol, which observes the skills developed in each district within a controlled setting: e.g., the District 3 male tribute in the Seventy-fourth Hunger Games who is able to reactivate the land mines that had originally surrounded the tributes' starting discs. Such knowledge would assist in predicting and controlling potential rebellion.

Because the tributes in the Hunger Games are subjected to heightened surveillance and spectacles of punishment, the Games' mentality of distrust, suspicion, and paranoia best illustrates the psychological effects of the panopticon. Katniss initially distrusts Peeta since she sees him as a foe, which foreshadows their relationship in *Mockingjay*— one forcibly engineered by the Capitol when their disciplinary controls are threatened by Katniss and Peeta's continued alliance. Haymitch's advice to Katniss and Peeta in the Seventy-fourth Games foregrounds this caution; he counsels that they should avoid parading their skills to the other tributes, saving displays for their private performances for the Gamemakers.

In particular, the dangers and deaths in the Hunger Games transform punishment into spectacle. Punishment that is publically enacted as a dramatic spectacle reinforces the absolute power and authority of the Capitol, particularly when ritualized. All the Hunger Games function as rituals of torture, prolonging life while maximizing the pain suffered before death and thus displaying the Capitol's power to impress its magnitude on the audience. The death of the victim marks the limit of the controlling power; with repeated spectacle, deaths must be delayed longer each time the spectacle is performed to allow the Capitol to maintain the fiction of its excessive power. Accordingly, of all the deaths in the Seventy-fourth Games, the final one takes the longest. The grotesquerie of Cato's tortuous, drawn-out death engrosses the audience while it reminds them of their own impotence. For Katniss and Peeta, whose rising fame might make them influential, Cato's experience inflicts psychological distress, eliminating any thought of anything else.

The Capitol's punishments, which are performed for an audience, have a physical and psychological impact on the immediate victim, but are constructed to affect the wider audience through the idea of punishment. As Bentham argues, the benefit of punishment is that it minimizes the pain to a single victim while acting upon all others — those for whom it is actually designed — through its appearance (193). The panoptic system privileges appearance over reality when more than one person needs to be controlled. Accordingly, much of the Capitol's punishment occurs publicly in the form of whippings, mutilations, and executions.

"Avox[es]" serve as silent reminders of the punishment for crimes (*HG* 77). Katniss feels shame and remorse when her recognition of Lavinia, the red-headed Avox, forces her to recall the moment when she betrayed Lavinia by not helping her escape from the Capitol's hovercraft. Unsuccessful in avoiding being observed by the Avox, Katniss feels Lavinia's penetrating gaze silently judging her and wonders whether the Avox will enjoy her upcoming public death. For Katniss, Lavinia functions as both a deterrent and a punishment for a perceived crime: the betrayal of another human oppressed by the Capitol. The punishment is increased when the following year, one of Katniss's friends from District 12 becomes the other Avox assigned to the tributes. Still later, Katniss's perception of her ultimate betrayal — her inability to protect her sister — causes her to punish herself by becoming a psychological Avox after her sister is killed. Temporarily unable to speak, Katniss has internalized panoptic control.

The more control that needs to be exerted, the more spectacular the punishment or the larger the psychological component. The escape from the Quarter Quell arena — which involves cooperation across districts, appears live on television, and includes audience favorites — elicits the dramatic bombing and destruction of District 12 a mere fifteen minutes after the extraction. Earlier, the Peacekeepers' beating and removal of Cinna in front of Katniss was meant to "unhinge" her prior to the start of the Quell (*CF* 267). The use of the jabberjays in the Quarter Quell arena works in a panoptic manner, as the jabberjays' echoes of real screams seem to tell Katniss and Finnick that their loved ones have been tortured.

In contrast to the open brutality and theatricality of the Capitol, District 13 first looks like a sanctuary. However, the early disclosure of District 13's infertility not only hints at its leaders' motives in welcoming the District 12 survivors, but also gestures toward the rigid controls imposed on and internalized by 13's inhabitants that prohibit them from conceiving original thoughts or actions. Ostensibly, District 13's panoptic structure is a survival mechanism initiated after its pact with the Capitol isolated it from the rest of the districts. District 13 threatened the Capitol with the nuclear weapons it manufactured, forcing an agreement: District 13 would cease to exist to the rest of Panem, and in return, the Capitol would relinquish control over District 13. But District 13's subsequent move underground and adoption of strict codes of conduct and a military culture mirror the invisible mechanisms of confinement and control that make this district a more effective and deadly panopticon than the Capitol.

Every District 13 citizen receives a daily tattoo with a mandated schedule; everyone over fourteen is conscripted. Access to areas are tightly controlled by electronic surveillance, elaborate security devices, and guards; decisions are issued from the appropriately named Command, District 13's war room, containing maps, monitors, control panels, and a large television screen, which signals the media's importance in disciplinary control. When Katniss is granted the rare privilege to hunt outside, she must wear a tracking device on her ankle and be escorted through an electrified fence, which reaches nearly as high as the fences surrounding District 11. Increasingly aware of the mechanisms of control, Katniss realizes that even the Capitol was slightly less controlling than District 13 in some areas. For example, the highly controlled distribution of food seems annoying but appropriate under the circumstances, but when Katniss finds her prep team abused and imprisoned in a sublevel of District 13 for taking a slice of bread, she accurately interprets it as President Coin's warning about who is in control and what will happen to those who disobey.

Coin herself embodies the characteristics of the panopticon she governs, serving the same function as Snow does for the Capitol. She speaks infrequently, perfunctorily, and primarily to issue orders; her rigidly controlled appearance mirrors the order enforced upon her citizens; she watches Katniss closely and often. She represents District 13's disciplinary modality of power that observes individuals, gathers and organizes data, and imposes its codes of conduct within society. Because of the ostensible function of protection and then war, this panoptic structure functions as Foucault's invisible net of disciplinary relations (203).

The Hunger Games and their arenas are designed for public consumption, illustrated in the way the arenas are constructed for and manipulated during the Games, as well as in their use after the Games as tourist attractions, memorial sites with reenactments of the Games' events that maintain their power to dissuade rebellion. Before and during the Games, the Gamemakers observe the tributes closely, modifying the arena and the events to maximize the impact on the audience and the control over the tributes. Viewers are aware that the location and dangers are designed for entertainment purposes; the designers modified future Games after one year in which many tributes froze to death, the "quiet, bloodless deaths" considered "very anticlimactic" (*HG* 39). Gamemakers do avoid the other extreme: a tribute who degenerated into cannibalism may have had his supposedly accidental death contrived by Gamemakers who worried about a negative audience reaction.

Katniss recognizes that the core of the Hunger Games is the opportunity to see tributes kill tributes, and that the Gamemakers manipulate the arena accordingly. They use fire in the Seventy-fourth Games to drive the tributes closer together, hoping to provide more entertainment for the spectators. They also introduce a change, allowing two winners if they are from the same district, allowing as well for heightened drama — which they achieve by revoking the change when only Katniss and Peeta remain.

As the Capitol's primary tool of control, nearly every aspect of the

Hunger Games is televised. The Capitol schedules replays of the district reapings to maximize the exposure of the Games to the districts it controls and mandates viewing of some events, such as the pre–Games interviews, the victor's celebration, and final highlights show. During the Games, the Gamemakers project the images of the dead tributes into the sky over the arena, not so much for the effect on the television audience, who would already be aware of the fatalities, but for the impact on the tributes. The Capitol carefully edits the broadcasts to present its story of the Games; in much the same way, a tribute's stylist and prep team cultivate an image for public consumption. Cinna, Katniss's stylist, orchestrates Katniss's fiery image and creates a series of costumes that communicate her inner strength and rebelliousness. In particular, his transformation of her wedding dress into the Mockingjay prefigures Katniss's adoption of the role. Beyond his adept crafting of her physical appearance, Cinna helps shape her performance, fabricating Katniss's required talent by creating the designs for which Katniss can take credit. When Katniss worries about the interviews before her first Games, Cinna offers himself as an audience, a friendly watcher whom Katniss might feel comfortable being observed by, so that her presentation truly reflects her hidden reserves.

Katniss's constructed persona becomes so influential that the rebels extract Katniss from the Quarter Quell and urge her to become the Mockingjay, the symbolic image of the rebellion. Her participation in staged spectacle is as carefully constructed by District 13 as it was for the Games, seen in her new, image-oriented duties, including speeches, public appearances, and propaganda spots. In Command's discussions of how best to cultivate audience sympathy, in Coin's use of Katniss for her own agenda, and in Plutarch's insistence that Katniss perform for the people of District 13 during the lockdown, Katniss serves as persona rather than person.

District 13 and the Capitol struggle for control over the broadcast, both sides realizing that control over this medium of communication means control over reality. Peeta is used as a puppet by the Capitol, just as Katniss is manipulated by District 13 during the battle for control of the airwaves. When Peeta manipulates the broadcast to warn District 13 of an attack, he is beaten off camera, but with the program still on the air so that everyone is aware of what has happened. A priority after the bombing of District 13 is to film another propaganda spot, demonstrating the importance of constructing fiction in the struggle for control. Katniss, Finnick, and then Peeta are assigned to a select group that District 13 intends to use as the public faces of the invading forces.

The Capitol and District 13 construct reality in the same ways that the penitentiaries that emerged about two hundred years ago "re-presented the sensible world (both to their inmates and to the public at large) in order to alter motivation, and, ultimately, to reconstruct the fictions of personal identity that underlie consciousness" (Bender 2). Foucault argues that the key to this reconstruction lies in the disciplining gaze, whose effects are so pervasive that subjects participate in their own subjection by their vigilance (203). Thus, Katniss and others, aware that they are always being watched and judged, internalize the normative gaze and are controlled by it. Katniss's evolution from a marginalized district's tribute to a full-scale rebellion's symbolic image occurs in part because of her increasing recognition of the function of surveillance and spectacle in identity formation and, ultimately, because of her manipulation of these factors. In particular, her transformations, many constructed for public consumption, exploit surveillance and spectacle.

The entry point for the Hunger Games, the reaping, coincides with an escalation in public spectacle and scrutiny. District 12's public reaping is compulsory, ensuring that all will view the spectacle and all will be viewed by others via the camera crews perched on the roofs of the buildings surrounding the square. Citizens turn out in their best clothes, and the square is decorated with banners. Despite the poverty of District 12 and others districts, broadcasts of the reapings and the Games are universally available on public viewing screens. At this stage, Katniss equates the cameras with self-control as she struggles to contain her tears so that she will not look weak to competitors during the evening replays of her district's reaping. Her early training in controlling her affect to avoid trouble for herself and her family also benefits her as she navigates the heightened media attention following her volunteering in her sister's place at the reaping. Her evaluation of Peeta's contrasting lack of control illustrates her internalization of the panopticism of the Games: when she observes his tears on leaving his family and his unwillingness to hide his reaction from the crowds and cameras, Katniss never considers the impact of the reaping on him or on his family. Instead, she assumes that his emotional reaction is a facade cultivated as a strategy to mislead his competitors.

Her own cultivated reticence becomes problematic, however, when she and Haymitch have difficulty creating a persona for her pre–Games interviews, crucial for gaining her possible sponsors. Katniss's discomfort with being the object of a gaze surfaces in her dismay when she realizes how much Peeta had observed about her in District 12, as well as how much she had noticed about him. Similarly, she initially resists being objectified despite her awareness that her visual appeal would reap benefits in the form of sponsors and helpful gifts. She grudgingly accedes to the makeover of her image and to the presentation training provided by Effie. Peeta also resists being transformed, hoping not to become monstrous because of his participation in the Games. The motives for their resistance distinguish the two prior to the beginning of the Games: Peeta wishes to show the Capitol that he cannot be owned or controlled fully; Katniss accepts that everyone is controlled by the Capitol.

Katniss struggles with the new identities created for her, but eventually performs for the cameras in both Games, knowing that success and punishment will be based on how she appears to be. She moves, therefore, from being unknowingly shaped by Panem's panopticon to actively participating in her own identity formation as her awareness of panoptic mechanisms increases. This evolution surfaces in her embrace of spectacle and costume and increasing sophistication in reading her environment.

As a tribute, she enters an arena that foregrounds the surveillance mechanisms that shape her world and her identity; the Games particularly emphasize panoptic control with the arenas' physical construction, the media broadcasts, sponsorship, and the emphasis on spectacle. Katniss is stunned herself by the beauty of Cinna's creation for their first opening ceremonies, and realizes that her image will be burned into the crowd's memories. Moreover, Katniss observes that she and Peeta get a larger-than-normal share of the filmed coverage of the opening ceremonies. Her own inclination to spectacle is seen in her fury at the Gamemakers' indifference to her fate at her private session before her first games. After shooting an arrow directly into the centerpiece of the Gamemakers' elaborate meal, she dramatically storms out of the room.

Katniss's manipulation of spectacle truly begins when, transformed and motivated by her anger with the Capitol's manipulations, she provides a wreath for Rue's body, knowing the cameras will have to transmit the image for all to see. She moves from accepting her role as a pawn to sharing Peeta's desire to demonstrate that despite the controls, part of the tribute cannot be touched. Her victory in the Seventy-fourth Games arises from her manipulation of the panoptic structure of the Games and Gamemakers. She knows that the Games must have a winner, and speculates that if both she and Peeta die, the Gamemakers are likely to be publicly tortured and executed (a prediction borne out when the Head Gamemaker is executed). Consistent with Bentham's model, only the perception of punishment — the suicide pact of Katniss and Peeta — is enough to ensure compliance.

Initially, Katniss's awareness of the function of panoptic devices is located in her knowledge of the Games. She knows, for example, when the cameras will be likely to focus on her, and so she performs for the audience and potential sponsors, allowing them to see her hunting ability and her feigned confidence, her stoicism in the face of injury, her spirit and sense of humor when confronted by other tributes, her gratitude to Rue's district when they send her food, and her caretaking of Peeta when he is injured. Katniss also closely observes her competitors during the interviews and training, looking for clues about their relative strengths and weaknesses, but also noting the images that were crafted for each of the tributes that emphasize a memorable characteristic. She knows from a "lifetime of watching the Hunger Games" (*HG* 175) that the arena has zones preset with booby traps and that another tribute's death will provide her with more time, as it will momentarily appease the audience.

Katniss's developing awareness of panoptic control allows her to receive and interpret Haymitch's advice through the content and timing of sponsored gifts. Moreover, she acknowledges her ability to discern the implicit message Haymitch sends with any gift he has arranged: "I'll see the strings attached to it" (*HG* 306). Similarly, she comprehends that Cinna's costume for her presentation as victor emphasizes her innocence and youth, signaling the danger she is in for her manipulation of the Capitol's control mechanisms. Haymitch warns her that the Capitol is angry about its public humiliation and consequent diminishment of power. She must perform in a new role: as an actor in the Capitol's story of the Games, a story that now includes the melodrama of both threatened suicide and romance.

Katniss's awareness of the increased danger to her and her family after her unorthodox victory makes her increasingly mindful of being watched: she mentions or thinks of being observed or monitored frequently. She increasingly monitors her own presentation, viewing the highlights reel through the eyes of the audience and gauging how her victory interview is progressing not by her own perception but by monitoring the reactions of the people in the room.

The escalation of punishment and surveillance by the Capitol coincides with her move to District 13 and concomitant transformation into the Mockingjay. Her real challenges appear when she realizes that District 13, instead of being a safe haven, is, in fact, a more insidious prison because its controlling mechanisms are disguised or hidden. When the captive Snow tells Katniss that Coin was the one who ordered the bombing of the children outside the President's mansion, he attributes his downfall to failing to see Coin's plan, which was to allow the districts and the Capitol to fight until the Capitol was weakened and easy to overthrow. He states that he "wasn't watching Coin. I was watching you, Mockingjay. And you were watching me" (*M* 357). Coin's manipulation of the panoptic gaze has led to the destruction of the Capitol and the near-destruction of Katniss.

Katniss's role and usefulness as the Mockingjay come to a conclusion when she is asked to publically and symbolically execute President Snow with her iconic bow. Katniss is acutely aware of the audience, noticing the large crowds with representative groups, hearing the spectators' reactions, and positioning herself as directed. However, her awareness that her efforts have resulted only in the substitution of one warden for another equally capable of sacrificing children spurs her decision to assassinate President Coin.

While Katniss is eventually pardoned, released, and returned to life with Peeta in District 12, the subsequent distress that colors her future demonstrates the panopticon's enduring hold. The long-lasting impact of the panoptic controls of the Hunger Games appears in the vivid nightmares that plague Katniss and Peeta and the memories that inspire Peeta's paintings. In the epilogue, set some twenty years after Katniss is pardoned, she admits that her nightmares will never disappear. She counters her recurring fears that what is good in her life will be taken away with a mantra of the good that she has seen people do, demonstrating her internalization of the panopticon. In the end, she continues to provide her own surveillance and control.

WORKS CITED

Bender, John. *Imagining the Penitentiary: Fiction and the Architecture of Mind in Eighteenth-Century England.* Chicago: University of Chicago Press, 1987. Print.

Bentham, Jeremy. *The Panopticon Writings.* 1791. Ed. Miran Bozovic. London: Verso, 1995. Print.

Collins, Suzanne. *Catching Fire.* 2009. New York: Scholastic, 2010. Print.

_____. *The Hunger Games.* 2008. New York: Scholastic, 2010. Print.

_____. *Mockingjay.* New York: Scholastic, 2010. Print.

Foucault, Michel. *Discipline and Punish: The Birth of the Prison.* 1975. Trans. Alan Sheridan. New York: Vintage, 1995. Print.

15

Fueling the Spectacle
*Audience as "Gamemaker"**

SHANNON R. MORTIMORE-SMITH

Pitted against a throng of armor-clad, murderous foes, Maximus, the hero of the box-office smash-hit movie *Gladiator,* triumphs in the arena through strength, determination, and a steady stream of quick and decisive blows. Moments later, however, standing amid the thick crowd of bodies piled at his feet, Maximus angrily surveys the roaring, bloodthirsty rabble — assembled to cheer on this death match — and hurls his sword at the tent of his "Gamemakers," crying, "Are you not entertained? Is this not why you are here?" As he motions to the lifeless carnage around him, his fiery words indict all who served witness to his brutal role in these "games": he did not act alone; the audience drew swords with him, elated and gratified as he flattened each foe. Yet Maximus's plea — intended to evoke conscientious pause in his spectators — is futile. It results only in fueling the bloodlust of the audience even more. Similarly, the "games" that Katniss must play in the Hunger Games arena in order to cheat death and confound her opponents commence the moment the cameras train themselves on her every move. Beginning with a full body wax and escalating with a flaming costume, a staged romance, and a fateful handful of berries, Katniss is transformed into the fan favorite, the future rebel leader whose actions unhinge the minds of Panem viewers. Reluctant to play this role, Katniss, spurred on by her cast of mentors, grudgingly accepts that her survival pivots upon fickle public favor. Only by achieving the "gaze" of her sponsors — by evoking the empathy and the bloodlust of her spectators — can Katniss truly triumph. Survival in the Hunger Games, then, depends more on Katniss's ability to fuel a clever deception than to exercise her precision with a bow.

*I wish to express my gratitude to Carson Glusco, Gary Malone, Tessa Gilson, Evan Smith, Bret Girton and Brittany Foulds, students in my spring 2011 Introduction to Literature class (Shippensburg University), for allowing me to present their insights in this essay.

Today, our "games" are less gladiatorial, yet they harbor the same voyeuristic gains for those who choose to watch them. It is inconceivable to fathom "arenas" large enough to house the millions of viewers who tune in from the comfort of their recliners each week to watch *American Idol, Survivor, Teen Mom,* and *Jersey Shore.* Yet these millions, with one hand planted firmly on the remote control and the other buried in a bowl of buttered popcorn, continue to influence the outcomes of those they observe. Like Capitol fans who watch the Hunger Games, insulated by their own apathy and far from any "real" danger or consequences, our audiences relish the ruin and humiliation, the unpredictability, and the spectacle that unfold in the lives of their beloved reality television stars. What's more, through their "sponsorship" of the advertisers who fuel this programming, viewers guarantee that the games will go on, perpetually titillating audiences with more, and increasingly shocking, episodes each week.

Panem's Games are engineered not only to ensure the docility and subservience of the twelve districts, but also to entertain a wide and voracious viewership. Indeed, from the makeovers to the personal interviews to the televised ratings of the tributes, the audience plays an integral role in ensuring that the brutality and the popularity of the Games continue year after year, despite the human cost. Hunger Games heroine Katniss is less the "sport" of her rival tributes than the "sport" of her spectators. Moments after her arrival in the arena, Katniss recognizes that there is no element of chance — no coincidence — in these games. Like pawns on a chessboard, the tributes are maneuvered through a series of deliberate encounters designed by the Gamemakers to maximize spectator engagement in the Games. What viewer would dare look away as the tributes dash for the treasures stashed in the Cornucopia? How could one possibly pry one's eyes from the telescreen as the tributes scramble to obtain meager fragments of weapons, sustenance, and shelter? From the opening pronouncement to the final cannon shot, the Gamemakers toy with the tributes, dictating each encounter and animating every move. Brief pauses in the action are punished with traps. The flames bearing down on Katniss in the arena are no accident; they are a mechanical snare designed with one specific purpose in mind: to flush the tributes into battle and force a confrontation that will ultimately result in ultra-color bloodshed. *This* is what the audience *wants* to see: tributes hurled into hungry packs of "[m]uttations" (*HG* 331), covered in swarms of stinging insects, tortured with third-degree burns, shrunken by exhaustion and starvation, and murdered at the hands of their peers. This is the only "sport" that will slake the spectators' thirst; anything less might bore the viewers into apathy, and this, as every television sponsor knows, "is one thing the Games must not do" (*HG* 173). A death match where the contenders deliberately abandon their will to fight is no death match at all. In order for the Games to go on, both viewer and viewed must play a part in the drama that unfolds on the public stage of the arena.

Under the direction of her team of advisors, Katniss is taught that abandoning herself to viewer scrutiny will win her the "gaze" of her audience and subsequently secure her survival. Exposing her bruises on national television, for example, advances her image as a tough contender. Waxing her legs and plucking her eyebrows improve her physical appeal to audiences. An elaborate, flaming costume evokes awe and elation in viewers, who gossip about this fiery tribute. And the grandest hoax of all — feigning true love — secures Katniss the empathy of her sponsors. According to Haymitch, "It's all a big show" (*HG* 135). It's not about what's *real;* it's the fabrication of reality that truly matters. Against her better judgment, Katniss reluctantly surrenders to this rationale, yet it is not until Rue's death that her power to manipulate the audience's gaze is fully actualized. Rue, the smallest and youngest of the tributes, seeks an alliance with Katniss to bring down the warring Careers. Like the mockingjays who mimic her joyful song, the bird-like Rue survives by hopping from tree to tree, spying on her opponents and listening to their plans — but she is finally ensnared by the Careers and mortally wounded. Comforting the dying Rue, Katniss vows to win the Games for both of them. In an act designed to dishonor the Capitol, Katniss decorates Rue's corpse with wildflowers. This tender and wholly unexpected act of humanity magnifies the brutality of the Capitol, whose viewers selfishly and insatiably "hunger" for more violence. As evidenced by the small gift of bread from the members of Rue's district, however, Katniss succeeds in arousing the emotions of at least some of the districts' viewers. In doing so, she marks her first act of rebellion against Capitol rule.

Katniss's creator, Suzanne Collins, has argued that "there's just too much of our lives we're putting on television" (qtd. in Hudson). In an interview with *Instructor,* Collins specifically describes the Games as "a reality television program." While Collins admits in her interview that this is an "extreme" interpretation of popular television culture in society today, she also notes that twenty-first-century audiences enjoy a "voyeuristic thrill, watching people being humiliated or brought to tears or suffering physically"— a thrill that is undeniably disconcerting to many of us (qtd. in Hudson). Collins, who advocates for a conscientious viewership, further argues in this interview that our "potential for desensitization" is the real tragedy. She wants her readers to understand that, despite the way the media attempt to anesthetize viewer perceptions of violence and war on screen, "the young soldier's dying in the war in Iraq" does not pause "at the commercial break" (qtd. in Hudson). The news footage we see — and often choose to ignore — is "not something fabricated," Collins argues. "It's not a game," she continues. "It's your life" (qtd. in Hudson).

Like the spectators of the Hunger Games, reality TV viewers "tune in" to "peer through the keyhole" into the lives of others (Gabler). We lick chocolate ice cream from a bowl while we watch contestants on *The Biggest Loser* step onto cattle scales, we laugh at Simon Cowell's infamous insults on *American Idol* and *The X-Factor,* we weigh the merits of our marriages against *Wife Swap* and *Trading Spouses,* and we discipline our children according to the *Supernanny.* Instead of practicing democracy at the polls, we exercise our "inalienable rights" by texting in votes for our favorite contestants on *Dancing with the Stars* and *America's Got Talent.* In every way, our "hand" plays a part in sculpting the direction of the entertainment we view; our participation is crucial to the reception and the success of these shows.

In his article "Watching Television Without Pity: The Productivity of Online Fans," Mark Androjevic argues, "In an era in which the mass audience is becoming increasingly visible thanks to a variety of increasingly sophisticated monitoring technologies, viewers are increasingly encouraged to climb out of the couch to embrace a more 'active' approach to their viewing experience" (25). Unlike the passive television programming of the 1950s, where viewers stooped over a dial with twelve channels to select singular episodes, twenty-first-century channel flippers surf nimbly among hundreds of programs, stopping only when their attention is titillated enough to warrant a momentary pause. Once an allegiance is forged between the viewer and the viewed, however, loyalties are paid in arenas that extend far beyond the one-sided television screen. Self-proclaimed fans tweet their feedback on Twitter and Facebook, where the "stars" of these shows — the viewed — entertain the spotlight of a *second* stage where they respond *en masse* to viewer comments and queries. Viewers solicit websites, comment on cast members' blogs, and loiter in "behind the scenes" video chat sites that allow them to lurk even further into the "real" lives of the viewed. The key to "reality" success is *interactivity.* Viewer and viewed operate in tandem with each other. The "actors" work cyclically with audiences to provide a brand of entertainment that not only simulates "real life" but, more pervasively, mirrors what the viewer demands to see. According to Neal Gabler, this particular brand of "voyeurism" reaches far beyond innocent peeping. In "Behind the Curtain of TV Voyeurism," Gabler argues that "[v]oyeurism isn't just peeking. It's a form of privilege" and that "[t]o watch unobserved is to appropriate lives and assert oneself over them. Those we observe become ours, hostages to our eyes." Each time viewers demand this privilege, they experience what Gabler calls "the thrill of subversiveness," a way of "safely exercising mischievousness in a society that allows few opportunities to do so."

In a recent survey of the ninety students I teach in "Introduction to Literature," a 200-level general education course offered by the university where I work, nearly all of my students admitted to actively viewing reality television programming. The program referenced the most by my students during in-class discussion and in their weekly written blogs was none other than the "GTL'ing" (Gym, Tan, and Laundry) and "Fist-pumping" MTV reality show *Jersey Shore*. Nearly half of my students reported that they watched the show weekly, with the remainder citing additional MTV shows like *Teen Mom* and *The Real World* as notable runner-ups. Unaccustomed to thinking critically about why they engage in reality television programming, these students initially cited the fistfights, binge drinking, hook ups, backstabbing, and entertainment — in a word, what they refer to as "drama" — as the characteristics that sealed their "sponsorship" of these shows each week.

In relation to our reading of *The Hunger Games* and Gabler's criticism of reality TV, however, I was curious to learn how my students rationalized their "participation" in these weekly "games." In order to elicit their perspectives, I asked them to write about the question that follows in their class blogs:

> What part do *we* play as viewers and fans in the "reality" of these programs? In what way do we (as the audience of these "games") influence the "games" themselves?

Many of my students struggled to answer this question. Several summed up their personal participation in these shows as insignificant; they felt their viewership made very little impact on the outcome of the programming itself. While they collectively acknowledged that very little "reality" exists in reality TV, they were, at the same time, reluctant to admit that a team of "Gamemakers" — writers, producers, and executives — deliberately devise and direct this programming to guarantee their future viewership. Most students believed the purpose of these shows to be "simple entertainment." They enjoyed, as Gabler suggests, making the actors their "hostages" and comparing their own lives to the lives of the actors on TV. By comparison, they rationalized, their lives were "so much better" than the ones they saw on screen. One group of students, however, constructed a thoughtful threaded discussion in their blogs that moved more directly to the heart of society's reality obsession and our very human desire to experience "peeking" as a form of "privilege":

> **Brittany:** Reality TV is popular because Americans [enjoy] watching [other people's] lives picked apart. We tune in each week to see what the latest gossip will be, and to find out what will happen next.... We are the reasons that shows continue on for seasons and seasons; we follow these people like they are real celebrities instead of random people off the street. We influence the "games" because networks [create] what we are most interested in viewing. When a couple or housemates fight that's when it *gets good,* or when people go out and drink and make a fool of themselves it's funny because *it's not us* that's doing it (emphasis added).

Instructor: Yes ... exactly! We're tuning in to watch the next "pile-up." ... We want to know when the next "car wreck" is going to happen.... Isn't that kind of ... well, sick? (and not in the sick=badass sense either).

Brittany: Thinking about it, yes it is sick. We are more interested in what will happen next in these people's lives than we are in our own lives. We get excited about how people's lives are torn apart and think nothing of it....

Gary: This is what people want to see. After [these] fights when you look on Facebook, it's what everybody [is] talking about.

Tessa: Haha! I agree with you....We are drawn to this because we like to see how these "real" people react to different situations. We are intrigued by how they react and handle what goes on in their lives, either [by] relating our own life to their scenarios or applauding how different they are....

Carson: I hate *Jersey Shore* to be completely honest. What does it say about us that we are so focused on the lives of reality TV stars that we don't even worry about our own lives? Are we so caught up in it that we can't even control our own lives anymore? To be so caught up in others' lives seems disturbing to me.

Brittany: No Carson (lol) ... I don't really think that's true.... If we're watching other people on TV how has that stopped us from controlling our own lives?

Carson: It creates a false sense of reality and doesn't allow us to put things in perspective if we watch too much of it. Essentially, it doesn't help, but you're right some people take it a lot further than others.

Bret: I'd have to agree that these people are getting paid to ... get drunk, hook up, fight, and do this over and over again night after night. But I [am] always thinking about this question. Do you think there are people out there who try [to] be just like these idiots? I mean, I hear the [*Jersey Shore*] saying all the time ... "It's T-shirt time!" And people like to fist pump.... I really think that some people try to be like *Jersey Shore* members.

Evan: Let's be honest, [Mike "The Situation"] is a pretty smart guy. The man is living the life right now, getting paid millions to do basically nothing, and he knows that the only way to keep his "job" at this point is to satisfy the audience. Ironically, the audience happens to be most drawn towards the violence, fights, and drama that he, himself (whether he wants to admit it or not), is seemingly starting on purpose. He knows what the audience wants to see and he knows what needs to happen for him to continue living the life he is now.

Bret: Many viewers are drawn to this type of show because we like seeing other people in a similar situation that we are in or could be in, even though some of the situations are wayyyyy over the top. The fact that people are getting paid for letting a camera follow them around is pretty sad. It is bad television and yet so many people love it. *It would not be on TV if it didn't have any viewers ...* (emphasis added).

Brittany's admission that it "gets good" when the "drama" begins and Tessa's observation that we are "intrigued" by how others "react and handle what goes on in their lives" clearly demonstrate the power of the spectator's gaze. What most viewers would consider to be *genuine* reality — cast members mundanely eating cornflakes, paying bills, sorting laundry, or ringing up customers at the cash register — is far less enticing than witnessing an argument that escalates into a drunken tirade, a theatrical arrest, and a sullen set of mug shots. It's the "drama" that the viewers want to see, the "subversiveness" and deviance of these acts that are, "in reality," a dramatic shift from the norm. Furthermore, Evan's and Bret's statements illustrate the cyclical relationship between the viewer and the viewed. If a good fight is what the audience demands to see, then it logically follows that Mike "The Situation" Sorrentino will secure his viewer's gaze by staging himself into incrementally violent "situations" each week. What's more, this cycle is self-perpetuating: the *Jersey Shore* cast uses the expression "It's T-shirt time!"—coined as a way to indicate when it's "Party time!"—and the slogan goes viral; even Mom is Facebooking it! Audience *interactivity* validates the phrase, and as a result, the cast members repeat it, over and over again. In addition, cast members who receive the most attention in tweets, fansites, Facebooks, and blogs, as Gary noted, are generally the ones who engage in the most backstabbing, fighting, drinking, and hooking up on the show. Consequently, the cycle of what Bret refers to as "bad television" endures, despite what most of us, as viewers, recognize to be our better judgment.

Like many young adult viewers today, the futuristic Capitol citizens who reside in the pages of Collins's cautionary tale are intentionally oblivious to the power of their gaze. Whether caught up in the "drama" of reality television or Panem's games, both real and fictional audiences alike are ensnared by the remarkable pageantry that accompanies each spectacle. Criticizing the cruel appetite of twenty-first-century viewers, Collins's dystopia forecasts the brutal outcome of any society that loses sight of the "reality" that drives its entertainment. In Panem's arena, children kill other children, and no amount of media sorcery can alter this cold fact. Furthermore, lavish lifestyles isolate Capitol viewers from any real empathy for the districts' poverty. Ironically, while the tributes are fattened up on rich stew and chocolates, residents of the Capitol drink a special tonic that allows them to vomit the contents of their stomachs in order to continue eating. Nothing satiates them; they persistently lust for more. For Capitol residents, tuning in to watch the Hunger Games is nothing short of Pauly shouting "It's T-shirt time!" on *Jersey Shore*. The Games are merely one more party to be enjoyed.

Additionally, while the Capitol elite parade about, flaunting the latest grotesque fashions, the tributes, far removed from such extravagant practice, are dressed for slaughter and paraded on television, prodded by their handlers like prize cattle charged with attracting a set of sponsors whose gifts might somehow delay their dark future. Even tributes who elect to be in the Games, whose training is a matter of honor in the districts they represent, eventually succumb to this dark reality. Like Mike "The Situation" Sorrentino, whose theatrics earn him the rapt attention of his fans, "the bad behavior" of Cato and the Careers entice viewers into the "drama" that unfolds in the arena.

Both believe that their actions secure them the "sponsorship" they need to survive. In the end, however, both Cato and Sorrentino are made what Katniss calls "lapdogs" for the viewers' pleasure (*HG* 161). Nothing matters more than maintaining the arousal of the spectator. In this way, sponsorship is secured and the cycle — the exchange between the viewer and the viewed — is perpetuated.

Contrary to what most believe, Katniss's final triumph in the end of *The Hunger Games* is not saving two lives; it's actualizing her power to turn tables on the Capitol's rule and play "Gamemaker" to her viewers' desires and demands. Like Maximus in the *Gladiator,* Katniss first seizes control when she spins her arrow into the gluttonous judges' roast pig. Outraged by their visible display of apathy and arrogance, Katniss fearlessly demands recognition and pause. Despite their disregard for her life and the lives of the tributes, Katniss refuses to be "upstaged by a dead pig" (*HG* 101). Her arrow, like Maximus's sword, declares her presence, her dignity, and her threat. Second, in her district salute — her respectful recognition of the tragedy of Rue's death — Katniss once again shifts the audience to her side. The simple of act of decorating Rue's body drives an arrow into her spectators' hearts. They, like the Gamemakers, not only served witness but also played accomplice to Rue's murder. And last, what the Gamemakers intended to be the "most dramatic showdown in history" — re-reversing the rules to pit two lovers against each other in a final, embittered battle to the death — becomes Katniss's definitive victory (*HG* 342). With a plan bold enough — and, more importantly, *dramatic* enough — to crumble the integrity of the Games, Katniss maneuvers her final pawn against the Capitol with a handful of berries and her viewers' empathy as her ally.

In this — Collins's climax — readers are no doubt entertained, but have they learned, like Katniss, the importance of practicing critical reflection and conscientious pause? In *Walden,* nineteenth-century transcendentalist Henry David Thoreau writes that "we are determined to be starved before we are hungry" (223), and two centuries later the viewer's "appetite" for *more* is visibly swelling bellies. Relishing their claim over the lives of those they view, twenty-first-century audiences — consumed with their next media fix — fail to recognize that they, too, have become hostages to the entertainment they watch. Only when we, like Katniss, begin to question our spectatorship in these "games" and recognize the role we play within them will we truly understand what it is we "hunger" for.

WORKS CITED

Androjevic, Mark. "Watching Television Without Pity: The Productivity of Online Fans." *Television and New Media* 9.1 (Jan. 2008): 24–46. Web. 10 Sept. 2011.
Collins, Suzanne, *The Hunger Games.* New York: Scholastic. 2008. Print.

Gabler, Neal. "Behind the Curtain of TV Voyeurism." *Christian Science Monitor* 92.158 (July 2000): n. pag. Web. 12 Sept. 2011.

Gladiator. Dir. Ridley Scott. Screenplay by John Logan. Perf. Russell Crow, Joaquin Phoenix, and Connie Neilson. Dreamworks, SKG, and Universal Pictures, 2003. DVD.

Hudson, Hannah Trierweiler, ed. "Sit Down with Suzanne Collins." *Instructor* 120.2 (2010): 51–53. *EBSCO.* Web. 8 Sept. 2011.

Jersey Shore. Prod. SallyAnn Salsano. MTV. New York, 2009. Television.

Thoreau, Henry David. *The Annotated Walden.* Ed. Philip Van Doren Stern. New York: Barnes, 1970. Print.

16

Simulacra, Sacrifice and Survival in *The Hunger Games, Battle Royale,* and *The Running Man*

HELEN DAY

Like two of its predecessors, *The Running Man* (1982) by Stephen King (as Richard Bachman) and *Battle Royale* (1999) by Koushun Takami, *The Hunger Games* trilogy is a dystopia set amid fearful games that the protagonists must survive. Beyond the games, what these texts share is the role of television as a repressive Ideological State Apparatus. While it is used sparingly but effectively in *Battle Royale,* in the other books television is no longer, as Baudrillard argues, a "spectacular" medium; instead, "TV watches us, TV alienates us, TV manipulates us, TV informs us" (*Simulations* 56). In the worlds of King and Collins, television screens frame the relationship between audience and those who participate in the terrifying games that are used to control the population. Each of the games functions like Baudrillard's conception of Disneyland (*Simulations* 25). The streets, arenas, and islands are there to conceal the fact that the entire country is violent and repressive even if some citizens feel more protected from the repression than others. The physical locations of the games, and the designated roles — tributes, Female Student No. 2, Gamemaker, instructor, President — disguise the fact that everyone is always already interpellated as a player. Witness the real-world Disney shops, toys, and television programs: simulacra leaking into the real, hijacking it so that little girls, for example, become convinced they really are princesses. If the games could be contained within their arenas, the players adhere to the rules, and the controllers remain "outside" events, all would be flawless. But there is always seepage: the head of the Network in *Running Man* wants Ben as his new Head Hunter; Sakamochi, the instructor of the Program in *Battle Royale,* kills one of the class prematurely; and the Head Gamemaker, Seneca Crane, gets carried away by the romantic drama he is portraying and allows Katniss to live. And the players — and viewers — can't seem to help sacrificing themselves for each other and the greater good.

The dominant Ideological State Apparatus (ISA) within *The Running Man,* rather than the Church or Education, is "Communications," the Media (Althusser 1489). By law, every Development apartment must have a Free-Vee. Like all ISAs, television functions not only by ideology but also by violence. Nowhere is this made clearer than in the Games Network (so dominant that it *is* the State Apparatus), a "huge and potent communications link to the whole world" (King 119). The Network exploits the poor and the desperate with games that exchange cash for health or even life: witness *"Treadmill to Bucks,"* *"Dig Your Grave,"* and, the *pièce de résistance, "The Running Man"* (King 12, 33, 35). The book opens with Ben's wife watching him watching the Free-Vee "with steady, vacant, concentration" (*RM* 1). Their daughter is dying of influenza, and with Ben having no job, his decision to apply to the Games Network seems "always already" determined (Althusser 1503). Although they never ordinarily watch the Free-Vee, Ben is now transformed by this new set of circumstances into a Free-Vee subject. In this brave new world, citizens like Ben can be "interpellated" or "hailed" by the ideological ritual of the application process, ready to make visual their place in the world within the *mise-en-scène* of the Free-Vee screen (Althusser 1504).

The recruitment process is designed to rob contestants of their individuality and any sense of power by first rendering them "stripped and anonymous" (*RM* 14) and then replacing their clothes with the Games uniform. "When the entire group was wearing them," states the narrator, "Ben Richards felt as if he had lost his face" (*RM* 20). Network head Dan Killian takes pleasure in telling Ben exactly why he has been selected by detailing his misdemeanors: not only being fired numerous times for insubordination but for adhering to the old-fashioned ideology of marriage. It seems that the show *The Running Man* is one of the "surest ways The Network has of getting rid of embryo troublemakers" (*RM* 39).

The rules of the Game are that Ben — or his surviving family — wins 100 New Dollars for each hour he remains free. He will be hunted by special operatives, the general public, and independent cameramen who win money for film and verified sightings. The Game is loaded from the beginning as Ben appears first to the crowds as a doctored image taken by hidden camera. His mouth is given a "jeering, curled expression by some technico's air-brush," transforming him into "the angel of urban death" (*RM* 53). The audience response is immediate and predictable: "Kill him! Kill the bastard!" (*RM* 53). Host Bobby Thompson entreats them to *"Remember his face!"* (*RM* 55, emphasis in original). *"They hate your guts"* Killian reminds Ben: "You symbolize all the fears of this dark and broken time" (*RM* 56, emphasis in original).

Killian's counsel that Ben stick near his own people proves good advice;

indeed, Ben's developing relationship with an intelligent teenager and his family is the first time Ben has any real understanding of who his "own people" are. Eighteen-year-old Bradley makes Ben aware of the suffocating conditions of his existence and the reason for his daughter's illness: "the pollution count in Boston" (*RM* 100). Bradley puts the blame squarely on Free-Vee, which he claims is used to "keep us off the streets so we can breathe ourselves to death without making any trouble" (*RM* 100). Bradley, it seems, has preempted journalist Michelle Conlin's description of reality TV shows as "weapons of mass distraction ... causing us to become ... more disengaged from ourselves and society." Ben is transformed from an individual rebel into part of a group: "There was no longer just himself, a lone man fighting for his family, bound to be cut down. Now there were all of them out there, strangling on their own respiration — his family included" (*RM* 116). His attempts, however, to use his compulsory video-messages for the Games Network to tell his audience of this "monstrous conspiracy" fail as his image is hijacked, growing obscene and screaming, "I'm gonna kill every pig I see" (*RM* 103, 104).

Realizing that the Games are doubly loaded and that his mailed clips are giving his location away to the Hunters, Ben takes a hostage, the middle-class Mrs. Amelia Williams. Amelia confirms that the beautiful chosen ones see Ben as a "cowardly little murderer" who took her because she is "defenseless" and "decent" (*RM* 155, 156). Ben's angry response is to question a decency that leaves Amelia with plenty of money to buy a car while his poverty-stricken daughter is dying of the flu. Despite declaring Ben an enemy because "[i]t says so on the Free-Vee" (*RM* 156), Amelia soon acknowledges that the cops also shot at her, collateral damage in their pursuit of the prize of killing Ben. "You can't kill hostages unless no one is watching," Ben tells her (*RM* 167). In due course, Amelia continues to change, realizing, as she does, that there can be no "his people" and "her people" when it comes to the Network's needs.

Those who do not have the luxury of this personal interaction with Ben as the Running Man remain stubbornly passive consumers, enjoying the pleasure offered by the Free-Vee show for vicarious and actual viewer participation: Ben is on view and is, therefore, "fair game" (*RM* 47). But Ben proves so adept at this Game that Killian attempts to commodify his dissent, inviting him to a fake execution that will be followed by his initiation into the team of Hunters. The Network head places his desire to provide the Game with fresh talent above his own and others' safety. With no control over how his image or words are broadcast, however, Ben chooses to hold the real images of his wife and daughter in his head while he drives the plane he has hijacked into the Network building. Unable to reach the people to start a revolution, his only option is a short-term solution: the violent and suicidal destruction of the image-making machine: "All over Harding, Free-Vees went white with interference and people stared at them with stupid, fearful incredulity" (*RM* 240).

In the show *The Running Man,* image is used to mask and pervert a basic reality, one that Ben Richards comes to understand but cannot communicate through the TV screen. If the "good middle-class folks" believe the screen reflects reality, perhaps all he can do is blank that screen, hoping it will interfere with the mirror, perhaps enabling viewers to turn away from the evil procession of images. *The Running Man* novel was published in 1982, before the success story of reality TV in the 1990s. Within the text, the middle-class audience of Free-Vee's *Running Man* is stereotypically passive, seemingly unaware of the way television "puts reality together" and how editing can create different degrees of reality (Schlesinger, qtd. in Hill 449). The viewers do not seem to distrust the visual evidence presented to them by the Games Network perhaps because they have little firsthand experience of the material conditions of Ben's "people." As Goffman indicates, when we do not have full information of a factual situation, we tend to "rely on appearances" (qtd. in Hill 461). Ben's identity is framed and presented by the host through distorted images and threats that, paradoxically, also reveal the real: while Ben is aware that he is projecting "exactly the aura of hate and defiance that they wanted him to project," he "could not help it" (*RM* 54).

In a similar way to the show *Running Man,* the "Program" in *Battle Royale* functions as a deterrent against the population of the Republic of Greater East Asia. Every junior high school student is aware of it as a battle simulation program instituted for research and security reasons. Fifty classes are selected, and classmates are forced to fight until one survivor is left. As a result of protests during the first year of its enactment, the Great Dictator gave his famous "April Speech" insisting that the Program was essential to prepare for invasion by "shameless imperialists prowling our republic, attempting to sabotage it" (*BR* 40). Such ideological propaganda convinces few; much more persuasive is the constant threat of violence against, and repression of, those who speak out of line. This ensures that, by their silence and inaction, everyone is complicit. Shinji's uncle, for example, whose death is officially reported as an accident, told Shinji that "you couldn't survive in this country if you really wanted to be good" (*BR* 200).

Shuya, the novel's male protagonist, remembers gazing at the television screen when the News presented a statistical report about a recently ended local Program in Kagawa Prefecture. What makes Shuya "inexplicably afraid" is the image of "the winner," her "twitching face" occasionally forming "what appeared to be, strangely enough, a smile" (*BR* 42). Shuya realizes that this was "the first time he had seen an insane person," and with every subsequent reference to the Program, "dark fear choked him up again" (*BR* 42, 43–44). Although this is the only image shown of the Program, it is a highly effective threat, working alongside the statistics from the autopsies: "17 from gunshot wounds, 9 from knife or blade wounds, 5 from blunt weapons, and 3 choked to death" (*BR* 43). The implications of the Program are left to the public's imagination: if a schoolgirl could kill and survive this, then what could we, our friends, our children be capable of? This is confirmed by the guard Sakamochi, who, when he thinks the Program has ended, confesses to the winner, Shogo:

> Why do you think we have the local news broadcast the image of the winner? Of course, viewers might feel sorry for him or her, thinking, the poor student probably didn't even want to play the game, but had no choice but to fight the others. In other words, everyone ends up concluding, you can't trust anyone, right? Which would extinguish any hope of uniting and forming a coup d'état against the government, hm? [*BR* 596–97].

Unlike *The Running Man,* where participants at least volunteer, all third-year juniors have an equal chance of their class being selected for the Program. The perverted equality of this society means that circumstances beyond your control, such as your family's wealth and position, have no bearing on whether you are chosen. Even those like Shogo, a previous winner, are not exempt. And yet, from the beginning of *Battle Royale,* the Program is framed, like *The Running Man,* as a game that has an entertainment function, even if the guards and government officials are the only spectators. The violence and killing in the Program are displaced, or perhaps framed, as spectacle. As she is attacked, Megumi hears a slashing sound like a lemon being cut, the knife really sharp and the lemon fresh, "the way they are on television shows, as in 'Today, we'll be cooking lemon salmon'" (*BR* 117–18). Equally, the students' behavior and the outcomes of battles are based on scenarios from television, movies, computer games, and novels. Shinji compares himself to The Terminator, while Mizuho copes by imagining herself as space warrior Mizuho. Mitsuko uses her sexuality to distract her killers: "Geez, this was turning into one of those adult videos titled *Fetish Special! Starring Real Junior High School Girls!*" (*BR* 441). The legitimacy of these little stories is ratified by the reality principle of genre and narrative itself.

The Program functions effectively because it relies on suspicion and lack of trust among the players. From the beginning, Sakamochi warns them that, although they may think that murdering their classmates is impossible, others would be willing to do it. From this moment something changes: "[E]veryone was looking around, glancing at the others' pale faces" trying to work out, by looking, who was ready to take part (*BR* 62). Noriko realizes that she does not really know her classmates, and she chooses to put her trust firmly in appearances, believing Shuya would never do anything horrible, a judgment based on "watching [him] for so long now" (*BR* 86). She also believes what she sees on the News. When Shogo tells her that the Dictator is only an actor, her response is disbelief: "[W]e see him on the news ... and on New Year's he makes an appearance in front of everyone at his palace" (*BR* 226). The entire political narrative of the Republic is predicated on falsehoods and second-order simulacra, masking and perverting reality.

With death so imminent, identity becomes little more than a series of memory flashes and fantasies. While at first it appears that using the full names of the students is an attempt to anchor their identity, it becomes clear that this makes it easier for both Sakamochi — and the reader — to keep a tally of who dies and who kills. The majority of students are referred to in the narrative as they are in the "Student List" at the beginning of the text by their full name, gender, and number on the list, for example, "Kazuo Kiriyama (Male Student No. 6)" (*BR* 25). This statistical reduction has an alienating effect on the reader that is compounded if the reader records the deaths by annotating the list and marking fatalities on the map provided, providing a simulacrum of the dots on the computer screen that Sakamochi is watching. Only the reader's access, through free indirect discourse, to the little stories, memories, and fantasies that substitute for the identity of each of the students prevents us from becoming totally dehumanized by our part in keeping the statistics of the game.

In the end, Shogo's advanced planning and manipulation of his audience defeat the game — but only with the unwitting assistance of Sakamochi's hubris. Unlike Shogo, the instructor first trusts in the authenticity of the conversations he overhears through the collars, even when he is reminded that someone hacked into the government computer before this Program. He interprets Shogo helping the injured Noriko as a magnificent bluff, believing that he alone knows Shogo and that it is impossible to escape. But Shogo is successful because, apart from lying about not being a computer whiz, he does not attempt a simulation by faking his friendship and conversations with Noriko and Shuya. Even when Sakamochi recognizes the quality of Shogo's performance and realizes Shuya and Noriko are still alive, he does not consider that he might be the one being played or that Shogo might be willing to sacrifice himself. Despite telling the students that entrance to this game is based on equality, Sakamochi never considers he could be part of it as anything other than the instructor. Ironically, if Sakamochi had understood and adhered to the rules of the Program, it might, indeed, have been flawless. Instead, Shuya and Noriko's attack on the boat enables Shogo to stab Sakamochi through the neck with one of the pencils on which the instructor forced everyone to write "We will kill each other" (*BR* 599).

Much like the show *The Running Man* and, to a certain extent, the Program, the rationale for the Hunger Games is both entertainment and "a deterrence machine" (Baudrillard, *Simulations* 25), designed to punish the districts for their past rebellion against the Capitol. In a similar way to *The Running Man,* the odds are in favor of the children of the better off, as the poor and starving like Katniss and Gale enter their names for the reaping multiple times in exchange for food. The "tesserae" (*HG* 15) are intended to create hatred between the starving and the well fed, ensuring that they never trust each other; trust and friendship are enemies of the state. Children are thus interpellated into the Hunger Games as already hungering subjects. However, Katniss volunteering to take the place of her younger sister, Prim, although allowed by the rules (perhaps because it creates tension and a better show), discloses the older sibling as a loving, sacrificing subject, an unfortunate byproduct of state-endorsed repression.

A further insult within this sacrifice of children is the requirement to treat the Games as a festive sporting event: entertainment. Watching the Hunger Games on TV is compulsory. In an even more complex way than in *The Running Man,* television is a repressive Ideological State Apparatus. While some in District 12 do indulge in betting, it is mostly the Capitol's citizens who produce and consume the Hunger Games for enjoyment. Since its well-fed children are not entered, the Capitol does not recognize the role of reality TV in anesthetizing its inhabitants to the real conditions of their existence: that in the end they might be no safer than those in the districts. Although we have only Katniss's point of view, in the first book her prep team seems to be the embodiment of luxury and artificiality, feeding off fashion and gossip, celebrity and image. They are passive viewers, unable to recognize that the children on their screens are more than images and will experience real deaths. Like Ben, Katniss is sickened by the prep team's excitement, yet she also attempts to understand how they are a product of the Capitol.

Katniss, too, is a product of her district. Although her initial experiences at the Remake Center leave her looking like a "creature" and feeling like "no-one at all," she is not a powerless, passive victim of reality television (*HG* 146, 143). She learns very quickly how to use the screen to control her image, able to put herself in the place of the audience and give them what they want. Her survival comes to depend on maintaining the viewers' interest and belief in her romance with Peeta. Since she has no experience to draw upon, she must simulate being in love, speaking in the special tone her mother used with her father and touching Peeta's cheek with her hand. She can't help interpreting Peeta's behavior in the same way, as a strategy to keep them alive, believing that the image he projects "masks and perverts reality" rather than reflecting real feelings (Baudrillard, *Simulations* 11).

A reliable narrator, Katniss repeatedly informs us that she cannot tell if her feelings for Peeta are real or simulated: whether she acts out of anger or decency, for survival, or because she really cares. She tries constantly to find her authentic self behind the words and images — self that the Capitol can't own or control — but she fears that maybe, unlike Peeta, the image *she* projects masks an absence. However, as Baudrillard suggests, simulation can reveal more than you think. Try to organize a fake holdup, he urges, to test the repressive apparatus to a perfect simulation. You won't succeed, as "the web of artificial signs will be inextricably mixed up with real elements," and you will find yourself "immediately in the real" (Baudrillard, *Simulations* 39). Katniss's simulated feelings for Peeta do become real, perhaps as a result of the simulation, of getting to know "the boy with the bread" (*HG* 362). Love is always already a simulation, in that it is "inscribed in advance in the decoding and orchestration rituals of the media"— the unlucky lovers beloved of television audiences (Baudrillard, *Simulations* 41). But it has real effects. "Let's find the most stunning Mockingjay look possible," exhorts Fulvia, preparing Katniss for the propaganda segments the rebels plan to use to hijack the Capitol's television screens, "and then work your personality up to deserving it!" (*M* 52).

Simulation, in this series, is always a temporary state: the real can be hijacked, but it always returns. Just as Peeta's mind is hijacked by aversion therapy and tracker-jacker venom to hate Katniss, so he eventually recognizes the shiny quality of simulation. There is a way to see the flaw in the arena force field and a way to find out that District 13 still exists by the repetition of the same mockingjay in every Capitol broadcast. Real and not real *are* two distinct options, and the hyperreal only a stage in discovering a real, safer future.

Katniss's act of rebellion in the first Games, threatening to eat poisonous berries with Peeta, exposes the war between ratings (which require the editors to show this climactic gesture) and deterrent (which requires the censorship of such an incendiary act). However oppositional these may seem, President Snow's power depends upon balancing them both. The people of the Capitol must be kept happy and anesthetized by the drama of reality TV. Seneca Crane, Head Gamemaker, finds himself caught up in the dramatic culmination of the Games and, rather than expediently assassinating Katniss, allows his audience to see her act of rebellion in full, forgetting the logic of deterrence he is employed to serve. Snow's response is to counter with the Quarter Quell, to show that even the strongest cannot win. While the image of one winner (like the girl Shuya sees in *Battle Royale*) broadcasts a message that anyone can kill so trust no one, the image of two survivors suggests that if they can defy the Capitol and walk away, so can anyone. Snow's execution of Crane is both an act of punishment and a threat, something Katniss uses to remind the new Gamemakers that no one is out of Snow's reach when she hangs a dummy of Crane in front of them.

The war for Panem is, in many ways, fought on and through the TV. While in the first Hunger Games Katniss uses the TV screen to manipulate her sponsors, she prepares for the second by watching recordings of previous victors to devise a strategy for survival. Meanwhile, the victors remind the Capitol audience of their supposedly special relationship in an attempt to manipulate them into acknowledging their part in the Games. Both sides use images for propaganda and to send direct messages to each other, as when Peeta warns District 13 of imminent attack. The Capitol broadcasts an interview with Peeta begging for a cease-fire; the rebels counter with a montage of the bombing of unarmed patients in District 8 and the message that they must fight on. The same images, it seems, can be used by the media for good or evil: "[I]mages can just as readily be employed to deceive as tell the truth" (Baudrillard, *Gulf War* 47). Images of bombing can be used as a deterrent or a call to arms. Television becomes the ultimate war-making machine. Image is war: the medium *is* the message (McLuhan 7). The Capitol audience is so seduced by the image that the viewers fail to acknowledge the tributes as real; Katniss too becomes so caught up in this game of images and war of words that it comes as a surprise to her, as it did to Ben, to actually meet her audience in the hospital in District 8. This face-to-face encounter is so strong that she no longer feels alone in her struggle and finally realizes her power to fire Panem's hunger for hope.

President Snow may be a powerful adversary, but he makes some fundamental mistakes. Firstly, like Sakamochi, he believes no friendship could exist that overcomes the desire to kill and win the Games. He sees Katniss's relationship with Peeta as scripted simulation and cannot conceive of the value of love and sacrifice. He is right, in part. Even though the victors hold hands before the Quarter Quell, the killing begins immediately once they are in the arena. But Finnick, Mags, Johanna, and others are willing to sacrifice themselves for the rebellion. While some of the victors are playing Snow's Game, others are playing the Game hijacked by Haymitch and Plutarch. Snow also cannot see that his circus has had real effects on the Capitol. Seeing their celebrities entered into the Quarter Quell reveals that the people have forged bonds with their victors, seeing them as friends and empathizing with their experiences. "Oh, not Cecelia," whispers a distressed Effie (*CF* 230). Like today's viewers of reality TV, they become invested in the victors' lives, choosing Katniss's wedding dress as they would that of a family member. When Peeta announces Katniss is pregnant, there are even calls for change.

Like Sakamochi, Snow's other mistake is to continue the Games even when they begin to fall apart, believing the odds are always in his favor. Even in the Seventy-fourth Hunger Games, it is Katniss's knowledge of the rules — that there must be a winner to satisfy the Capitol — that allows her to manipulate the Gamemakers. Understanding the rules of the game — that the collars in the Program are recording devices, and that Ben is being kept alive to replace the Hunter who failed to capture him — means you can hijack the game for your own purpose. Even when Katniss reminds Snow of the fragility of his system, which can be brought down by "a handful of berries" (*CF* 26), he does not seem able to play in any other way. Take away their bread (as supplies dwindle) and circuses (by killing off their celebrities), and the Capitol begins to turn against him. Hijack his hovercraft to bomb children, and support is lost forever. Snow uses up his limited number of moves and, without new Gamemakers, is stuck in a loop. He fails to realize in time that whatever move he makes can be hijacked by the rebels.

President Coin's misjudgment, also like Sakamochi and Network head Dan Killian, is to believe that, as leader, she is outside the Hunger Games, able to use Katniss as a piece in her political games while remaining herself immune to their effects. Coin's supreme arrogance is her undoing as she fails to realize not only that Katniss has seen the logic flaw in the bombing of the Capitol's children but also that the Mockingjay inspires loyalty and sacrifice in the leader's own people.

Katniss's strength comes from recognizing that she is always a part of the Hunger Games. She knows the rebels are manipulating her and using her image, and understands the implications of the fact that the streets of the Capitol are rigged like a Games arena: "Let the Seventy-sixth Hunger Games begin!" she mocks (*M* 293). The Hunger Games arenas have a vital function in Panem. After the Games, they are turned into historical theme parks where vacationing Capitol residents can rewatch, tour, and even take part in reenactments. Like Disneyland, the arenas, as they were in the Games, serve now as ideological blankets covering a third-order simulation. To paraphrase Baudrillard, each new arena is there to conceal from the people of the Capitol the fact that it is the "real" Capitol, and all of "real" Panem, which *is* an arena (Baudrillard, *Simulations* 25). The arenas are originally presented as places of violence in order to make the Capitol citizens believe that they are safe, to conceal the fact that violence and repression are everywhere. Of course, they cannot fool those in the districts, who are faced every day with the signifiers of violent repression (the Peacekeepers, electric fences, and public whipping posts), but they do partly explain why those in the Capitol seem so easily taken in. And while Coin believes that the Hunger Games are somewhere else and that a Gamemaker is not a player, she is vulnerable to Katniss's arrow of reality.

In *The Running Man,* Ben cannot hijack the image-making machine, so he destroys it: there is no indication of what comes next. The reader is almost entirely passive, required to do little but follow Ben on his journey of suicidal discovery. In *Battle Royale,* image is used sparingly and effectively as a deterrent, but the report of Sakamochi's death and close-up images of Shuya and Noriko as dangerous adversaries on the giant screen at the railway station are an acknowledgment, of sorts, that the Program can be beaten. In Takami's text the careful reader has little choice but to become actively involved in the Program, vacillating between the role of instructor and the only friend some of these children have, alone with their memories, fears, and violent deaths. This is acknowledged in the epilogue, where we are reminded of our interpellation: "'2 students remaining.' But of course they're part of you now" (*BR* 616). In *The Hunger Games* trilogy, image is manipulated by everyone, used to disguise the real, hijack the real, reveal the real, and finally become the real. The last image the reader has is of Katniss and Peeta's children playing in the Meadow over the graves of District 12. Katniss knows that eventually she will have to acknowledge the real of her past to her children, to prevent it ever returning or being hijacked by the next power-hungry leader. Between the seduction of the Games and the excessively reliable Katniss, however, the reader really does have to work hard to turn her head away and consider whether *she* could be part of the Hunger Games, and what ideological comfort blanket she is using to get through the day.

WORKS CITED

Althusser, Louis. "Ideology and Ideological State Apparatus." *The Norton Anthology of Theory and Criticism.* Ed. Vincent B. Leitch et al. New York: Norton, 2001. 1483–1509. Print.

Baudrillard, Jean. *The Gulf War Did Not Take Place.* Trans. and introd. Paul Patton. Sydney: Power, 2009. Print.

_____. *Simulations.* Trans. Paul Foss et al. New York: Semiotext(e), 1983. Print.

Collins, Suzanne. *Catching Fire.* London: Scholastic, 2009. Print.

_____. *The Hunger Games.* 2008. London: Scholastic, 2009. Print.

_____. *Mockingjay.* London: Scholastic, 2010. Print.

Conlin, Michelle. "America's Reality-TV Addiction." *Businessweek.com.* Bloomberg, 30 Jan. 2003. Web. 4 Aug. 2011.

Hill, Annette. "Reality TV: Performance, Authenticity, and Television Audiences." *A Companion to Television.* Ed. Janet Wasko. Oxford: Blackwell, 2005: 449–67. Print.

King, Stephen [writing as Richard Bachman]. 1982. *The Running Man.* London: Hodder, 2007. Print.

McLuhan, Marshall. *Understanding Media.* 1964. London: Routledge, 2002. Print.

Takami, Koushun. *Battle Royale.* 1999. Trans. Yuji Oniki. San Francisco: VIZ, 2004. Print.

PART IV.

Thematic Parallels and Literary Traditions

17

The PR Wars

The Hunger Games *Trilogy and*
Shakespeare's Second Henriad

CATHERINE R. ESKIN

O, for a muse of fire that would ascend
The brightest heaven of invention!—*Henry V,* Prologue

Avid readers of *The Hunger Games* trilogy cannot help but imagine Katniss Everdeen as they read the opening lines of William Shakespeare's history play. Like Shakespeare, Suzanne Collins provides her readers with images to "ascend / The brightest heaven of invention." Media-frenzied Panem and war-torn fifteenth-century England and France may seem an unlikely pair, yet they offer powerful examples of "PR Wars." PR, public relations, is a modern and postmodern discipline; during the early modern period in England it would have been called rhetoric or policy. Viewed with suspicion laced with curiosity, rhetoric and PR are equally ambivalent as methods of political manipulation. They generally require a spokesperson or image to present the message being proffered. Collins and Shakespeare both demonstrate the necessity of such a figure by creating characters who effectively win the hearts of the audience. While those characters are the focal point of my study, I will not argue for the parallel roles of Katniss Everdeen and Prince Hal (later King Henry V); instead, this essay will consider the ways an early modern and a postmodern population can be manipulated by the effective utilization of personality.

The motivation for seeking out persuasion is undeniably power. In both the later Henriad (*1 Henry IV, 2 Henry IV,* and *Henry V*) and *The Hunger Games* series, that power is essentially political. The arc of power in the Henriad is straightforward: we watch Hal plan and then take his place as prince in *1 Henry IV;* recognize the threat to his family's monarchical legitimacy in *2 Henry IV,* then meet that threat with a successful play for internal union under his rule; and, finally, unite the diverse strands of Britain through shared hardship and masculine action. *The Hunger Games* trilogy is less easily deciphered: Katniss is, throughout, a pawn of the brokers who vie for power in Panem. The Capitol, under President Snow, maintains its stranglehold on the districts by using the draconian Hunger Games; Katniss's emergence as a victor undermines the very basis of Panem's political structure, revealing the space for popular rebellion. In the second book, Snow acknowledges the fragility of his system and voices his desire to use Katniss's rhetorical power to his own advantage; but the failure of both the Victory Tour and the Quarter Quell to reify Capitol power spells the end of Katniss's collusion with his corrupt government. The rebels, who have surfaced first through rumor, claim their figurehead: Katniss as the Mockingjay. The last installment of the series offers the most complex struggle, using public manipulation as Snow and rebel President Alma Coin battle for political control of Panem. Ultimately, both lose.

Within the arcs we see the dominance of image: Hal's powerful beacon of hope in the darkness of civil unrest and the cultivation of Katniss's personality as an "every-girl" with a difference; she is both calculating and pure of motive. Hal, according to Donald Hedrick, is an "advantage-mongering" hero (481). He is the creator of his own *sprezzatura*: "a certain nonchalance, so as to conceal all art and make whatever one does or says appear to be without effort and almost without any thought" (Castiglione 32). Katniss's inborn rhetorical skills, on the other hand, make her a political pawn (though they also keep her alive). While Hal runs his own PR machine, Katniss is co-opted by the PR machines of Panem, which recognize and exploit her uncanny ability to epitomize the mockingjay. One of the *"muttations"* (*HG* 42, emphasis in original), the mockingjay began as a jabberjay, created by the Capitol as a weapon and then abandoned when it had no further tactical use. The bird stubbornly survives by mating with mockingbirds to become a symbol of resistance and adaptability. Shakespeare's Henry recognizes his need to symbolize legitimate (native) and popular power: his father was a usurper, leaving Hal's legitimacy as a prince in question. For Katniss, a naive and clever teenager living in poverty, her sister's ill luck thrusts upon her an opportunity for symbolic power she is unprepared to control — though more experienced managers are keen to capitalize upon her natural genius.

The Hunger Games *and* 1 Henry IV: *"Wisdom Cries Out in the Streets and No Man Regards It"* (I Henry IV)

Prince Hal speaks this line to Falstaff early in Act I (I.ii. 194–95) when he observes the ways common sense is disregarded in Henry IV's London.

Katniss, who lives the senselessness of District 12's daily existence, remains unaware of how her own survival skills might offer an alternative. Hal is Machiavellian in both his analysis of his father's creation of royal identity and the stylized image he wants to create for himself. When Collins's Gale Hawthorne, attracted to and awed by Katniss, suggests that the two might survive happily in the woods, she refuses to seriously consider the implications of his idea: that she might be desirable or that her personality might inspire hope. In the first installments of the trilogies we see not the parallel characters of Hal and Katniss, but the parallel creation of a public aesthetic. Hal consciously recognizes the importance of image making — his own. Katniss creates a persona, too, one that will captivate a nation, yet her participation in that fashioning is intuitive and lacks Hal's willfully political self-interest. Hal will "imitate the sun" so "he may be more wondered at" (*1 Henry IV,* I.ii. 300, 304); in contrast, after her fiery debut through the streets of the Capitol, Katniss recognizes only that she has been given a tactical advantage by her stylist, Cinna, seeing it as "hope" for her chances in the Games rather than an unforgettable entry into the political arena (*HG* 70).

Katniss's image — and its construction on screen throughout her first Hunger Games — is manipulated by others: Cinna and Haymitch Abernathy, her mentor. Working for her survival, her public relations team fires up the country. As willing participants in the District 12 tributes' rise to prominence, neither Snow nor his Gamemakers realize the political implications of her growing popularity. Nor, frankly, does Katniss, whose involvement in the marketing of her image is such an astonishing demonstration of the theories of *sprezzatura* and self-fashioning that her intelligence in most things makes her ignorance in this realm frustrating to readers. During private sessions with the Gamemakers that will result in her ranking as a tribute, Katniss becomes so angry at "being upstaged by a dead pig" that she lets loose an arrow at the offending dish (*HG* 101). Her temper earns her a nearly perfect score. In the arena, Katniss's wild-card behavior makes her a star with viewers. Choosing the diminutive and seemingly weak Rue as an ally, Katniss makes what will become a thematic choice: a combination of calculated and gut-driven decisions that earn her the sympathy and approval of a nation. Though she may not recognize the long-term impact of her choices, Katniss does realize that, as she sings and then covers the fallen Rue's body in flowers, she is creating a picture the Capitol cannot erase. As always, she is driven by her emotions rather than a desire for political power. Her verbal message — "*Here is the place where I love you*" — is in concert with her floral and gestural message (a farewell movement of her left hand) before she allows the hovercraft to collect Rue's body (*HG* 235). Katniss uses the unwritten rules of indebtedness among the lower echelons of Panem society, invoking and transcending the regionalism that the Capitol uses to divide the districts.

Hal is more deliberate in his desire to win a broad base of support. Unlike his father, Henry IV, who reminds his eldest son that he stays seldom seen so that "like a comet" he can be "wondered at" (III.ii.1870), Hal has found love and acceptance among the inhabitants of Eastcheap by being often among them. Yet Shakespeare's goals are very different from those of Collins. Hal must publicly regret his lack of class consciousness in order to counter the power of his father's favorite, the "gallant Hotspur" (III.ii.1964). A modern audience may see Hal's method of contrast as forced, but an early modern one would recognize the political necessity of social singularity. Hal's conscious efforts at control contrast sharply with his rival, Hotspur, the man (like Katniss) "on fire" (IV.i.2343). The ideal early modern ruler is able to control his emotions and use people as assets: Hal secures the loyalty of his tavern friends by delegating responsibility for the mustering and leadership of foot soldiers to Falstaff. Ultimately, however, Hal's goal in this first play is to gain the loyalty of the aristocracy and emerge as a worthy prince: "I may speak it to my shame, / I have a truant been to chivalry" and now would "Try fortune with [Hotspur] in a single fight" (V.i.2716–17, 2723). As the chivalrous knight who would save the lives of his patrician liegemen by sacrificing his own, Hal wins the approval of the ruling class: Vernon relates Hal's offer in such loving terms that Shakespeare's audience cannot miss the preview of the future Harry V: "England did never owe so sweet a hope, / So much misconstrued in his wantonness" (V.ii.2841–42).

Hal's insistence to the mocking Hotspur that "Two stars keep not their motion in one sphere, / Nor can one England brook a double reign / Of Harry Percy and the Prince of Wales" (V.iv.3023–25) is echoed by the voice of Claudius Templesmith, whose last-minute announcement revokes the rule change that would have allowed both Katniss and Peeta to survive the Games as champions. Harry's world expects a single victor, while Panem's rank and file dreams only of collective triumph. Hal's promise to steal all of Hotspur's glory sounds sweet to Shakespeare's audience: a single hero, unabashedly male, honorable in praise of the fallen Hotspur. Katniss's moment is far different.

The shaken adolescent recognizes first that in order for the Hunger Games to work, the Capitol needs a single victor, or the system might "blow up in the Gamemakers' faces" (*HG* 344). She also recognizes the impossibility of surviving (emotionally or socially) outside the arena without Peeta; the people of Panem would never forgive her. Her solution, the berries, is an impressive display of political acumen. Katniss's focus on simple survival effectively uses affective narrative appeal through the "subject's radical disadvantage before some oppressive force" (Hedrick 472). The political implications of the victory — the Games can be beaten, and by extension the Capitol — are missing from her personal radar.

Two distinct public figures emerge from the opening installments of the trilogies. In the process, we recognize the fault lines in existing political power and the disruptive/emergent power of Katniss and Hal. Henry IV and Snow underestimate the potential of the rabble, the ways popular opinion will support or reject political figures based on their appeal. Shakespeare's world is bound by the auspices of monarchical and patriarchal power; it requires a royal ruler. In Panem's dystopia, a world so contrary to the postmodern audience's sense of personal and patriotic responsibility, rulers must at least *appear* responsive to the popular will. Katniss is not only responsive; she is proactive in her protection of the weak and in her willingness to sacrifice herself. Hal, by contrast, deftly ensures his own political survival, having "redeemed [his father's] lost opinion" (V.iv.3003) by using *sprezzatura* as a PR strategy. Hal has clearly not reached his full potential: he is still a prince, still on probation. And war is still looming. Collins's heroine, revealed as both unlikely and unwilling to be a political contender, struggles emotionally with her public coup. Instead of a sense of victory, Katniss, in the last sentence of book one, dreads actually having to "let go" of Peeta's hand (*HG* 374). Unlike the Prince, who has created his persona, Katniss is a shell-shocked teenager whose naïveté about the implications of her political role makes her a perfect symbol of a nation on the brink of civil war.

Catching Fire *and* 2 Henry IV: *Rumor as Induction*

Shakespeare opens the second part of *Henry IV* with "Rumour," the play's "induction" trumpeting the "pipe / Blown by surmises" (*2 Henry IV,* Induction.16–17). A kind of initiation into the action, an induction's function is persuasive. As the media wars continue — for both Hal and the competing forces in Panem — the authors make clear that reaching the people is only part of the battle. The public relations teams must control the message. Hal is no longer aiming just to play the prince; he needs to be a king. Katniss has undergone a sea change: she now holds a position in Panem's social structure, a position complicated by her on-air relationship with Peeta. Not until her pivotal conversation with Haymitch does she realize the implications and scope of the role she must play. "[J]ust help me to get through this trip," she pleads to Haymitch (*CF* 43). The exchange concludes with her devastating realization that her romance with the baker's son is not just a seasonal obligation; the "act" must be her reality. Rumor is a threat to the dissemination and maintenance of an image. Underground communication — integral to civil unrest — cannot be fully controlled, especially when the "still-discordant wav'ring multitude" is undecided and dangerous (*2 Henry IV,* Induction.20). So Hal will — sometimes sullenly but with an increasing sense of duty — take up the charge of self-fashioning, while Katniss will become both victim and designer of herself as media phenomenon. Though reaching some cognizance of her effect, Katniss is still painfully naive regarding the ways her every action is read and interpreted by her audience and then culled and used by competing PR teams. As Stephen Greenblatt reminds us, "Theatricality ... is not set over against power but is one of power's essential modes" (447).

As the history play opens, Shakespeare's "Rumour" promises to confuse the populace by bringing "smooth comforts false, worse than true wrongs" (*2 Henry IV* Induction.41). The lower classes, represented as more prone to the dissemination and influence of gossip, are revealed as media savvy; Falstaff teaches Hal that "our English nation, if they have a good thing ... make it too common" (*2 Henry IV* I.ii.549–50). Hal's resulting education makes him "exceeding weary" with the political world he will inherit (*2 Henry IV* II.ii.945). We don't see the depressed and bitter Hal until Act II, when he emerges from his political lethargy to declare, "I feel me much to blame / So idly to profane the precious time" (*2 Henry IV* II.iv.1671–72). In *1 Henry IV,* Hal was making the rumors; now, he indulges in a self-pity that threatens to undermine the successful self-fashioning of Part One.

Reputation and public image are also vital for Katniss, who returns to her new house in the Victor's Village to face the chilling President Snow in the opening chapter of *Catching Fire.* Now seventeen, Katniss feels guilt and confusion about her first kiss with Gale. By thwarting rumors on the upcoming Victory Tour and convincing Snow and the nation of her devotion to Peeta, she hopes to save Gale and those she loves. Katniss erroneously believes that an innocuous love story will be enough to satisfy the viewers and maintain the status quo. Readers realize — when they meet the runaway citizens of District 8 in the woods of District 12 — that rumor has already rippled the waters. Those waters rise alarmingly at the very first tour stop, District 11. Wanting to express her deep sense of indebtedness to the families of Thresh and Rue, Katniss offers her thanks in a poetic and symbolic speech. She refers to mockingjays, invoking the symbol with no consideration of its implications. The explosive scene that follows illustrates a growing unification against the Capitol: the crowd salutes the District 12 victors with their left hands. Katniss admits that she has "elicited something dangerous" (*CF* 62). The Capitol, quickly shifting PR gears, recasts Katniss and Peeta as the tragic victims of the third Quarter Quell. But Collins — through the brilliant and caring Cinna — continues to focus on the image of the mockingjay, the "creature the Capitol never intended to exist" (*CF* 92).

Both Katniss and Hal are phoenix-like creatures: born of the ashes and devastation of nations muddled in civil unrest. Through his brilliant design, Cinna turns Katniss's pathetic wedding dress into a flaming mockingjay costume; the hopeless love affair marketed by the Capitol becomes a strategic image victory for the rebels. But *sprezzatura* is a delicate business. Before the on-air triumph, Katniss's fellow victors eye her dress with mixed anger and admiration. That doubt is present, too, as the playgoer watches Hal's impatient choice to grab the crown of his father — a dramatic trick that is an ambivalently received public relations move. Henry IV seems determined to see the worst in his son: "Harry Fifth is crowned. Up, vanity!" (*2 Henry IV* IV.v.3015). The other PR option is John of Lancaster, Hal's cold and emotionally detached younger brother. Yet the audience clearly prefers Harry, merciful and thoughtful in his consideration of the task which lies before him: kingship. And in spite of misgivings, Henry IV is resolved to see his elder son a king, advising Harry to "busy giddy minds / With foreign quarrels" (*2 Henry IV* IV.v.3009–10). Hal is assured of success partly because of his self-fashioned legitimacy; he will "rightfully maintain" the crown he will inherit (*2 Henry IV* IV.v.3120).

The endings illustrate how both the limits and variety of public relations strategies are inherent to the challenge of waging a PR war. Although after his coronation, Henry V is the "sad" son of Henry IV, "Harry lives that shall convert those tears / ... into hours of happiness" (*2 Henry IV* V.ii.3297, 3308–09). The hours in the clock-inspired arena of the Quarter Quell remind Katniss of both her self-appointed task — to keep Peeta alive — and her unconscious sense of political/personal justice. Hal is very conscious of the implications of his inheritance: "I survive / To mock the expectation of the world, / ... to raze out / Rotten opinion" (*2 Henry IV* V.ii.3373–76). "Rumour" has not been overcome; she has been effectively converted. Katniss, an equally inspiring figure for Panem, is guilty of self-delusion as she willfully ignores the growing evidence of her power. The contrast with the new King Henry is striking. Hal's cold answer of "I know thee not, old man" to Falstaff's "my sweet boy" is a frustrating assurance to John of Lancaster that the younger son will never be king (*2 Henry IV* V.v.3640, 3635). A postmodern audience might cringe at the new king's calculated treatment of the fat knight but, like an early modern one, recognizes the political necessity of disposing of a liability. Katniss struggles, amid gore and tension, to look beyond expediency and self-interest to a larger moral imperative: "*remember who the enemy is*" (*CF* 378, emphasis in original). Once the Games end and Katniss wakes, she finds that she is still a pawn in the play for political power. Now she has been duped not by a repressive Capitol but by those she trusted. So Hal, now Henry V, is ready to use his image unabashedly to serve his patriotic turn. Katniss, mired in guilt and pain, is determined to give up, but the author won't let her go.

Mockingjay *and* Henry V: *"Not a Boy Left Alive"*

While my reference to the killing of children is literal for both works — the camp boys are killed by the French army in *Henry V,* and the children of the Capitol are killed by a hovercraft's silver parachutes in *Mockingjay*— the final installments of the trilogies also end any innocence that might be left in the wars' survivors. Can there be *sprezzatura* among combat veterans? Collins opens the final book in the charred remains of District 12, where Katniss revisits her failure to protect either Peeta or her district. Shakespeare, in his spectacular prologue, reinforces the already awesome image of "the warlike Harry" (*Henry V,* Prologue.6), but immediately reminds the audience that Henry V is still young: in I.i, bishops debate ways to distract the new King from taxing or confiscating Church holdings. Harry is confident in his position, if inexperienced; Katniss has deep doubts about her worthiness and about the sincerity of the rebel leaders who want her to become a more conscious participant in their PR war. The problems of image are addressed first by her sister, Prim, then in a posthumous appearance by Cinna, and finally by Haymitch, who proves to the combat-ravaged young girl and the rebel PR team that her rhetorical skill is *extempore* (a *sprezzatura* for which courtiers would have killed). While the issue of her handlers' motives remains in doubt, Katniss comes to terms with her power and chooses to use it. Now both heroes work to unify the still dissentious people.

The opening scenes explore the dimensions of constructed image to bring populaces together for a cause — the limits, essentially, of a PR machine. The slight offered King Henry by the Dauphin of France, a coronation gift of tennis balls, allows the King to issue a warning that will echo within his country as well as in France:

> I have laid by my majesty
> And plodded like a man for working days;
> But I will rise there with so full a glory
> That I will dazzle all the eyes of France [I.ii.426–29].

Notice the use of contrast, the same rhetorical method the young Hal employed for his rise to power. Words such as "dazzle" and "rise" broadcast how Henry's maturity is increasingly based in his overt masculinity. Once in France, Harry's now-famous "Once more unto the breach, dear friends, once more" (III.i.1092) challenges his soldiers to prove their manhood with him as "friends." He reinforces the new image as he charges the enemy to open their gates or hear their "shrill-shrieking daughters" and see their "naked infants spitted upon pikes" (III.iii.1307, 1310). Henry V's cold violence illustrates his development from a prince of the people to a sovereign apart. His growth begins before he sails for the fields of France: losing "his bedfellow" and experiencing personal/political betrayal leave "a kind of blot" on his soul that is like "Another fall of man" (II.ii.641, 774, 778). With his commitment to power, Harry loses any remnant of uncomplicated innocence to the creation and maintenance of his image as a masculine warrior king.

As for Katniss, only in the putrid air of a makeshift hospital does she finally realize a feminine power she has never before accepted. As a tool for the rebels' PR machine, she is an unpredictable wild card. Carefully made up for the cameras, she fails to convince; with her clear face close to the dying victims of Capitol violence, she shines. Her avenging power in combat separates her from the healing power of her mother or sister. Directly disobeying the orders of her handler, she takes down Capitol fighters. Yet Katniss must watch, helplessly, as the hospital she visited burns. Instead of the stale line agonized over by the rebels' team, she becomes the bitch goddess and shouts a rallying cry born of her outrage: "[I]f we burn, you burn with us!" (*M* 100). Her maturation finally allows her to appreciate the contributions of the PR professionals who transform her front-line appearance into propaganda for national television.

Finding moments for unity is essential in the PR wars of both Panem and fifteenth-century England, though success in that campaign does not mean unilateral victory. Shakespeare creates a national regiment — Jamy (Ireland), Fluellen (Wales), MacMorris (Scotland), and Gower (England)—who talk about being of a "nation" (III.ii.1250). They act as a cheering section for the work of the King. The idea of nation is more difficult in the postmodern District 2, where the rebels try to crack the impenetrable stronghold of the Capitol's war machine. The siege warfare that seems unproblematized in *Henry V* is painfully scrutinized by Collins. Katniss watches burn victims pour out after the mountain explosion, convinced that both she and they are dupes of the Capitol. Her poetic and well-performed speech arguing for solidarity ends abruptly when she is shot. The audience now has an inkling that her inability to stomach the cruelties of war makes the role she is playing tragic. Harry is not so squeamish, though he is not without personal concerns. As the author of his own image, Henry V does not have to face the criticism and personnel choices of a PR team. Katniss, after the unification of the districts, realizes that a martyred Mockingjay might do just as well as a live one.

So enter the most striking parallel images between *Henry V* and *Mockingjay:* the dead children who litter the final battlefields. Shakespeare uses the death of the boys to demonstrate the moral superiority of the English over the French. Collins, who has illustrated the ethical ambiguity of war, does not provide an uncomplicated message. Katniss is broken after watching her younger sister die; unlike Henry, who shows infinite resiliency, Collins's heroine is unable to escape reality as seen through her personal, heartbreaking lens. Her last-minute decision to shoot Coin rather than Snow cannot be compared to Henry's desire for revenge after finding the bodies of the boys. Henry's moment becomes awash in triumph as the French herald announces "The day is yours" (IV.vii.2068). In contrast, Katniss hears a "gurgling cackle" as Snow chokes on his own blood (*M* 373). Yet Harry's loss is no less keen:

in securing the nation, he has lost his *joie de vivre* and, we know, will not be able to prevent the suffering of the War of the Roses. Stephen Greenblatt makes clear that Hal's position is always already "grotesque and cruelly unequal" (452). Greenblatt believes, "The rulers earn, or at least pay for, their exalted position through suffering, and this suffering ennobles, if it does not exactly cleanse, the lies and betrayals upon which this position depends" (452). After her *in absentia* trial, Katniss is presented to the public as a shattered, insane victim of the Capitol. And, in a move commensurate with the wooing scene that ends *Henry V*, Katniss is invited to perform on a new singing program Plutarch Heavensbee has created for television, "something upbeat" (*M* 379).

But "upbeat" is inappropriate to these trilogies about war. In spite of their chronological occurrence in the middle of the works, I have saved the hanging scenes for my conclusion because I believe they illustrate beautifully the conflicting effects of PR. Katniss and Henry provide us with examples of *sprezzatura,* yet only Henry consciously employs it. The angelic voice of Katniss rings out in the forlorn woods outside District 12 as she sings to the mute Pollux about a hanging tree. The scene is emblematic: the rebel propaganda team sits eating lunch, on break from a tense filming session. Katniss notices a mockingjay in a nearby tree and points it out to her companion. After a request to sing, she launches into the haunting song. For Katniss, a close reader if there ever was one, the song represents personal and political conundrums. Ultimately, she concludes that political power is not worth its human cost. The blockbuster audience agrees. The early modern audience of *Henry V* sees hanging as a necessary evil; Fluellen describes the execution of Bardolph, an old mate of Hal's, with approval: "his nose is executed" for "robbing a church" (III.vi.1571, 1566). Without missing a beat, the king agrees: "We would have all such offenders so cut off" (III.vi.1572). Henry V is charged with holding back the chaos of civil war, and his people love him for it. Pistol, despite his anger at the death of Bardolph, admits of his king, "I love the lovely bully" (IV.i.1894).

Henry V is an eternal symbol of hope to the English people. He is marched out at times of national crisis (e.g., Laurence Olivier's film version in 1944). The enduring image of Katniss is equally complicated. In the epilogue, Katniss and Peeta's children play in the field where people died; there is hope among the ashes. Yet what will be the cultural consequence when the war has been of personality rather than for humanity? After all, years before, when Katniss sang "The Hanging Tree" with heartrending sweetness, Plutarch Heavensbee listened with shrewd mastery. "Are you ... / Coming to the tree[?]" asked Katniss, retreating into her memories and critical consideration of the lyrics while Pollux cried softly (*M* 123). When the song ended and the cameras stopped rolling, Plutarch laughed merrily and asked, "Where do you come up with this stuff?" (*M* 126).

WORKS CITED

Castiglione, Baldassare. *The Book of the Courtier: The Singleton Translation.* Ed. Daniel Javitch. New York: Norton, 2002. Print.

Collins, Suzanne. *Catching Fire.* New York: Scholastic, 2009. Print.

_____. *The Hunger Games.* New York: Scholastic, 2008. Print.

_____. *Mockingjay.* New York: Scholastic, 2010. Print.

Greenblatt, Stephen. "Invisible Bullets: Renaissance Authority and Its Subversion, *Henry IV* and *Henry V.*" Rpt. in *Shakespeare: An Anthology of Criticism and Theory, 1945–2000.* Ed. Russ McDonald. Malden: Blackwell, 2004. 435–57. Print.

Hedrick, Donald. "Advantage, Affect, History, *Henry V.*" *PMLA* 118.3 (May 2003): 170–87. Print.

Shakespeare, William. *King Henry IV, Part 1. OpenSource Shakespeare.* George Mason University, 2003. Web. 14 Nov. 2011.

_____. *King Henry IV, Part 2. OpenSource Shakespeare.* George Mason University, 2003. Web. 14 Nov. 2011.

_____. *King Henry V. OpenSource Shakespeare.* George Mason University, 2003. Web. 14 Nov. 2011.

The Masks of Femininity

Perceptions of the Feminine in The Hunger Games and Podkayne of Mars*

RODNEY M. DEAVAULT

Writer David Brin asserts that much science fiction and fantasy writing (SFF) is obsessed with the Romantic past, "some lost golden age when people knew more, mused loftier thoughts and were closer to the gods — but then fell from grace" (9). While such a rearview mirror look at yesteryear can seem both naive and optimistic, Brin also points out that "Romanticism never made any pretense at equality. It is hyper-discriminatory, by nature" (7). Brin's assertions are made evident in the portrayal of heroines within the SFF genre. Casting a critical eye at J. R. R. Tolkien's *Lord of the Rings,* widely considered the model trilogy of the SFF genre, Lev Grossman notes that "the Fellowship is still as much a boys' club as the Augusta National" (4). In fact, director Peter Jackson had to reallocate lines from male characters just to give Liv Tyler's Arwen something to do in the film versions.

The predicament in which Jackson's version of Arwen found herself is quite similar to that of many other SSF heroines. Despite the additional lines and screen time, Arwen remains (as in the *LOTR* novels) an enchanting maiden whose entire identity is defined by her beauty and position as her kingly father's daughter or as Aragorn's wife and queen. She is conspicuously absent from the battles for Middle Earth and, in the end, relinquishes her family, her powers, and her immortality for romantic love and marriage. Given her scant presence in the novels, Arwen's position as beautiful object of desire is her chief importance to the trilogy. Since Elrond refuses to give her in mar-

---

*An earlier version of this essay was presented at the 32rd International Conference on the Fantastic in the Arts (March 2011) in Orlando, Florida.

riage to Aragorn until he is high king, Arwen becomes a prize to be won and thus the catalyst for Aragorn fulfilling his destiny. Arwen's beauty is a powerful force, but not one that she is allowed to control. Instead, it is part of a transaction between father and husband, leaving her voiceless.

Regarding the employment of beauty as an indirect route to power, Naomi Johnson notes that "Western culture has extended these same norms to increasingly younger girls, often under the guise of 'empowerment'..." (58). Through representations of female beauty, the SFF novel often gives authoritative voice to the heroine and then calls for her to sacrifice it, along with her ambition and identity, then return to the domestic space. Robert A. Heinlein's 1963 juvenile, *Podkayne of Mars*, stands as a prime example of this paradigm. Although Podkayne Fries, Heinlein's female protagonist, subverts the myth of commoditized beauty and uses it to gain knowledge, at the novel's conclusion she is unable to remain in the space she has carved for herself. In contrast to Podkayne, Katniss Everdeen, protagonist of Suzanne Collins's *The Hunger Games* trilogy, emerges as a heroine who also manipulates the beauty myth and manages to find autonomy through controlling her image. The parallels and distinctions between these two heroines and between their actions serve as a schema for determining precisely how the concept of feminine heroism is broadening in YA literature.

Comprehending that beauty constitutes social currency, both characters attempt to discover agency through manipulating the perception of their feminine identities. Podkayne's mastery of her perceived femininity illustrates the difficulties that female characters face balancing personal desires and societal expectations. Katniss's facility with manipulating this concept enables her to make the transition from a girl not included in the handling of her image to a young woman making informed decisions about how that image will be employed. In fact, Katniss's survival over the course of the trilogy is often predicated on her ability to perform femininity, the practice of which she initially scorns.

Although *The Hunger Games* and *Podkayne of Mars* take place in the distant future and were written well over forty years apart, traditional gender roles and expectations nonetheless remain intact in both novels. The female characters in Katniss's home district are largely dependent, nurturing, and emotional. Katniss is the only female character who remains unconfined within the domestic space. Even characters who are compelled to earn a living, such as Mrs. Everdeen, mostly do so from within the home, where they can tend to their children and mind their work. Similarly, in *Podkayne of Mars*, the reader may infer that a woman's proper place is in the home with children. Podkayne's Uncle Tom upbraids her mother for her absentee parenting, saying that "building bridges and space stations and such gadgets is all very well ... but that a woman has more important work to do" (*PM* 213).

Given the examples presented to them, both protagonists are vociferous in their initial rejection of the conventionally feminine role of motherhood, which they view as a form of societal enslavement. Podkayne's sole female role model is her career-obsessed mother, who regards children as chores to get out of the way. Described as having no sentimental feeling, Mrs. Fries, a brilliant and consummately logic-minded engineer, is habitually away from home and constantly leaves the teenaged Podkayne as custodian of her younger brother, Clark. Sorely neglected by both parents, Podkayne views marriage and motherhood as confining. Instead, she focuses on becoming a pilot. Katniss's negative view of traditional femininity leads her to become gender neutral, possessing aspects of masculinity and femininity while fully embodying neither. After her father dies, Katniss forsakes the domestic space for the forest, assuming Mr. Everdeen's responsibility of breadwinner by hunting wild game as he once did. By her own admission, she is uncomfortable sitting at the hearth with her dainty mother and sister, preferring instead to be in the woods, where she is unencumbered by gender norms or the expectation to conform to them. Forswearing both romantic love and motherhood, Katniss remains content with the knowledge that she could at any point flee into the woods and leave District 12 forever.

While both girls reject traditional womanly roles, Podkayne, unlike Katniss, revels in the power she knows her lush feminine appearance will afford her. Standard images of traditional female beauty imbue blonde hair with greater feminine approbation than red or brown hues. Deidre Johnson, referencing *The Last of the Mohicans,* draws upon James Fenimore Cooper's comparison of the blonde-haired Alice with her darker-complected sister Cora to exemplify this trope (13–14). Although Cora has more fortitude and passion, she envies the golden-haired and blue-eyed Alice, whose "soul is pure and spotless as her skin" (*LM* 333). In the opening pages of her story, Podkayne provides a detailed description of her own blonde hair and blue eyes, bust, waist, and leg size, enshrining herself as the ideal of feminine prettiness. In doing so, Podkayne acknowledges the entrenched societal commoditization of female beauty, evincing an early understanding of the gender performance concept that Katniss has yet to learn. As Podkayne's mother once says, "One works with available materials" (*PM* 4). Deliberately understating her own beauty, Podkayne finds her own materials "adequate" (*PM* 4). In contrast to Podkayne, whose blonde looks invoke the feminine angelic, descriptions of Katniss's physical appearance compared with that of her more overtly feminine mother and sister further separate her into a gender-neutral category. Katniss, with straight black hair, olive skin, and gray eyes, bears an uncanny resemblance to Gale, her male hunting partner; while her mother and sister, blonde-haired, blue-eyed beauties, always look out of place, both in contrast to Katniss's swarthier features and to the coal-mining denizens of District 12.

At this stage in the trilogy, Katniss is neither entirely "masculine" nor "feminine"; she is a new, "othered" category, a blank slate upon which a gendered identity can be crafted. While she is at ease in a masculine position as provider, Katniss cannot entirely divest herself of the nurturing feminine role into which society posits her. She deeply resents Mrs. Everdeen, who after her husband's death became catatonic with grief while her children slowly starved. This maternal defection has forced Katniss into the role of family protector, and she equates the classic feminine pursuit of romantic love with violence and danger. Her views of motherhood are similarly bleak. Since children from the districts are sent to the Capitol for televised slaughter, she views motherhood as the ultimate form of powerlessness.

Despite verbally eschewing motherhood, Katniss, nonetheless, becomes a surrogate mother to Mrs. Everdeen and Prim, who might as well be her children since they rely on her for sustenance. For love of Prim, Katniss leaves the gender-neutral haven of the forest and enters the televised Hunger Games, in which she is forced to proclaim some sort of definitive public gendered identity. While her circumstances are far less dire than Katniss's, Podkayne is also pulled into a situation that necessitates a gendered identity and performance. A space trip to Venus with Uncle Tom serves as her introduction to the realm of gender politics. Engaging intellectually and socially with male spaceship officers, Podkayne discovers that "when I wrinkle my nose and look baffled, a man is usually only too glad to help me..." (*PM* 4).

In the implementation of public feminine performance, Katniss emerges as the more audacious of the two heroines, succeeding in achieving true autonomy, where Podkayne falls short of her goal. Katniss, unlike Podkayne, is a character for whom gender performance is more or less devoid of sexuality, a concept that she and her entourage acknowledge as beyond her capacity for understanding. After two tributes make sexual jokes at Katniss's expense, Peeta, her constructed love interest, accuses her of being too "pure" (*CF* 216). For Katniss, commoditized femininity and its performance have nothing to do with sex; it is a type of coded language used to ensure her survival.

Podkayne, however, enacts only one specific type of feminine performance, that of the innocent yet knowing virgin, a performance that relies mostly on her sex appeal. Katniss manipulates men's emotions; Podkayne plays to their egos and libidos. By using her "best astonished-kitten look" (*PM* 71), Podkayne wins over Captain Darling "with the idea that I was awfully sweet, even younger than I am, terribly impressed by him and overawed ... and not too bright" (*PM* 70). She also charms her way into the ship's cockpit and observes pilots firsthand. From second officer Mr. Savvonavong, Podkayne learns to program a ballistic computer, while the junior officer, Mr. Clancy, has all of the study and reference books that she requires but would otherwise have no access to. In under a week, Podkayne becomes "the unofficial ship's mascot, with free run of the control room — and I am almost as privileged in the engineering department" (*PM* 71). By pandering to what Heinlein, a product of a male-dominated culture, sees as the officers' sense of masculinity, Podkayne gains access to the tools and knowledge she seeks while laughing at the gullibility of the male ego.

For Katniss, survival is predicated on her ability to appear traditionally feminine rather than fully embodying the concept. As a Hunger Games tribute, Katniss realizes that her physical appeal to viewers is as intrinsic to her survival as her hunting ability since viewers sponsor the tributes they find most engaging, sending gifts to aid them during the Games. The sponsors require more of a female tribute than mere endurance; they demand a hybrid of survivor and show-woman, who can slit a man's throat one moment and giggle and blush like a decorous female the next. Katniss, who has never had time for fussing over her appearance, is at a considerable loss. Knowing this, the men in her life — her mentor Haymitch, her fellow contestant Peeta, and her stylist Cinna — craft a feminine persona and place it on Katniss without her initial consent. In doing so, Cinna asserts that femininity and gender can be either a code of conduct or a performative construct, with costumes and masks to be donned and discarded as necessary. Katniss's status as gender-neutral "other" remains unchanged; instead, she is taught to act out the audience's idea of femininity.

In Cinna's hands, she becomes an indelible icon. When Peeta and she are presented in the Capitol, her image burns as brightly in the spectators' consciousness as her flaming cape and gown do. Cinna crafts different feminine images for Katniss to wear before the crowd, each designed to excite, tease, or charm. Her second look transforms her into a coquettish princess whose shimmering gown gives the appearance of being consumed by flames. This marks the first time Katniss respects the power of feminine appearance. As Katniss twirls prettily during her interview, the crowd erupts in applause at the image of girlish femininity being presented, and she finally acknowledges the hold her radiant appearance has over the throng.

As opposed to Katniss, whose mutable and artificial portrayal of femininity garners her increasing acclaim, Podkayne's innocent yet sexy approach ultimately limits her effectiveness and upward mobility. Her limitations are due in part to the pre-second-wave feminist period in which Heinlein wrote the novel, but also to her overreliance on her feminine appearance. She is seen as a pet by the starship officers and a silly girl by her genius younger brother. Although she gains knowledge, Podkayne has limited choices for implementing it. When comparing herself to Dexter, a male suitor also intent on pilot training, Podkayne realizes that "Dexter's chances are a hundred times as good as mine. He's as smart as I am, or almost; he'll have the best education for it that money can buy.... But the clincher is that Dexter is twice as big as

I am and male" (*PM* 153). Katniss, in contrast, combines a more masculine lethal physical aggression with a pleasingly feminine public countenance. Everyone, from her competitors in the Hunger Games to President Snow, takes her seriously.

Podkayne's choices are either to be desexualized as her mother is or to be like Theodora and Catherine the Great, who could "[l]et a man boss the job ... then boss that man" (*PM* 153). Despite her efforts to forge a space between these two extremes, in the end the point is moot. Near the close of her story, Podkayne nurtures a baby fairy and ends up comatose protecting it, becoming the very angel her looks suggest she is, "emotional, selfless, and submissive" (Boyle and Combe 167). Yet Podkayne's story, interestingly enough, has two possible endings. The first published version of *Podkayne of Mars* ends with her lying comatose while her injuries heal. Heinlein's original ending, however, kills Podkayne off, leaving her younger brother to narrate the novel's conclusion. The 1995 Baen edition of *Podkayne* contains both endings, along with a collection of essays debating whether Podkayne should have survived; again, it is a moot point since both endings rob Podkayne of her narrative voice and, therefore, her power of choice.

For Katniss, who is neither overtly masculine nor feminine, the path towards autonomy lies in learning to channel aspects of both traits. When Peeta weaves a romantic narrative for the audience, casting himself and Katniss as lovers forced to compete against each other, she upbraids him, angered that she was not consulted and insisting that the narrative makes her appear weak. Survival and the crowd's favor depend on how she is perceived, Haymitch warns Katniss, reminding her that she was "about as romantic as dirt" (*HG* 135) until Peeta proclaimed his love for her. Only after his declaration does she become desired by the masses.

As she looks at the screens in the stadium, Katniss sees they are all filled with images of her and Peeta, the perfect couple whose love is being ripped asunder by the Games, and the audience falls desperately in love with the carefully crafted portrait of romantic tragedy. Witnessing this spectacle, Katniss understands that her gender performance is part of a dialogue between herself and the crowd. She can get what she needs by giving them what they want. As a stealthy masculine-influenced hunter, Katniss has the ability to survive; as the girl in danger of losing the boy, she needs material tools for their survival. While the cameras are on her, she learns to merge the two spheres of influence without changing her core identity. During the Hunger Games, when Peeta is critically injured, Katniss plays the grief-stricken lover to manipulate sponsors into sending her the materials necessary to nurse him. She can almost hear Haymitch exhorting her to take clearer ownership of the charade, reminding her that Peeta is dying and she is supposedly desperately in love with him. In her mind, Haymitch is telling her that to get what she wants, she must "Give me something I can work with!" (*HG* 261). Katniss, a stranger to romantic love, draws on memories of her mother and father together to guide her conduct, and suddenly the love she previously denounced as weak is potent in her eyes.

At that moment, Katniss achieves a perfect blend of her actual personality with the performance contrived for the Games. She arms herself for battle with the weapons she wields most adeptly but takes the time to maintain the facade of a feminine lover. She may be a consummate warrior, but she understands that her moments of fragile femininity are what keep the audience riveted. In fact, this ruse works with Katniss precisely because she is a gender-neutral character and views the world differently from Podkayne, who is more traditionally romantic in temperament. Katniss possesses a predatory intuition that only Gale and Haymitch, staunchly male characters, share, an intuition that allows them to communicate without words. Katniss knows, for instance, that the sleep syrup Haymitch sends isn't something to ease Peeta's pain but a signal to play up the romance and a ploy allowing her to go into battle without Peeta's interference. Curling into Peeta's arms, vowing that he is her only love, earns the pair a feast when they are close to starvation. Katniss admires Peeta's sincerity and compassion, which, combined with her chameleon-like ability to perform, ensure their mutual survival. Katniss becomes so adept at gender performance in the final battle of the Hunger Games that she is unsure whether her love for Peeta is genuine or part of her elaborate performance.

At the end of the first novel, Katniss takes control of the image fashioned for her and uses it to blackmail the Capitol into giving both her and Peeta victory. When, at her instigation, Katniss and Peeta threaten a double suicide and so beat the Capitol at its own game, she manipulates the image of the thwarted lovers, pitting the audience's voyeuristic thirst for a televised romantic climax against the Capitol's need to assert dominion. Finally, Katniss Everdeen learns to generate her own flame. Unfortunately for Katniss, having gained power at the Capitol's expense, her only hope for survival is to maintain the love-struck facade she has now perfected.

In *Catching Fire*, Katniss's public image makes the transition from beribboned girlishness into womanhood. Forced back into the arena by the Capitol, Katniss and Cinna craft a more mature fire-inspired identity. As an expression of her lethal rage, this more mature Katniss permanently discards her "flickering flames and bejeweled gowns and soft candlelight frocks. She is as deadly as fire itself" (*CF* 207). Scowling at the cameras, Katniss relishes the opportunity to "be myself at last" within the facade she and Peeta are maintaining (*CF* 212). Unfortunately, in *Podkayne of Mars*, the tragic ending deprives Poddy of a similar moment of self-discovery. Podkayne's embracing of her maternal instincts and her increasing determination to still have a career evidence some maturation on her part, but her untimely coma/death prevents her from making any mature life decisions. Unlike Katniss, who is propelled into adulthood by circumstance, Podkayne is deliberately frozen in her adolescent state, as passive and beatific as Sleeping Beauty.

In *Mockingjay*, Katniss becomes the symbol of the districts' rebellion, and with this transition, she finally takes full ownership of her image and performance. The costume is designed as usual by Cinna, but Katniss is not shown the costume until she decides to be the Mockingjay of her own volition. Finally accepting the power of her own performance, Katniss becomes a galvanizing force whose televised image blends the child she once was with the young adult she has become. *"Fire is catching!"* (*M* 106, emphasis in original) she tells President Snow in a televised broadcast, turning both his media and her public image against him. Katniss's role as the Mockingjay, which does not rely on gender performance, is proof of her having come into her own. Having first drawn power through performing femininity, Katniss progresses beyond the Capitol's vision of what she should be.

The epilogue of *Mockingjay*, however, takes a curious turn by placing Katniss in the role of wife and mother. Given her violent bid for autonomy and independence throughout the trilogy, relegating Katniss to the domestic sphere seems to do her a grave disservice by destroying the power of her "other-ness." Unlike Podkayne, however, who ends up either dead or enclosed within the household in angelic repose, Katniss's ending affords her the luxury of creating and controlling her domestic space. Both characters eventually embrace their maternal instincts, but the dual endings of *Podkayne of Mars* seem to punish Podkayne for having aspired to a vocation other than motherhood. For Katniss, who is battle-weary at the end of *Mockingjay*, motherhood seems to be almost a reward for her hard work and sacrifice, a way for her to find peace. Disillusioned with humanity's cyclical capacity for self-destruction, Katniss chooses to walk away from an active role in government, deciding that people can make her beautiful and design weapons for her, "but they will never again brainwash me into the necessity of using them" (*M* 377). Instead, she plans to become her children's teacher, using her personal history to prepare them for what may lie ahead. In this way, she maintains her autonomy and identity long after the action of the trilogy has concluded.

Suzanne Collins's complex treatment of Katniss refutes Uncle Tom's scathing implication that motherhood is more significant than any other job that a woman can take on. In her own way, Podkayne, who ponders the difficulties of having a career and motherhood, is a pioneer for being brave enough to seek both. Collins takes Katniss a step further, allowing her to fight for her autonomy and her family, and ultimately have both on her terms. Female characters no longer have to choose between saving the world and attending to maternal duties. Katniss Everdeen is more than capable of accomplishing both.

Works Cited

Boyle, Brenda, and Olivia Combe. "Gender Lies in Stars Hollow." *Gilmore Girls and the Politics of Identity.* Ed. Ritch Calvin. Jefferson: McFarland, 2008. 159–74. Print.

Brin, David. "We Hobbits Are a Merry Folk: An Incautious and Heretical Reappraisal of J. R. R. Tolkien." *Tomorrow Happens.* Ed. Deb Geisler. Framingham: New England Science Fiction Association Press, 2003. Print.

Collins, Suzanne. *Catching Fire.* New York: Scholastic, 2009. Print.

_____. *The Hunger Games.* New York: Scholastic, 2008. Print.

_____. *Mockingjay.* New York: Scholastic, 2010. Print.

Cooper, James Fenimore. *The Last of the Mohicans.* 1826. New York: Signet, 1962. Print.

Grossman, Lev, et al. "Feeding on Fantasy." *Time.com.* Time Inc., 2 Dec. 2002. Web. 10 Mar. 2010.

Heinlein, Robert [A.]. *Podkayne of Mars.* 1963. New York: Ace, 2010. Print.

_____. *Podkayne of Mars.* 1963. Wake Forest: Baen, 1995. Print.

Johnson, Deidre. "Nancy Drew—A Modern Elsie Dinsmore?" *Lion and the Unicorn* 18:1 (1994): 13–24. *Project Muse.* Web. 30 June 2011.

Johnson, Naomi R. "Consuming Desires: Consumption, Romance, and Sexuality in Best-Selling Teen Romance Novels." *Women's Studies in Communication* 33 (2010): 54–73. Web. 3 Mar. 2011.

19

The Child Soldier and the Self in *Ender's Game* and *The Hunger Games*

SARAH OUTTERSON MURPHY

Much has been made of the remarkable levels of violence in Suzanne Collins's *The Hunger Games* trilogy: in a 2010 blog post, a book buyer complained of "not only children killing children; we have electrocution, drowning, burning, stabbing, being injected by virulent venom and more torture than I can recall in any young adult novels I've ever read" (Cotleur). Do portrayals of children combating evil and saving the day glorify violent solutions to complex problems, desensitize readers to the suffering of others by presenting violence as entertaining spectacle, or even justify violence by presenting it as revenge for suffering? In other words, is the hero myth by which violent power represents courage and progression toward maturity really a moral message for young readers? Such criticisms, however, miss the way Collins's trilogy actually subverts these myths of violence. If violence in the standard hero myth serves at its core as an allegory for the youth's journey from weakness and victimization to independence and power, then *The Hunger Games* questions the assumption that this journey to adulthood is worth pursuing in such a violent world. The extent of the trilogy's subversion of the adult world becomes clearer in light of another YA novel about the violent games that adults play with their child heroes: *Ender's Game* (1985). Understanding these stories as allegories of how adults and children perceive each other — adults as violating, deceitful, and manipulative; children as unknowably alien, unruly, and dangerously powerful — suggests that perhaps the most crucial story told here is the conflict between children and the adults they may become.

Ender's Game is one of Orson Scott Card's earliest novels, an adaptation of his 1977 short story about an extraordinarily gifted boy, Ender Wiggin, who wins every battle, both alone against bullies and as a game commander at his military school in space, albeit at great emotional cost. Through a battle "simulation" that turns out to be real, Ender's teachers use his military skill to destroy the insect-like alien race that has attacked humanity. At the end, when Ender discovers that the last remaining alien queen actually seeks peace with humans, he sets off on a quest to find a planet where she may one day awaken and rebirth her species. Like *The Hunger Games,* this book became immensely popular immediately on publication, winning the Hugo and Nebula awards for science fiction and launching Card's career; it remains a cult favorite today for many children, adolescents, and adults.

Both narratives are notable for the way their child protagonists' violence is manipulated by the adult world. Although Ender's and Katniss's main narratives range respectively from age six to fifteen and sixteen to seventeen, I use the term *child* here because of the stories' emphasis on the contrast with adults. While neither Katniss nor Ender is an orphan, both are abandoned or betrayed by the older generation at a formative age — a common motif in children's literature, with obvious narrative value. Ender is given up by his parents at age six for what promises to be years of training. Because Ender's very existence, as a "Third" child in a population-controlled world, was permitted only because the government was hoping for a military genius, his parents' feelings toward him are complicated, and he is told that they will not miss him long. When, at age ten, he is given the chance to visit them, he turns it down. When Katniss is eleven, her father dies in a mining accident, at which point her mother becomes catatonically depressed and unable to provide for Katniss and her sister. After Katniss becomes the primary caretaker of the family, her attitude toward her mother is reserved and cynical. Laura Miller notes the practical narrative value of such detachment from parents in her review of *The Hunger Games,* arguing that "adventure stories" like these require a less safe environment than "the world of our hovered-over teens and preteens" (132). Yet the emotional detachment that Katniss and Ender experience not only makes them adventuresome child protagonists; the weakness and irrelevance of parental figures in these stories also sets up a larger pattern of deliberate, purposeful violence and injury inflicted on children by representatives of the adult world.

This violence, significantly, is designed to turn these children into ferocious killers — a disturbing and unusual motif for children's literature, and very rarely made as explicit as it is in these books (in contrast with, for example, the way Dumbledore's Machiavellian plotting in the Harry Potter series is never called out as such by the narrator). Ender's teachers repeatedly place him in physical danger from bullies and manipulate his reality in order to shape him into a perfectly self-reliant and ruthless killer, a precociously powerful hero who can defeat aliens for them. Like Ender, Katniss is the victim of deliberate and calculating adult manipulation of children's violence for political purposes, and she knows it: "Forcing [kids] to kill one another while we watch — this is the Capitol's way of reminding us how totally we are at their mercy" (*HG* 18). The Capitol sacrifices Panem's children for the sake of political power. Furthermore, the later books in Collins's series explore Katniss's own increasing power as a symbol of the rebellion against the Capitol — power gained through the violence inflicted on her. Katniss feels increasing horror at the Gamemakers' influence on her emotions and character, even as her pain is used by District 13 for propaganda purposes in the war. Her emotional isolation, suffering, and manipulation by government operatives on both sides all contribute to the violence that everyone demands from her.

Still, this kind of story can be seen as morally problematic in terms of shifting responsibility for violence onto others. Some readers have taken issue with *Ender's Game* for this reason. One particularly descriptive reviewer writes that Ender, as an unrealistically perfect character, is essentially "porn" for two "fetishes," wish fulfillment and self-pity: "After every victory comes an equally cathartic bout of self-pity, as Ender wracks his soul in ecstatic remorse over his situation. Even in this area, he excels. No one can self-pity like Ender!" (Bond). John Kessel argues that the novel presents a morality in which intention alone matters; such a morality is dangerous because it can lead to atrocities as a means to a higher end. Ender's violent actions are justified by presenting them as a blameless response to violence, effectively telling the child reader that "your mistreatment is the evidence of your gifts. You are morally superior. Your turn will come, and then you may severely punish others, yet remain blameless. You are the hero" (Kessel 96). Thus, the narrative's construction of Ender as inherently righteous and helpless to avoid committing violence would justify that violence in a disturbing way. Similar issues resonate in *The Hunger Games*. Katniss's violence could be seen as problematically justified by the violence inflicted upon her because, like Ender, she has precocious skill in combat (e.g., her infallibly lethal aim) and because her actions are initially reluctant and committed only in self-defense. Katniss, again like Ender, experiences wracking episodes of grief, regret, and self-doubt concerning her role in the violence swirling around her. Do the helplessness and the suffering of the child heroes justify their violence?

An alternative interpretation is the child messiah motif, in which the child's sacrificial suffering ultimately gives him or her the power to redeem humanity. In an essay about the "doomed child messiah" in children's fantasy of the last thirty years, including *Ender's Game*, Radhiah Chowdhury identifies a pattern in which child messiahs are "fated to sacrifice everything for a world that may be less than deserving" with a "relentless, inevitable pull towards their own destruction" (108). Chowdhury distinguishes this pattern from that of earlier fantasy stories whose endings are "celebratory, not tragic" for the

Chosen One (107). By contrast, Ender "is not permitted to stay in the world that he has saved" and leaves Earth forever on a spaceship (Chowdhury 110). Similarly, by the end of *Mockingjay,* Katniss's grief sends her to the fringes of society to live in the remains of District 12, an ending marked by loss despite the rebels' victory. This sacrificial "messiah" plot, of course, is exactly what Card's critics find so disturbing about Ender as a model for supposedly moral violence: "No one is that special; no one is that innocent" (Kessel 97).

Yet both attacks on Ender and Katniss as heroic justifications of a "morality of intention" and explanations of their sacrificial roles as child messiahs miss the satirical and allegorical significance of their situations as child soldiers. Both narratives closely mirror the pattern by which real-life child soldiers are created: the child is emotionally isolated and subjected to violence that is closely linked to forcing the child into committing acts of violence against others. In an account of the reintegration into society of child soldiers in Mozambique, Alcinda Honwana describes how "young boys and girls were initiated into violence through a deliberate process of terror. Terrified themselves, they were prepared to inflict terror on others" (65). In one example, a ten-year-old boy was captured in 1985 by rebels, along with his father and sister. When the three attempted to escape, they were caught, and "as punishment, and for his own life to be spared, Marula was ordered to kill his father. And so he did" (64). In these accounts, there "were not two separate phases in which boys were first brutalised by soldiers and then forced to brutalise civilians"; rather, the experiences of suffering and inflicting violence were "intertwined and mutually reinforcing" (65). Victimized children make the most ruthlessly violent soldiers.

Part of the way each book works is by tricking the reader into initially believing the very lies about violence and irresponsibility that the books are designed to combat; for example, the satirical critique of the Capitol's insatiable consumption of Katniss's violence would fail without the reader first responding to that violence as entertaining. Later, Katniss's and Ender's disgust at their violence compounds our shame. These stories force a rethinking of the tropes of the heroic violence we expect; the protagonists are neither self-pitying child Hitlers nor self-sacrificial child messiahs, but child soldiers whose vulnerability produces violence. While Katniss is a good deal older than Ender, whose young age is emphasized by Card, Katniss is even more dependent on others' help than Ender, and her physical danger is more vividly painted, producing an equivalent effect of vulnerability. Both stories link childhood's innocence, especially a desire not to fight, with unexpected violent power.

While most of Ender's time at Battle School is spent fighting laser-tag training battles, rigged to be increasingly impossible but which he nevertheless always wins, his success makes him a target for one last bully, who plans to kill him. Camera surveillance is ever-present at Battle School (just as in

Panem's arena), reminding us that the teachers once again choose not to intervene. Ender taunts the boy into facing him one-on-one and then incapacitates and (unknowingly) kills him ruthlessly, recognizing that the teachers will never help him and that this is "the only way to end things completely" so that he doesn't have to fight bullies anymore (*EG* 212). Here is the deadly self-justification that Kessel finds so disturbing. However, what Kessel misses is that Ender's desire not to fight (in conjunction with his pity and guilt afterwards) is not simply an excuse after the fact but rather the essential secret of his success.

Later that day, Ender is given one last battle, in which he will be ludicrously outmatched by a force double his own: "Everything they can do to beat me, thought Ender. Everything they can think of, change all the rules, they don't care, just so they beat me. Well, I'm sick of the game. No game is worth Bonzo's blood pinking the water on the bathroom floor. Ice me, send me home, I don't want to play anymore" (*EG* 215). Because Ender no longer cares about playing, he comes up with the one move that can possibly win him the battle. Instead of winning as usual before passing through the enemy's gate on the other side of the battleroom as a final formality, Ender sends a few soldiers straight to the gate and wins even as the rest of the room begins the impossible fight. When a teacher enters the room, Ender speaks directly:

"I beat you again, sir," he said.
"Nonsense, Ender," Anderson said softly. "Your battle was with Griffin and Tiger."
"How stupid do you think I am?" [*EG* 219].

Ender wins his battles because he realizes that no one will help him; therefore, he can depend only on himself for his survival.

This is only the first iteration of the pattern by which Ender realizes and rejects adults' violence against him. In Ender's final test against the "battle simulator" (which is, unknown to him, actually the alien fleet in space, light-years away), the enemy outnumbers him by five or ten thousand ships to eighty. His reaction is to laugh, rejecting any desire to pass the exam. Instead of trying to fight strategically to eliminate the enemy ships in pitched battle, he sends a suicide mission to explode the alien planet, thinking, "If I break this rule, they'll never let me be a commander. It would be too dangerous. I'll never have to play a game again. And that is victory" (*EG* 293). Ender has come to this point through adult manipulations that make him increasingly violent and increasingly horrified at himself, culminating in a rejection of the adult world. Paradoxically, however, this disillusionment with adult violence gives him the tactical insight that results in his unknowingly committing the most violent act of all: genocide.

Katniss undergoes a similar repeated process of realizing how her violence and power are actually created by the adults in charge. This realization leads her to question the purpose of that power. Although from the very beginning she recognizes that the Games are a sick method of control and that the Capitol is an oppressor, Katniss nonetheless refers to Peeta and the other children in the arena as her "enemies" or the other "tributes"—both terms suggesting the Capitol's perspective (*HG* 114). However, at the emotional moment when Katniss is grieving over the death of her ally and surrogate sister Rue, after having avenged her by killing her attacker, Katniss unexpectedly redirects her anger away from the boy who speared Rue toward the Capitol (*HG* 236). Like Ender, she realizes who the real enemy is—not her peers but the adults overseeing it all.

Furthermore, the awareness of her surveillance by a manipulative adult audience gives Katniss the tools to succeed. Just as Ender's awareness of the adults' manipulations allows him to win their games, Katniss's recognition of the manipulated nature of her environment gives her crucial clues. When she desperately needs water, she realizes that her mentor must be choosing to save the gift because water is close by. Later, Katniss deliberately initiates kisses and intimate conversation with Peeta in hopes of rewards that help preserve their lives. Katniss's awareness that she is being manipulated ultimately forces her, like Ender, to reject the parameters of the game entirely in order to escape it. She must remember who the enemy is, as when she bluffs the Gamemakers with her suicidal berries at the climax of the first book, or when in the second she shoots the force field in order to destroy the arena. Just as Ender does, Katniss wins games by maintaining sight of the adult game designers as the true enemy. Both protagonists realize that these designers' stories are just lies told to direct the child players' violent power for the adults' own purposes. Once they realize that they are not only being made violent but being used to perpetuate the adults' cycle of violence, they either stop that cycle (in Katniss's case) or make reparation for it (as Ender does). Both do whatever violence is necessary in order to escape from having to commit more violence.

At this point, an additional paradox becomes evident: these characters gain their power not only because of their suffering but also because of their empathy; yet the same empathy that makes them powerful makes their violence painful. Part of Ender's traumatic discovery at the end of the novel is the revelation that his capacity for loving and understanding others is what made him such a brilliant strategist—as long as he didn't know that the killing was real. Innocence can be deadly, and it is clear that intention isn't the only thing that matters, after all: Ender's empathy does, in fact, make him good at war, and such violence is terrifying and even evil, whether he likes it or not. In a psychological computer game and in dreams, he finds himself killing creatures who attack him but who have the faces of his friends and beloved sister (a combination reminiscent of the tribute mutts in Katniss's first Hunger

Games), while a mirror shows him only the face of his hated, psychopathic older brother. When he tries to tear that mirror down, snakes devour him; thus even before the final discovery that the battle simulations are real, Ender reveals an increasing self-hatred.

Katniss faces a similarly complex situation during *The Hunger Games,* as her empathy and emotions become sources of both power and danger. The key psychological aspects of Ender's violence are his despair and horror at his violent self, the empathy that provokes this despair, and the tactical insight that these feelings of despair and horror consistently provide him. Katniss experiences all of these, especially in her attempts to understand her relationship with Peeta, which has been marked by shared suffering but also by her readiness to use violence toward him, and her despair at that coldness within her. Realizing that Peeta is yet another casualty of adult practicality when he's left behind at the Quarter Quell, Katniss states, "[I]t takes more than [an IV] to keep a person going once she's lost the will to live" (*CF* 389). Her statement mirrors the way Ender gives up whenever he is overcome by despair at the way he is manipulated by adults. And just as Ender's empathy is a cause of his power as well as his suffering, Katniss's love and emotion become a source of power that cannot be artificially created or imitated, as the rebels discover when they try in vain to script her propaganda speeches. Instead, Katniss has the most emotional impact — the most power — when she is left to do her own thing.

As the rebels use Katniss's real love for those who are victimized to energize the rebellion, they also attempt to use her love for her sister to control and manipulate her. When Katniss's sister, Prim, is killed at a final moment of the battle in the Capitol, Katniss realizes that a thirteen-year-old medic would not have been on the front lines without approval from high up. President Coin, hoping to punish the Capitol by instituting a new Hunger Games, has sought to win Katniss's support through her desire for revenge on Prim's supposed killers. Coin thinks Katniss's love can be turned into a weapon against the Capitol. But, in fact, Katniss's certainty that no good government would have put Prim in danger helps her understand that the old and new governments are turning out to be interchangeable. She realizes that, like Peeta in his prescient and misunderstood calls for peace while in captivity, she cannot trust the rebellion to be any different from the government that she has just helped to take down.

Katniss's mental confusion before this decision represents the existential crisis she has been experiencing since the first book, pulled between vengeance and compassion as much as between Gale and Peeta. Ultimately, Katniss's role as media symbol and her love for her sister — both of which remain authentic, despite attempts at manipulation — give her the insight to vote for the new Hunger Games. Her vote "for Prim" may startle and even successfully fool many readers, but it actually provides Katniss with a chance to have weapons in President Coin's presence, the last opportunity to avert a repeat of the dictatorial regime of the Capitol (*M* 370). Symbolically conflating the adults of the Capitol and of the rebellion, Katniss uses the violent power given her by both sets of adults in order to destroy their cycle of violence. Katniss's insight comes from her emotional strength and ability to see past revenge to empathy for the future children of the Capitol.

After killing Coin, Katniss knows that she will accept even death before any more manipulation and violence. Despite the heroic glory of the weapons designed for her, she declares that those in charge will "never again brainwash" her "into the necessity" of violence (*M* 377). Katniss extends her condemnation of her own violence to a condemnation of all humans, finding governmental justifications for violence (efficiency and expediency) unacceptable if they produce "a creature that sacrifices its children's lives to settle its differences" (*M* 377). She even rejects the concept of kinship with human beings, calling them "monsters" (*M* 377). Imagining a similar group who approved the first Games, Katniss recognizes the relationship between individual vengeance and governmental violence. Crucially, she is able to come to these insights by rejecting a shortsighted allegiance to one side in a war, realizing that the children of the Capitol no more deserve to be sacrificed than she or Prim did. Katniss rejects humanity, certainly, but she rejects her own human self first, repudiating her violent power and contemplating suicide. Her moral vision here seems despairing, but the despair obscures how, by loving her sister, Katniss has actually expanded her sense of the self to include those who had been emphatically Other.

Ender experiences a similar expansion of the human in his final reconciliation with his alien enemies. In the fantasy game, finding no way to destroy the mirror with his brother's face on it, he reaches down and, somehow, kisses the mirror instead. It turns into his sister, who opens a door in the wall to free him. The psychological story the game tells him is that Ender's two siblings represent two selves for him, one evil and one good; although he cannot kill the evil one in the mirror without dying too, by kissing what he fears, he finds the self he thinks of as good, and as a result becomes free. While Ender fears his own violence, he can escape it only by loving and accepting the part of him that is terrifying, violent, and powerful. After he has won the war and discovered the horrible truth of what he has done, he takes one of the first colony ships out to explore the planets left empty by the death of the alien queens. There, Ender discovers a replica of the fantasy game landscape, telepathically taken from his own mind and constructed long ago for him to find one day. There is even a crude mirror with a human face scratched into it. Ender expects a deadly trap, the aliens' long-delayed revenge. But, like Katniss, he is no longer afraid of death. He has done the worst he can imagine and faced it in the mirror — and so he now takes this literal mirror down. Behind it, he finds a cocoon, the last infant queen. The aliens — unable to communicate otherwise with the humans bent on destroying them — have entrusted the last survivor of their species to Ender.

Ender's recognition of himself in his enemy is a mirror image of Katniss's realization of her complicity in adult violence. In prison after Coin's death, Katniss's singing — an act connected with both her beloved father and Peeta's life-bringing artistry with paint — marks the hope arising from the death of her heroic self. Later, when Peeta's primroses remind Katniss of the rose Snow left her, she realizes that the "evil thing is inside, not out" (*M* 383); her purging of the unnatural rose still inside her house represents her awareness of the evil inside her as much as in others. Katniss also ultimately reconciles with Buttercup the cat, who, like Haymitch, has been presented as quite similar to Katniss despite their mutual dislike. Like Ender, Katniss learns to recognize herself in her enemy and her enemy in herself.

The stories of Ender and Katniss demonstrate the connection between experiences of suffering and inflicting violence. In these stories, there is no easy way to overcome violent power with empathy and innocence: empathy produces the capacity for the tactical insight that can make violence effective, while good intentions, lack of knowledge, and inability to communicate provide the dangerous rationale under which such violence seems to be necessary. Ultimately, while a child (or any other innocent, such as Katniss's childlike prep team or Ender's thoughtless aliens) may not be responsible for beginning a violent situation, these two stories make clear that such a child has an opportunity and moral obligation to come to terms with his or her own complicity in that violence. Thus, even as Ender and Katniss become aware that their power is being created and used by adults, they become even more horrified at themselves. The profound psychic distress they experience is not simply posttraumatic stress disorder or anger at the adult world but a realization of their own participation in the violence they fear. Ender and Katniss must challenge the conception of the self and expand it to include those previously considered enemies, learning even from their own violence to forgive the violence of others. If the child is going to become an adult one day without ending up hating and rejecting either self, these two violent species must learn to understand each other. As war stories, as allegories of adolescence, *The Hunger Games* trilogy and *Ender's Game* provide both cautionary and hopeful images of reconciliation with the enemy inside and out.

WORKS CITED

Bond, Stephen. Rev. of *Ender's Game. Plover.net,* 28 Aug. 2008. Web. 21 May 2011.
Card, Orson Scott. *Ender's Game.* 1985. New York: Tor. 1994. Print.
Chowdhury, Radhiah. "A Chosen Sacrifice· The Doomed Destiny of the Child Messiah

in Late Twentieth-Century Children's Fantasy." *Papers: Explorations into Children's Literature* 16.2 (2006): 107–11. Print.

Collins, Suzanne. *Catching Fire.* New York: Scholastic, 2009. Print.

_____. *The Hunger Games.* New York: Scholastic, 2008. Print.

_____. *Mockingjay.* New York: Scholastic, 2010. Print.

Cotleur, Sheryl. "Hunger Games Trilogy: Questioning the Violence." *Shelf Awareness.* 26 Aug. 2010. Web.

Honwana, Alcinda. "Children in War: Reintegrating Child Soldiers." *IDS Bulletin* 40.1 (2009): 63–68. Print.

Kessel, John. "Creating the Innocent Killer: *Ender's Game,* Intention, and Morality." *Foundation: The International Review of Science Fiction* 33.90 (2004): 81–97. Print.

Miller, Laura. "Fresh Hell: Dystopias for Young Readers." *New Yorker* 14 June 2010: 132–36. Print.

20

Apples to Oranges
The Heroines in Twilight *and* The Hunger Games

AMANDA FIRESTONE

When *The Hunger Games* was published, comparisons between heroines Katniss Everdeen and *Twilight*'s Bella Swan became inevitable. Both narratives are young adult fiction, centering on the fantastic experiences of an adolescent girl. Drawing from tenuous similarities between the two characters, popular opinion has elevated Katniss to a modern feminist heroine. Bella, on the other hand, has been derided as Katniss's antithetical representation of traditional femininity. A brief article titled "Bella Swan vs. Katniss Everdeen: What Does Empowerment Look Like?" on the webpage *AfterEllen.com* reveals a conversation thread that references the way many readers place Katniss well above Bella as a feminist heroine. The author, noted only as "The Linster," first cites Laura Miller's *Salon.com* article, which immediately asks: "Is Katniss Everdeen the Antidote to Bella Swan?" At the end of her article, Miller articulates that, for all of her faults, Bella knows what she desires in her world and at least attempts to get it. In contrast, Miller finds Katniss to be passive-aggressive, making decisions only when forced to. The Linster attempts to refute Miller's observations:

> I'm not sure what books Miller read, but in my copy of the *Twilight* series Bella is sort of a wimp, subject to the wishes of Edward. She will literally give up her life to be with her man. True, Katniss is subject to the will of other people, but she has no real choice in the matter. When she realizes that she can actually be an inspiration to people, she steps into the role, albeit reluctantly.

This kind of exchange is common between the two fan allegiances, as demonstrated by the comments following The Linster's article. Interestingly, there are many who post to the thread who admit they have not read all of the books in question, yet some nonreaders have clearly chosen a "team" (The

Linster). Take for example the post by "andshescreamed": "Bella is the opposite of female empowerment. Totally and completely.... I cannot think of one instance where I admired Bella.... I haven't read the *Hunger Games* book though, but from what I've read on here she seems to have a lot more going for her than Bella...."

What neither Miller and The Linster, nor any of the thread commenters on their articles, have investigated, is whether or not these two characters *can* be compared. It seems few people are wondering if their respective fictive universes prohibit comparisons. Sarah Seltzer published an article in the Summer 2011 issue of *Bitch Magazine* concluding that it isn't helpful to impose polarized binaries on readers, particularly young ones (42). She explains that many feminists would deride ideas about making binary comparisons between adult literatures such as speculative fiction by Margaret Atwood and paranormal romance by Charlaine Harris, let alone lump all female protagonists into one heap (Seltzer 42). As Seltzer explains, "To stack them against each other without context, while tempting, assumes that all popular books for female readers with female protagonists must compete in the same category" (42).

Seltzer makes tentative touches with ideas about genre conventions and YA literature as an overarching category, but more explicit connections need to be made. A brief history of the YA category first contextualizes the genres that fall within its purview. Romance and postapocalyptic/dystopian fiction can then be explored as literary genres. Finally, examinations of the individual genres' conventions and requirements will shed light on the comparability of Katniss and Bella in the context of their own worlds. For the purposes of clarity, examples drawn from both series are confined to the initial texts, *The Hunger Games* and *Twilight,* as they function as complete narratives in their own right, presenting consistent characterizations for both heroines that later carry through their respective fictive universes.

"Young adult" as a literary category was popularized during the late 1960s by the publishing industry as a way to strengthen sales and section off the market to a specific demographic (Ramsdell 208, 212). The term *young adult* is ambiguous at best. While some might define a young adult as a teenager, others insist that children as young as eight are included in the blanket term (Ramsdell 208). However, chronological age is not necessarily the deciding factor in what is appointed as young adult. Rather than an age, the term applies to the "transitional period of one's life that children enter at varying ages and from which adults emerge" (Ramsdell 208). The transitions, or rites of passage, concern the bodily changes brought on by puberty, the growth of independence from parents, the awareness of the self in a social structure with peers, and the development of a specific moral code (Cline and McBride 6–10). This basically amounts to an extended period of liminality, and for Kristin Ramsdell, YA literature functions to help young readers "survive" that tumultuous period (209).

The increasing popularity of the YA genre ensures an abundance of texts for readers and a canon that will always be in flux. YA authors continually add to and push the boundaries of existing fiction subgenres such as steampunk and fantasy. This also is the case for YA narratives that include supernatural elements. Typically, these stories include components of myths, legends, and folklores that help young readers understand how certain cultural threads tie together (Cline and McBride 157). Such threads are common to supernatural fiction, and *Twilight,* with its references to Native American legends, old worlds, and impossible creatures, makes an excellent example. However, because *Twilight* also is firmly planted in the romance genre, it is accessible to readers who may not necessarily favor traditional supernatural fiction (Latrobe and Drury 104).

Popular romance fiction is defined by Pamela Regis as "a work of prose fiction that tells the story of the courtship and betrothal of one or more heroines" (19). Regis emphasizes the heroine, turning courtship and betrothal into active events, marking a departure from how romance has traditionally been coded (22). This definition allows for works from a variety of historical contexts to be analyzed and compared in terms of what exactly makes a romance (Regis 22). According to genre conventions, the focus of the narrative is the love story building between the main characters, and while this often is problematized by outside events, it remains the central driving force of the plot (Ramsdell 4). Regis identifies eight specific conventions that are essential for a text to be recognized as a bona fide romance: "Society Defined" (31), "The Meeting" (31), "The Barrier" (32), "The Attraction" (33), "The Declaration" (34), "Point of Ritual Death" (35), "The Recognition" (36), and "The Betrothal" (37).

Regis does not explicitly denote a sex scene as one of the requirements for a romance text, even though modern romance narratives often insist that some kind of sexual relationship be visible to the reader. While Regis acknowledges that sexual desirability is sometimes the crux of "The Attraction," it is typically just one component of something that may also include "friendship, shared goals or feelings, society's expectations, and economic issues" (33). For the YA category, this is appealing because it offers the opportunity for readers to become invested in a slow-building romance that doesn't necessarily involve sex (Ramsdell 209).

Ironically, while YA readers are encouraged to interact with texts in order to help them cope with growing pains associated with adolescence, romance as a genre requires readers to interact with texts in order to be successful. According to Teresa Ebert, historically, the romance genre has been written primarily for female readers (19). Ebert explains that romance narratives are by and large reproductions of patriarchal, masculinist fantasies, despite the fact that the majority of romances are written by women (5). At the end of many romance novels, the heroine must "[deny] her independent goal-oriented action outside of love and marriage" (Regis 10). This reinforces traditional, rigid gender roles and potentially subtextually advises female readers to accept their fate as eventual lovers, wives, and mothers (Radway 207).

Postapocalyptic/dystopian fiction appears, at first glance, altogether different from romance. For Claire P. Curtis, postapocalyptic fiction gives readers the ability to surmise just how people would come together and "create a new social contract" in the face of disaster that has effectively destroyed "functional government, food distribution, organized medical care, and the infrastructure on which we rely for most of what we do" (8). The causal disaster can be precipitated by any number of things: nuclear war, plague, environmental collapse, science and technology gone awry, or natural disasters (Curtis 16, 17). As the social contract is renewed, Kay Sambell notes that many authors "pull no punches" when depicting totalitarian societies resulting from the crisis that operate around government brutality, violence, and enforced inequalities between those who have rights and those who do not (247).

Like postapocalyptic narratives, dystopian future tales are didactic, subtextually warning readers of a possible future if humanity continues along its course (Curtis 34). In contrast to romance, it is usually a hero rather than a heroine who must quickly reconcile how he is to ensure his survival given the abject circumstances post-catastrophe (Broderick 362). Postapocalyptic/dystopian future fictions bypass the actual events that lead to a complete restructuring of society, and so these events become steeped in mythology (Broderick 362, 363), allowing the hero to face a foe of epic proportions in a David-and-Goliath showdown. The additional reading of the hero as the often reluctant everyman heightens the drama (Booker and Thomas 254). The skills the hero acquires to survive are employed in the eventual battle, making him more spectacular because he has no superpowers. While the hero may win in some fashion, the happy ending is never guaranteed and, in fact, is unlikely, particularly in a dystopian world.

As evidenced by their genres, the fictive universes Bella and Katniss inhabit are governed by significantly different rules. While the overarching category of YA creates a potential context where the two characters could go toe-to-toe, that context would be superficial. Both girls are in their mid-teenage years, ages seventeen and sixteen respectively, as their narratives begin. They're both slight in build with long dark hair and eyes that seem to miss nothing. Their similarities seem to end there, making every other aspect of their characters binary opposites.

Physically, Bella is "so clumsy [she's] almost disabled" (*T* 210). Katniss is athletic and nimble, accustomed to moving through forested areas quietly and efficiently. While Bella is book smart and has an affinity for literature, Katniss learns survival skills and knows how to skin a lynx. Bella seems to make choices that deliberately put her in harm's way; Katniss is thrust into dangerous situations. Neither young woman lacks male attention, with both soon facing the decision between two plausible suitors. Where Bella is consumed by the drama surrounding her romantic life, Katniss remains largely ambivalent about it. If any significant comparisons are to be made, then it is essential to go beyond the girls' activities and emotional displays to explore their genres as factors for characterization.

In general comparisons between the two characters, Bella is largely associated with traits considered traditionally feminine, and Katniss is associated with empowerment usually destined for men in the form of activity and perceived agency. Even Laura Miller, who advocates for Bella, admits that Katniss "is in many respects an improvement on the passive, besotted Bella." In a comment responding to The Linster's post, "Woolysocks" asks, "[H]ow many times over would Bella be dead if it weren't for Edward? Whereas Katniss saves herself AND the dead weight Peeta." While Woolysocks's observation is fair, it neglects to note the moments when Peeta displays strength, which Katniss admits when she says, "*Peeta Mellark just saved my life*" (*HG* 194, emphasis in original).

Indisputably, Katniss is more physically active than Bella. She has skills and coordination that Bella can never achieve in her human lifetime. Still, Katniss's physical abilities are necessitated by the world in which she belongs. Had she grown up in District 11, like Rue, she'd likely be more accustomed to a life of farm work rather than hunting. According to genre conventions, the reluctant heroine must figure out exactly *how* she and others are going to survive. Katniss's world is one that Bella can never conceive of: a place where people regularly starve to death, where sometimes the only thing available is boiled water and mint leaves. The skills Katniss learns and hones are a result of living in a home where there is no longer a male provider. She is unable to behave selfishly, because she has the responsibility of caring for her mother and younger sister.

Bella also is constructed as a caretaker in her text. In relation to her mom and dad, she exhibits traditional domestic behaviors such as cooking dinners, cleaning up, and generally organizing their lives. Still, her narrative arc is reliant on her relationship with Edward Cullen. The love story is the central driving force of her world, which is set in a small town in twenty-first-century America. There's no food shortage (in fact, Bella's quite a cook), and she spends most of her days navigating high school society rather than setting snare traps. All eight of Regis's requirements for a legitimate romance text are part of *Twilight*. While the paranormal elements present in the text shape the story line, Bella and Edward's relationship is the locus of the narrative.

When conflict separates them, Bella spends much of her time agonizing over how and when she and Edward will be together again, which is how it *must be* in order for the romance to succeed. The couple's forced separation while Bella is being hunted by the story's antagonist, James, heightens the suspense for readers and increases their desire to see Bella and Edward reunited. Additionally, it heightens the enjoyment of the happy ending, which largely takes place at the high school prom. Their reunion at prom, which substitutes for the traditional marriage or fete in romance, also reaffirms the couple's love and the authenticity of Bella's concern for Edward's safety.

If Bella spent most of her time pretending to love Edward to achieve her own motives as Katniss does with Peeta in the arena during the Hunger Games, readers probably wouldn't be able to successfully symbolically interact with the text through Bella. Readers ultimately might reject the text because the romance would be disingenuous and there would be no happy ending. Contrastingly, the conventions of Katniss's world do not require her love for Peeta to be true, nor do they require her to have a happy ending. Conventions for dystopian fiction dictate that Katniss's main goal must be to survive at any cost. Her genre sometimes uses romantic relationships to spur the heroine into action but not necessarily for the purposes of saving or strengthening a relationship. More often than not, any relationship may teach the heroine something that will be relevant to her survival even if the relationship ends.

Perhaps the largest criticism of Bella is that she is perceived as a helpless victim and, potentially worse, as an example of Mary Sue fiction gone wrong. A character construction first acknowledged in the fan fiction world, Mary Sue is a term for a character that appears as the idealized literary representation of the author (Bacon-Smith 94). Essentially, the writer creates a perfected pseudo-self who represents all the characteristics the author would like to have, and, according to Camille Bacon-Smith, "the Mary Sue story taps into deep emotional sources" (99). Unfortunately, this writing style is usually derided as lazy or inept. Blogger Maureen O'Danu defines Mary Sue as "a heroine ... who is too perfect to be true — who has special powers or exactly the right personality traits to get through whatever the author throws at [her] without batting an eye or tripping over those three inch stilletto [sic] heels." Bacon-Smith acknowledges that Mary Sue characters "meet emotional needs" for female writers, often allowing them to navigate adolescent experiences that more intellectual approaches to writing do not (100).

The negative connotations associated with Mary Sue and her über-perfection transfer to Bella, making possible the charge that she may be Meyer's idealized representation of herself. Bella simultaneously is independent and strong (e.g., her decision to move to Forks and later offer herself up as a martyr) while also totally dependent and weak (e.g., her suffocating relationship with Edward and physical awkwardness). However, Katniss does not seem to be associated with Mary Sue. Many of the comments in The Linster's thread agree that she is empowered, self-motivated, and capable. Still, O'Danu's definition implies that Katniss could potentially be a Mary Sue character as well. No matter the circumstances, she seems to have acquired the necessary skills to be successful. Her father teaches her to hunt, and when he dies unexpectedly, she has the knowledge that ensures her family's survival. When she discovers that Peeta's been infected with tracker jacker venom, she's learned the trick to draw the poison from his system. Repeatedly, Katniss finds a way to manage any given situation because she's learned a particular skill or lesson. She has all of the necessary tools that allow her to continue on her journey.

If her skill set is not enough to peg her as a Mary Sue, then her familiarity with geographic adversity might. Growing up in District 12, Katniss learns early on to navigate all sorts of terrain, including wide-open fields and thick forests. She's already skilled in hiding and can move through a variety of landscapes, leaving few tracks and making little noise. Upon her arrival in the arena, she quickly discovers that the landscape is remarkably similar to her home district. After escaping the bloodbath at the Cornucopia, she runs for the trees. The forest she encounters is so much like the one back home that all of her survival skills are transferable. Even Katniss admits that she would be in trouble if the Gamemakers had chosen different terrain like the scorching desert or frozen wasteland of previous competitions.

Not only is the land similar, but a bow with arrows — her weapon of choice — is visible at the Cornucopia. Katniss cannot help but think that it was put there especially for her, that she can survive the arena because it's "the weapon that might be [her] salvation" (*HG* 149). Before the Games, Katniss remembers an arena where the tributes had only "spiked maces" to use as weapons, further legitimizing her feeling that the bow is there for her (*HG* 39). Collins has given her heroine, either directly or through the aid of other characters, every single tool she might need to successfully navigate any problem in the narrative, including Katniss's emotionally closed-off demeanor that allows her to cope with extreme situations such as her father's death, Peeta's wounds, and Rue's demise. Her skill set, familiarity with the land, and cool emotional state makes Katniss the ideal competitor and winner in the Hunger Games. This certainly complies with standard definitions of Mary Sue characters, making her an excellent candidate for the title.

Those who would argue otherwise might cite Katniss's activeness as making her better than the standard Mary Sue. Although a multifaceted and complex character, the perceived empowerment from her action, particularly compared to Bella, is merely on the surface. There's a tremendous difference between activity and agency. Agency is the ability to make decisions and effectively enact those decisions to achieve specific results, whereas activity simply denotes physical action that doesn't necessarily require intense thought. Although Katniss has lethal skills with a bow and arrow, using them in survival situations doesn't necessarily assert her agency, by my definition.

In fact, it is as Miller suggests: Katniss does not make active decisions but rather reactive ones. Her decision to hunt to feed her family is a reaction to her father's death and her mother's inability to step into the role of provider. After Peeta gives her the burnt bread and she sees the dandelion in the school yard, she instinctively knows how the family will continue to eat. Hunting essentially becomes an obligation and not an active choice. While she does sometimes display her agency (e.g., when she decides to destroy the Careers' food source), whenever Katniss is faced with a monumental change in her life, her course of action often appears before her without her needing to make a concrete decision.

Bella, however, attempts to exercise agency at every turn, but her genre disallows her from becoming both an active and effective agent. It is Bella who pushes Edward from the beginning to acknowledge the love growing between them despite their radical differences as human and vampire. He resists her but eventually exerts his own agency, dictating the conditions of their relationship and smothering her potential activity with his patriarchal superiority. Nonetheless, she consistently attempts to push the boundaries of their relationship. When she wants to become more physical with Edward, it is he who must enact their first kiss. When Bella attempts to deepen the kiss and move closer, he physically restrains her and "with irresistible force, push[es] her] face back" (*T* 282).

From the beginnings of their courtship, Bella insists that she must become a vampire to complete their relationship. Yet, during a moment when her human life hangs in the balance and vampirism is in her grasp, her known desire to turn is thwarted when Edward draws the venom from her blood, halting the change and forcing Bella to remain human. When Bella questions him in the hospital after the incident as to why he didn't allow the change to happen, Edward's answer is that he was not prepared for her to become a monster or to steal her soul. While he may have valid concerns, Edward constantly refuses to open the topic of her transformation.

Repeatedly in the text, Bella attempts to assert her agency. The only time she succeeds is when she decides to go to the ballet studio to meet James alone so that the Cullen family will remain safe. Here, Bella willingly offers herself as a sacrifice for the people that she loves. It is no coincidence that, when she has the ability to make her plans come to fruition, Edward is not nearby. At that moment, she's being guarded by two of his "siblings," Alice and Jasper. The reader knows that both Alice and Jasper have extrasensory powers in the form of future visions and empathic abilities respectively, legitimizing Bella's agency without Edward's interference. She manages to get away from a fortune-teller and an emotional barometer with no hindrance. Of course, in accordance with the conventions of romance, Edward arrives at the ballet studio in the nick of time to ensure her (human) survival.

Bella's actions are consistently minimized by the fact that Edward's agency exceeds her own. His ability to enact and realize his decisions hampers Bella's ability to get the things she wants when she wants them. In stark contrast, Katniss rarely, if ever, uses her agency, although she appears to have the ability to do so. While Bella is a struggling agent quelled by her specific genre's conventions, Katniss is an agent who seems to refuse her agency, instead allowing her actions to be dictated by her reactions to what is happening around her. Point in case, both women choose to sacrifice themselves for someone they love. Bella actively plans her escape from Alice and Jasper and then puts it into motion while considering the ramifications of her decision and the implications for those she'll leave behind. When Katniss moves to take Prim's place at the reaping, she gives no thought to her action; as she takes her place on stage, her thoughts drift away from her family, moving toward preparation for the Games and her memories of Peeta. She doesn't think about the consequences of her snap decision until later.

It is more than tempting to compare the two characters based on their similar ages and the way they both seem to find themselves torn between two men. Such comparison is, however, implausible and impractical because the characters' respective genres require vastly different things from them as protagonists. Bella eventually must submit to the conventions of the romance (and desires of the readers) and be with Edward, effectively taking her place in the gendered symbolic order. Katniss must act according to what will ensure her survival, as well as that of the community she's surrounded herself with. Both characters are constrained by their genres; to call one feminist and the other antifeminist without considering their genre traditions is to attempt to compare apples to oranges simply because they are both fruits grown on trees.

WORKS CITED

Andshescreamed. "Not Bella." *AfterEllen: The Pop Culture Site That Plays for Your Team. AfterEllen.com,* 7 Sept. 2010. Web. 16 Aug. 2011.

Bacon-Smith, Camille. *Enterprising Women: Television Fandom and the Creation of Popular Myth.* Philadelphia: University of Philadelphia Press, 1992. Print.

Booker, M. Keith, and Anne-Marie Thomas. *The Science Fiction Handbook.* Chichester: Wiley-Blackwell, 2009. Print.

Broderick, Mick. "Surviving Armageddon: Beyond the Imagination of Disaster." *Science Fiction Studies* 20.3 (Nov. 1993): 362–82. Print.

Cline, Ruth K. J., and William G. McBride. *A Guide to Literature for Young Adults: Background, Selection, and Use.* Glenview: Scott, 1983. Print.

Collins, Suzanne. *The Hunger Games.* 2008. New York: Scholastic, 2009. Print.

Curtis, Claire P. *Postapocalyptic Fiction and the Social Contract: We'll Not Go Home Again.* Lanham: Lexington, 2010. Ebook.

Ebert, Teresa. "The Romance of Patriarchy: Ideology, Subjectivity, and Postmodern Feminist Cultural Theory." *Cultural Critique: Popular Narrative, Popular Images* 10 (Autumn 1988): 19–57. Print.

Latrobe, Kathy H., and Judy Drury. *Critical Approaches to Young Adult Literature.* New York: Neal-Schuman, 2009. Print.

The Linster. "Bella Swan vs. Katniss Everdeen — What Does Empowerment Look Like?" *AfterEllen: The Pop Culture Site That Plays for Your Team. AfterEllen.com,* 7 Sept. 2010. Web. 16 Aug. 2011.

Meyer, Stephenie. *Twilight.* 2005. New York: Little, 2006. Print.

Miller, Laura. "'The Hunger Games' vs. 'Twilight': Which Young Adult Crossover Hit Series Has the Most Empowered Heroine? You'd Be Surprised." *Salon.com.* Salon Media Group, 5 Sept. 2010. Web. 16 Aug. 2011.

O'Danu, Maureen. "Killing Mary Sue." *Am I the Only One Dancing? Join the Dance.* N.p., 27 June 2011. Web. 8 Sept. 2011.

Radway, Janice A. *Reading the Romance: Women, Patriarchy, and Popular Literature.* Chapel Hill: University of North Carolina Press, 1991. Print.

Ramsdell, Kristin. *Happily Ever After: A Guide to Reading Interests in Romance Fiction.* Littleton: Libraries Unlimited, 1987. Print.

Regis, Pamela. *A Natural History of the Romance.* Philadelphia: Universtiy of Philadelphia Press, 2003. Print.

Sambell, Kay. "Carnivalizing the Future: A New Approach to Theorizing Childhood and Adulthood in Science Fiction for Young Readers." *Lion and the Unicorn* 28.2 (Apr. 2004): 247–67. Print.

Seltzer, Sarah. "Hunger Pangs: Hunting for the Perfect Heroine." *Bitch Magazine: Feminist Response to Pop Culture* 51 (Summer 2011): 38–42. Print.

Woolysocks. "Oh Sweet Lord, Twilight." *AfterEllen: The Pop Culture Site That Plays for Your Team. AfterEllen.com,* 7 Sept. 2010. Web. 16 Aug. 2011.

From the Boy Who Lived to the Girl Who Learned

*Harry Potter and Katniss Everdeen**

MARY F. PHARR

To a Millennial YA audience, J. K. Rowling's Harry Potter series is iconic: a children's narrative that is at once *Bildungsroman,* fantasy, and epic. Indeed, despite the quotidian fact that *Harry Potter and the Philosopher's Stone* first appeared in Britain some fifteen years ago, most Potterites feel as if they've known about Hogwarts all their lives. While that feeling is just a whimsical conceit for older readers, it's effectively the truth for young adults. At its best, Rowling's work touches an even higher truth, its reflexivity echoing the universality of ancient genres: witness the way the series captures the spirit of the epic in the increasing intricacy and gravity of Harry's struggles to grow from "the boy who lived" (*SS* 17) to a man willing to die so that others might live. Elsewhere, I've noted how ingeniously Rowling turns this struggle, with Harry surviving "by giving into death," Voldemort dying "by longing too much for life," and stability returning "to the wizarding culture through the restoration of mortality" ("Paradox" 9). Through such turns, the Potter septet subtly links the contemporary obsession with fantasy to the ancient, epic need to ponder the cost of fighting evil in any form. Since the epic is, in J. B. Hainsworth's words, "the longest-lived and most widely diffused of all literary forms" (3), its inclusion in the fabric of contemporary literature is apt, most particularly when considered against the crises and challenges of the new millennium.

And now, the next step in the postmodern reinvestment of the epic has been taken. In 2008, the year after Rowling's series concluded in print,

*An earlier version of this essay was presented at the 32rd International Conference on the Fantastic in the Arts (March 2011) in Orlando, Florida.

Suzanne Collins published *The Hunger Games,* the first novel in a trilogy that not only evokes the complexity of the epic spirit but also convincingly demonstrates the ambiguity of action — any action — within the hellish context of war. Set in the futuristic dystopia called Panem, the series follows Katniss Everdeen's transformative journey from someone the Capitol regards as a poverty-stricken nobody to the heroic symbol of a rebellion against tyranny. In this respect, the series may seem like just a variant of the Potter books. But the structural and thematic differences are significant, ultimately giving the Everdeen trilogy a unique gravity that the Potter series reaches (appropriately for a *Bildungsroman*) only in its concluding volumes. Despite being published by Scholastic and slotted into the "Children's Best Sellers" section of *The New York Times Book Review,* Collins's narrative is not intrinsically a children's story. Its exploration of both the doubtful ethics within social crisis and the epic ambiguity of war reaches adolescents in a way the Potter series cannot, reminding every reader of the inherent tragedy in all violent action, even for those whom legend will call heroes.

The Potter and Everdeen series diverge initially in their narrative pacing, with Collins's storyline moving with an intensity that Rowling's work eschews. Katniss's transformative journey takes less than two years, meaning that Collins seldom gives her protagonist the delightful downtime that Harry sometimes has during his seven years of magical education. For all the sorrow of his orphaned past and the burden of his uncertain future, the Harry that readers know at Hogwarts does experience exuberant moments in his schoolboy present: with his friends, with animals, with sports, and with the escapades that prove both his inherent empathy with all living creatures *and* his ever-increasing prowess as a wizard. Katniss, however, gets very little time to relax during her journey toward legend. As a citizen of the impoverished District 12, she has struggled against death her entire life; as a sixteen-year-old thrust unexpectedly into the Hunger Games in Chapter 1 of the first novel, her struggle intensifies exponentially, rushing forward initially into a public display of sanctioned violence and then on into unsanctioned warfare — time compressed into episodes of increasing violence. By nature and experience, Katniss is a suspicious loner, and in the swiftly changing, increasingly brutal world of Panem, she holds in most of the stress that she constantly feels. Unlike Harry, Katniss has neither time nor occasion to be surprised by joy.

Both Rowling and Collins are masters of world building, but they build very different worlds. There's something inherently charming about the details Rowling provides Harry right from the first time he boards the Hogwarts Express, the vast supply of magical food and trinkets creating a cornucopia of imagined delights for the reader. This magical cornucopia can be justly interpreted as what Karin E. Westman calls "a fantasy of consumer purchases" offered within the wizarding culture (311); in context, however, it reads like a child's holiday fantasy: less harmful than hopeful. For readers of *The Hunger Games,* the word *cornucopia* develops an entirely different meaning, referencing a place that promises tributes refreshment and resupply but that also delivers entrapment and death. In effect, the arena's Cornucopia is a caricature of the false premise on which Panem is built: the Capitol promises its citizens a well-regulated life organized by the government but actually gives them a short and highly restricted existence eked out everywhere except within its own domain. In contrast, Rowling eschews most references to socially (rather than individually) induced pockets of poverty within the magical England she presents. The variances she does present within her social system seem primarily based on familial connections. Even Rowling's nonmagical England appears overwhelmingly middle class. Both Englands are in peril, but their plight is not clearly evident to most people — wizards or Muggles.

Of course, as representations of the greatest of the good, Dumbledore and his adherents do understand the danger inculcated in the recent dark past that takes Harry and his companions to the edge of an even darker future — but only to the edge. Rowling allows goodness to triumph, a satisfying conclusion to a series that can first be approached by grade-school students. Writing for an older audience in a changing time, Collins presents a society that *is already trapped in darkness.* In Panem, only the denizens of the Capitol are oblivious to their country's misery and oppression. Worse yet, since the country has been ruled by fascistic corruption for three generations, even the oppressed cannot clearly distinguish the light of moral certitude. And though Katniss is pivotal to the rebellion against her country's worst brutalities, she is as prone as everyone else to the ambiguity that is at the core of her society. Like every epic hero, she is the balance in the struggle of right against wrong. What she cannot do, however, is change human nature and the uncertain truth of war. Ambiguity creates a specter of tragedy that looms over Panem throughout its history — not always on the attack but always present. Such a specter also approaches Harry's England but (if the epilogue is to be taken seriously) is obliterated by the forces of light.

Thus, the Potter books tend to be cautious in their exploration of the dark side of human nature. The Dursleys, for example, are child abusers who have made Dudley into a minor monster; even so, the family comes across initially as such Dickensian caricatures that they are more humorous than threatening. And Dudley redeems himself in his final farewell to Harry, acknowledging his cousin's true heroism. Rowling is also circumspect about the war that breaks out in the last volumes of the series. Innocents definitely suffer and die — but their creator keeps the combat perspective primarily focused on both the personal and the positive. We mourn the loss of individuals such as Tonks, Lupin, and Fred rather than groups such as the population of District 12. And Rowling often (though not always) offsets these individual losses with a balancing triumph of goodness that bodes well for the future of the wizarding world. Hence, not only do Tonks, Lupin, and Fred die in a right cause that will reopen a free Hogwarts, but they also leave behind a new baby and a twin brother who will be their living verification of a peaceful society. Like Harry himself, Britain survives Voldemort with a permanent scar rather than a lingering wound. Built on postapocalyptic ruins, Panem survives its latest war to find only the season of rest that is the traditional ending of an epic. Like Katniss, the country can never be sure that the past, darkened by human rather than monstrous nature, will not return in the future.

Pointedly, while we learn much about the culture of magic in Rowling's epic, we learn little about the political structure of the domain that holds that magic. Panem's infrastructure, in contrast, is crucial to Katniss's transformative journey. Panem had a major rebellion some seventy-five years before the crux of the story, and its current government uses both draconian laws and a set of annual death games to remind its citizens that their home districts must never again rebel against the supposedly all-powerful Capitol. Broadcast to everyone in the country, the Games rely equally on fantastic technology and human ingenuity, but the metaphor being broadcast is simple: no matter how brave or inspiring, all the players soon die in agony — except a single winner, who thereafter becomes a pawn of the government, controlled by atrocities both threatened and committed against his or her loved ones. In an essay originally published after France had surrendered to Germany during World War II, Simone Weil famously observed that the "true subject matter" of the epic *Iliad* "is force" (44), for it is force that simultaneously terrifies and controls humanity. The Capitol understands this dictum, and the rules of the Games that define Panem's dystopia are supposed to be proof against the independent action that is the core of epic heroism. In other words, the consistent breaking of rules that Harry Potter repeatedly pulls off at Hogwarts is, in theory, impossible in the arena. But when Katniss and Peeta break the "unbreakable" rules anyway and together win the Games on live TV by using their own physical and emotional force, they become national heroes who threaten a system that — in direct opposition to the one at Dumbledore's Hogwarts — denies the possibility of true individual worth.

Beyond their overt symbolism as proof of power, the Games also serve the Capitol as a covert symbol of humanity's fundamental corruption. The government calls each of the twenty-four teenagers chosen to fight to death in the arena a *tribute*— a reference both to Roman structure and to the eternal debt all the proletariat districts owe the Capitol, whose privileged citizens are exempt from providing tributes — making the Games far more popular in the absurdly decadent Capitol than anywhere else. Class privileges and restrictions certainly exist as well in the Potter books, strictures controversial enough that

Julia Park can justly say of the wizard world, "what a rigid, structured world it truly is" (180), a world bound by Rowling's own "middle-class worldview" (188). But a middle-class worldview often includes a sense of fair play and upward mobility, concepts crucial to the inclusion of talented Muggles like Hermione in the wizarding educational system. Fair play and upward mobility, however, are concepts the Hunger Games essentially invert with their focus on victory through violence, deceit, and high-level connections (this last emblematized by the sponsor gifts literally dropped from the skies to favored tributes).

The gifts are a twist designed to keep the Games interesting for the mandatory TV audience, a little something extra to make the arena a break from the grinding routine of the watchers' daily life (itself just a slow death). Viewers are supposed to be thrilled when one of their home district's tributes wins — despite the inevitable death of the district's other contestant. As if to confirm everyone's corrupt complicity in the death of their own young, the Capitol provides the winning district extra rations — this in a land where most people slowly starve no matter how hard they labor. Hainsworth notes that the epic genre is able both to "explore and question" (6); Collins's trilogy investigates and interrogates the way the human need for food and entertainment diminishes the human ability to make clear judgments about right and wrong. This diminution of judgment is itself a kind of ethical starvation, gradually destroying whatever is most humane among humans.

Katniss herself quickly realizes that she belongs to her root society. When she impulsively volunteers to substitute for her sister, Prim, in the Games, she does so out of a desperate love, an innate belief that Prim is not only a vulnerable child but also a better human being than Katniss will ever be. Katniss's sacrifice is more instinctive than calculated — but it makes an impression on the TV audience that neither the Capitol nor Katniss initially expected. Then once she's in the surreal atmosphere of the Games, Katniss and her partner, Peeta, prove themselves truly the children of the Panem into which they were born. They lie to that same TV audience about being romantically involved, a Romeo/Juliet deception that gains them public sympathy and those much-needed sponsor gifts. It also infuriates President Coriolanus Snow, who sees that these two hick tributes have pulled a trick the Capitol was unprepared for and one it cannot block as long as the lie is a ratings winner. Ironically, Katniss is a far less comfortable liar than Harry Potter, who also repeatedly uses mendacity as a survival technique. The larger distinction here is the guilt that Katniss feels at lying, a guilt that substantially exceeds Harry's own qualms at stretching the truth. And it should. After all, Harry never has to mislead the people — both decent and decadent — of an entire nation.

All epic heroes have companions and mentors. But Katniss's supporting cast is more emotionally complex than Harry's — more troubled, more vulnerable, finally more realistic and so less likable than Harry's team. Harry has Dumbledore as his most important mentor; he also has Ron and Hermione, along with a host of others, as protective companions. Part of Harry's maturation process involves the discovery of some hard truths about Dumbledore, most especially his refusal to tell Harry everything he knows about the prophecy that links Harry to Voldemort. Even so, from first to last, Harry remains "Dumbledore's man" (*HBP* 348), just as Ron and Hermione always return to Harry as their leader — allies as faithful supporters. The bonds among Rowling's protagonists serve them well against the solipsism that dominates the Dark Lord and the prejudice that defines the Deatheaters. But Katniss, though supported by allies throughout the Games, rarely feels this level of bonding with her companions. Haymitch Abernathy, her official mentor, is a middle-aged dipsomaniac who knows much but initially seems to believe in nothing — least of all Katniss. Even so, Haymitch does all he can to keep his accidental protégé alive, but mentor and tribute seem incapable of forming the kind of poignant connection Harry shares with Dumbledore — a connection that may be impossible to sustain in Panem. The pre-arena Katniss does have a close friend in the dashing Gale; they are, however, relentlessly driven apart by Katniss's ever-intensifying relationship with Peeta and by her own increasingly complex attitude toward the new rebellion that she unwittingly ignites and that he helps take to increasingly violent levels.

Gale is a natural leader, but he's never in the arena, where everyone is required to be an enemy of everyone else. Some of the tributes, known as Careers, are obviously professional young warriors trained for the Games, while other tributes are true victims of the Capitol. As for Katniss, although she is a natural hunter, she still needs allies in the arena — allies who must die if she is to survive. Even as she develops real feelings for Peeta, she reminds herself that they cannot both win by Capitol policy, so she tries to reject her own emotions. Yet after she watches a very young ally named Rue die brutally at the hands of a Career (whom Katniss kills in return), she suffers survivor's guilt over the inevitability of each succeeding death. That guilt, based not just on the arena's paradox but also on her increasing awareness that everyone associated with her is in deadly danger, keeps Katniss in a state of suspended emotion — unable to connect to others except when they are being taken from her. Thus, Peeta and Katniss's initial triumph becomes an ironic illusion since the Romeo/Juliet story is itself an act — at least on Juliet's part. Even more than Harry, Katniss needs help to be a hero, but her heroism is built on blood and deception as surely as it is created from the clothes Cinna styles for her. Harry suffers genuine ups and downs in his relationships with his beloved allies, but only rarely does he feel the awful ambiguity Katniss carries constantly as she performs a public role she cannot justify privately.

The Gamemaker who grants Katniss and Peeta mutual victory in the Seventy-fourth Games is quickly killed by President Snow, who understands the frailty inherent in a society of lies. When Snow meets Katniss privately, they agree, in a mixture of loathing and fascination, not to lie to each other. Even so, neither tells the other anything like *all* the truth they know. Such is the dark spirit of Panem. One truth Katniss omits is her determination to one day kill the über-killer Snow. But because he has her friends' and family's lives at his disposal, she continues to play his Games, this time on a Victory Tour. There she realizes she has become a legend as one who flouted the Capitol and lived. The mockingjay pin that she wore in the arena as her district's symbol has evolved into a unifying icon of defiance against the dystopia that is destroying both the bodies and souls of Panem. Like the infant Harry, like all epic heroes, the teenage Katniss has her destiny thrust upon her. Like all epic heroes as well, she accepts that destiny and confirms her heroism; but she does so with no heartfelt passion. Even before she is drafted into the larger game of war, she feels the hollowness at Panem's core.

As the logo for a second major rebellion against the fascistic Capitol, Katniss sees firsthand that there is no such thing as a good war and that no one is immune from the warping that dystopia and war produce. Aware of increasing instability, the Capitol forces most of the surviving Hunger Games victors to play a series of ferocious Quell Games, obviously designed to thin out the ranks of those who have proven resistant to Panem's policy that no individual can outshine the state. The techno-sadism of this second set of Games defines cruelty — and forces the rebellion, led by Alma Coin, out into the open. But even as the rebel army rescues Katniss from the arena, Peeta is captured and brainwashed by the Capitol. Engulfing all Panem, the war obliterates District 12, leaving Gale a bitter rebel hero who saves the district's survivors, and leaving Katniss a reluctant icon who performs propaganda broadcasts from war zones as the all-inspiring Mockingjay. As herself, she feels more guilt than ever. When Gale and Coin advocate terroristic bombing, Katniss realizes that the savagery of the war has caused the same physical, emotional, and ethical deterioration seen in the Games — but on a larger and much less entertaining scale. Panem has finally made its favorite reality show reality for everyone.

Charles McGrath has noted the connection between *The Hunger Games* and both the television show *Survivor* and Shirley Jackson's classic story "The Lottery," stating that Collins's work "taps into the same themes of anxiety and fear of elimination" (10). Yet Collins internalizes those themes in a particularly significant way. All three books are narrated in a rolling present tense by Katniss herself—dissolving the distance between her reality and the reader's. In contrast, while Harry's perspective dominates Rowling's series, the third-person voice Rowling uses (along with the memory of the magic

Pensieve) allows other perspectives — even that of Voldemort and the Death-eaters — to be offered on occasion to the reader. But we can never escape Katniss's point of view or the pressure of the role she has accepted. As she grimly struggles with the savage violence of all-out war, she finds herself faced with choices that are anything but clear, especially when the rebels prove themselves as ruthless as President Snow. Worse yet, no good deed seems to go unpunished. Impulsively, Katniss tries to talk mutual peace to a group of combatants — and gets shot for her trouble. On recovery, she returns to her early decision to kill Snow as the root of the evil — but is caught in a bombing that slaughters both a cluster of children and her beloved Prim. Later, Snow (who never lies to Katniss) declares that the bombing was designed by the rebels so that he would be blamed for an unspeakable atrocity. On her own, Katniss realizes that the bombing was, indeed, in line with the terroristic strategy advocated by Gale, now working for Coin and "the greater good" of ending the war.

The strategy is a success. Almost immediately, the war ends, the rebels having won over the rest of Panem with their bloody "evidence" of Snow's insane butchery. But Coin plans to continue the Hunger Games, using Capitol children to feed the public's need for both vengeance and entertainment. Like her predecessor in power, Coin instinctively understands that "Force wielded by others dominates the soul like an excessive hunger, since it comprises an unending power of life and death" (Weil 50). By aligning the literal misery of hunger with the metaphorical horror of force as a hunger that warps the soul, Suzanne Collins has done more than show that war wreaks havoc on innocents; she has cut through the Gordian knot of wartime propaganda to demonstrate the ultimate corruption of power itself. As the war's most famous hero, Katniss is selected to execute Snow on live TV, but impulsive as ever, she chooses to assassinate Coin instead. Snow still dies, but he dies laughing. Katniss is exonerated, in absentia, at a televised trial — as a "hopeless, shell-shocked lunatic" (*M* 378). The new government, free of Snow *and* Coin, bears the much-diminished Mockingjay no ill will; it even ends the Games in favor of a different kind of reality show, one where contestants sing rather than kill. Katniss, however, is first suicidal and then fundamentally traumatized by her own continued survival in a world of strategy rather than empathy. She has learned too much about human nature and political vagaries not to believe that the Games may yet return.

Left on her own, Katniss is fraught with nightmares: the dead — tributes, allies, soldiers, children, friends, and enemies — reminding her that every choice has consequence beyond intention. As Jennifer Lynn Barnes notes, "Katniss never gets to sacrifice herself. She doesn't get the heroic death. She survives — and that leaves her doing the hardest thing in the world: living in it once so many of the ones that she loves are gone" (26–27). Choice is, of course, crucial in the Potter epic as well, but Harry's most important choice is between his human desire to live and his faith in the truth of something beyond his own desires. He is Christlike — though it is the Christ of the "Dream of the Rood" rather than the New Testament — in his final combat with Voldemort. At the very last, Harry even tries to save the final remnant of Tom Riddle's tortured soul, telling the startled Voldemort to "try for some remorse" before their final duel (*DH* 741). At seventeen, Harry has achieved an inner peace that Katniss will never feel. Her decision to kill Coin seems to have been instrumental in ending the Hunger Games, but Gale might say the same of the terror tactics. Truth remains ambiguous.

In this sense, it's easy to read *The Hunger Games* trilogy as a tragedy at its core rather than an epic, but ultimately, the epic reading stands *if* the reader accepts the *Iliadic* proposition that epics often comprise elements of the tragic. In a solemn epilogue that has little in common with the frivolous comedy in the epilogue to *Deathly Hallows*, Katniss, now married to a mostly recovered Peeta, does acknowledge that national peace has come to the Panem that their children live in — but she knows its cost and its uncertainty. Beyond Rowling, Collins pushes her heroine into knowledge of something even more frightening than the necessity of fighting evil; she pushes Katniss into an awareness of the awful ambiguity of human action in conflict. This is truly the somber side of the epic: the knowledge that however noble a warrior may seem from a distance, however clear a cause and shining its weaponry when seen from afar, no one and nothing really shine in actual war. War can be necessary, and sometimes good does win, but it's never a clean win. Achilles comes to accept this grim truth in the *Iliad*, and Harry gropes toward it in his struggles, but Katniss learns it fully and has to act upon the knowledge — as though Collins had combined Harry Potter and Severus Snape. With her knowledge of ambiguity, Katniss will never be as loved as the boy who lived, but as the girl who learns, she is even more consequential for the adolescents becoming adults in an uncertain world.

WORKS CITED

Barnes, Jennifer Lynn. "Team Katniss." *The Girl Who Was on Fire.* Ed. Leah Wilson. Dallas: Smart Pop-BenBella, 2011. 13–27. Print.

Collins, Suzanne. *Mockingjay.* New York: Scholastic, 2010. Print.

Hainsworth, J. B. *The Idea of Epic.* Berkeley: University of California Press, 1991. Print.

McGrath, Charles. "Teenage Wastelands." *New York Times Magazine* 20 Feb. 2011: 9–10. Print.

Park, Julia. "Class and Socioeconomic Identity in Harry Potter's England." *Reading Harry Potter: Critical Essays.* Ed. Giselle Liza Anatol. Westport: Praeger, 2003. 179–89. Print.

Pharr, Mary. "A Paradox: The Harry Potter Series as Both Epic and Postmodern." *Heroism in the Harry Potter Series.* Eds. Katrin Berndt and Lena Steveker. Farnham: Ashgate, 2011. 9–23. Print.

Rowling, J. K. *Harry Potter and the Deathly Hallows.* New York: Scholastic, 2007. Print.
_____. *Harry Potter and the Half-Blood Prince.* New York: Scholastic, 2005. Print.
_____. *Harry Potter and the Sorcerer's Stone.* New York: Scholastic, 1998. Print.
Weil, Simone. *Simone Weil's The* Iliad *or The Poem of Force: A Critical Edition.* Ed. and
    Trans. James P. Holoka. New York: Lang, 2003. 44–69. [Essay originally pub. in *Cahiers
    du Sud* (Marseilles): Dec. 1940–Jan. 1941.] Print.
Westman, Karin E. "Specters of Thatcherism: Contemporary British Culture in J. K. Rowl-
    ing's Harry Potter Series." *The Ivory Tower and Harry Potter.* Ed. Lana A. Whited.
    Columbia: University of Missouri Press, 2002. 305–28. Print.

Dystopian and Postapocalyptic Fiction and Criticism

A Core Bibliography, with Emphasis on Young Adult Works

LEISA A. CLARK

FICTION

Atwood, Margaret. *The Handmaid's Tale.* Toronto: McClelland, 1985. Print.

Bradbury, Ray. *Fahrenheit 451.* 1953. New York: Random House-Ballantine, 1987. Print.

Butler, Octavia. *Parable of the Sower.* 1993. Boston: Grand Central, 2000. Print.

Carey, Anna. *Eve.* New York: HarperCollins, 2011. Print.

Carmody, Isobelle. *Obernewtyn.* New York: Tor, 1999. Print.

Condie, Ally. *Matched.* Boston: Dutton, 2010. Print.

DeStefano, Lauren. *Wither: The Chemical Garden Trilogy, Book One.* New York: Simon & Schuster, 2011. Print.

DeVita, James. *The Silenced.* New York: Harper Teen, 2007. Print.

Dunkle, Clare B. *The Sky Inside.* New York: Ginee Seo, 2008. Print.

Grant, Michael. *Gone.* New York: Tegen, 2008. Print.

Hall, Teri. *The Line.* New York: Speak, 2011. Print.

Hegland, Jean. *Into the Forest.* New York: Dial, 1998. Print.

Higson, Charlie. *The Enemy.* New York: Hyperion, 2009. Print.

Hocking, Amanda. *Hollowlan.* Seattle: CreateSpace, 2010. Print.

Hoover, H. M. *Children of Morrow.* Columbus: MacMillan, 1973. Print.

_____. *This Time of Darkness.* New York: Viking, 1980. Print.

Huxley, Aldous. *Brave New World.* 1932. New York: HarperCollins-Harper Perennial Modern Classics, 1998. Print.

Jordan, Sherryl. *Winter of Fire.* Bel Air: Point, 1993. Print.

Karl, Jean. *But We Are Not of Earth.* New York: Laurel Leaf, 1984. Print.

Karr, Julia. *XVI.* New York: Speak, 2011. Print.

Kress, Nancy. *Crossfire.* New York: Tor, 2004. Print.

Lawrence, Louise. *Children of the Dust.* Cambridgeshire: Tracks, 1985. Print.

Lewis, C. S. *That Hideous Strength.* 1945. New York: Simon & Schuster-Scribner, 1996. Print.

Lowry, Lois. *The Giver.* New York: Bantam, 1993. Print.

Malley, Gemma. *The Declaration*. New York: Bloomsbury USA, 2007. Print.
Mariz, Rae. *The Unidentified*. New York: Balzer & Bray, 2010. Print.
Marsden, John. *Tomorrow, When the War Began*. Sydney: Pan Macmillan, 1993. Print.
Nelson, O. T. *The Girl Who Owned a City*. 1975. Minneapolis: First Avenue, 1995. Print.
Ness, Patrick. *The Knife of Never Letting Go (Chaos Walking: Book One)*. Somerville: Candlewick, 2008. Print.
Oliver, Lauren. *Delirium*. New York: HarperCollins, 2011. Print.
Orwell, George. *Nineteen Eighty-Four*. 1949. New York: Penguin-Plume, 2003. Print.
Pearson, Mary E. *The Adoration of Jenna Fox*. New York: Henry Holt, 2008. Print.
Pfeffer, Susan Beth. *Life as We Knew It*. Boston: Graphia, 2006. Print.
Reeve, Philip. *Fever Crumb*. New York: Scholastic, 2010. Print.
Rosoff, Meg. *How I Live Now*. New York: Lamb, 2006. Print.
Roth, Veronica. *Divergent*. New York: Tegen, 2011. Print.
Ryan, Carrie. *The Forest of Hands and Teeth*. New York: Delacorte, 2009. Print.
Shelley, Mary. *Frankenstein*. 1818. Atlanta: Intervisual, 2010. Print.
Shusterman, Neal. *Unwind*. New York: Simon & Schuster, 2007. Print.
Simmons, Kristen. *Article 5*. New York: Tor Teen, 2012. Print.
Stephens, J. B. *The Big Empty*. New York: Razorbill, 2004. Print.
Takami, Koushun. *Battle Royale: The Novel*. 1999. Trans. Yuji Oniki, 2003. 2nd ed. Introd. Max Allan Collins. San Francisco: VIZ, 2099. Print.
Tolan, Stephanie S. *Welcome to the Ark*. New York: Harper, 1998. Print.
Treggiari, Jo. *Ashes, Ashes*. New York: Scholastic, 2011. Print.
Wasserman, Robin. *Skinned (Skinned Trilogy)*. New York: Simon Pulse, 2008. Print.
Wells, H. G. *The Time Machine*. 1895. New York: Tor, 1992. Print.
Westerfeld, Scott. *Uglies*. New York: Simon Pulse, 2005. Print.
Weyn, Suzanne. *The Bar Code Tattoo*. New York: Scholastic, 2004. Print.
Wyndham, John. *The Chrysalids*. 1955. New York: NYRB, 2008. Print.
Young, Moira. *Blood Red Road (Dustlands)*. New York: McElderry, 2011. Print.
Zamyatin, Yevgeny. *We: A Novel of the Future*. 1921. Trans. Gregory Zilboorg, 1924. Piscataway: Transaction, 2000.

CRITICISM

Armitt, Lucie. *Where No Man Has Gone Before: Women and Science Fiction*. London: Routledge, 1991. Print.
Baccolini, Raffaella. "The Persistence of Hope in Dystopian Science Fiction." *PMLA: Special Topic: Science Fiction and Literary Studies: The Next Millennium* 119.3 (2004): 518–21. Print.
Baccolini, Raffaella, and Tom Moylan. *Dark Horizons: Science Fiction and the Dystopian Imagination*. New York: Routledge, 2003. Print.
Becker, Manuel Benjamin. *Forms and Functions of Dystopia in Margaret Atwood's Novels*. Saarbrücken: VDM, 2008. Print.
Berger, James. *After the End: Representations of Post-Apocalypse*. Minneapolis: University of Minnesota Press, 1999. Print.
Booker, M. Keith. *The Dystopian Impulse in Modern Literature*. Westport: Greenwood, 1994. Print.
Bradford, Clare, Kerry Mallan, John Stephens, and Robyn McCallum. *New World Orders in Contemporary Children's Literature: Utopian Transformations*. Basingstoke: Palgrave, 2008. Print.
Busch, Justin E. A. *The Utopian Vision of H. G. Wells*. Jefferson: McFarland, 2009. Print.
Claeys, Gregory. *The Utopia Reader*. New York: New York University Press, 1999. Print.
Cole, Pam B. *Young Adult Literature in the 21st Century*. Boston: McGraw, 2009. Print.

Cooper, Susan. *Dreams and Wishes: Essays on Writing for Children.* New York: McElderry, 1996. Print.

Curtis, Claire P. *Postapocalyptic Fiction and the Social Contract: We'll Not Go Home Again.* Lanham: Lexington, 2010. Print.

Donawerth, Jane L., and Carol A. Kolmerten, eds. *Utopian and Science Fiction by Women: Worlds of Difference.* Syracuse: Syracuse University Press: 1997. Print.

Dowling, David. *Fictions of Nuclear Disaster.* Iowa City: University of Iowa Press, 1987. Print.

Dunn, Thom, and Karl Hiller. "Growing Home: The Triumph of Youth in the Novels of H. M. Hoover." *Science Fiction for Young Readers.* Ed. C. W. Sullivan. Westport: Greenwood, 1993. 121–31. Print.

Freedman, Carl. *Critical Theory and Science Fiction.* Hanover: Wesleyan, 2000. Print.

Gresh, Lois H. *The Hunger Games Companion: The Unauthorized Guide to the Series.* New York: St. Martin's Griffin, 2011. Print.

Hambouz, Annissa, and Katherine Schulten. "Dark Materials: Reflections on Dystopian Themes in YA Literature." *The Learning Network. New York Times* 6 Jan. 2011. Web. 17 Aug. 2011.

Haraway, Donna. *Simians, Cyborgs, and Women: The Reinvention of Nature.* New York: Routledge, 1991. Print.

Hintz, Carrie, and Elaine Ostry. "Monica Hughes, Lois Lowry, and Young Adult Dystopias." *Lion and the Unicorn* 26.2 (2002): 254–64. Print.

_____. *Utopian and Dystopian Writing for Children and Young Adults.* New York: Routledge, 2003. Print.

Hunt, Peter. *Children's Literature.* Malden: Blackwell, 2001. Print.

James, Edward, and Farah Mendlesohn, eds. *The Cambridge Companion to Science Fiction.* Cambridge Companions to Literature. Cambridge: Cambridge University Press, 2003. Print.

James, Kathryn. *Death, Gender, and Sexuality in Contemporary Adolescent Literature.* New York: Routledge, 2008. Print.

Jones, Katharine. "Getting Rid of Children's Literature." *Lion and the Unicorn* 30.3 (2006): 287–315. Print.

Katerberg, William H. *Future West: Utopia and Apocalypse in Frontier Science Fiction.* Lawrence: University Press of Kansas, 2008. Print.

Latrobe, Kathy H., and Judy Drury. *Critical Approaches to Young Adult Literature.* New York: Neal-Schuman, 2009. Print.

Lurie, Alison. *Don't Tell the Grown-Ups: The Subversive Power of Children's Literature.* Boston: Little, Brown, 1990. Print.

McGrath, Charles. "Teenage Wastelands." *New York Times Magazine* 20 Feb. 2011: 9–10. Print.

Miller, Laura. "Fresh Hell: What's Behind the Book in Dystopian Fiction for Young Readers?" *New Yorker* 14 June 2010: 132–36. Print.

Mosle, Sara. "The Outlook's Bleak." *New York Times* 2 Aug. 1998: SM34. Print.

Moylan, Tom. *Scraps of Untainted Sky: Science Fiction, Utopia, Dystopia.* Boulder: Westview, 2000. Print.

Olander, Joseph D., Eric S. Rabkin, and Martin H. Greenberg. *No Place Else: Explorations in Utopian and Dystopian Fiction.* Carbondale: Southern Illinois University Press, 1983. Print.

Ostry, Elaine. "'Is He Still Human? Are You?': Young Adult Science Fiction in the Posthuman Age." *Lion and the Unicorn* 28.2 (2004): 222–46. Print.

Pintér, Károly. *The Anatomy of Utopia: Narration, Estrangement and Ambiguity in More, Wells, Huxley and Clarke.* Critical Explorations in Science Fiction and Fantasy. Jefferson: McFarland, 2010. Print.

Reber, Lauren L. *Negotiating Hope and Honesty: Rhetorical Criticism of Young Adult Dystopian Literature.* M.A. Thesis, Brigham Young University: April 2005. *Mountain West Digital Library.* Web. 17 Aug. 2011.

Reddish, Mitchell G. *Apocalyptic Literature: A Reader.* Peabody: Hendrickson, 1995. Print.

Reeve, Philip. "The Worst Is Yet to Come." *School Library Journal.* 1 Aug. 2011: N. pag. Source Media. Web. 18 Aug. 2011.

Rosen, Elizabeth K. *Apocalyptic Transformation: Apocalypse and the Postmodern Imagination.* Lanham: Lexington, 2008. Print.

Sambell, Kay. "Carnivalizing the Future: A New Approach to Theorizing Childhood and Adulthood in Science Fiction for Young Readers." *Lion and the Unicorn* 28.2 (2004): 247–67. Print.

Seed, David. *A Companion to Science Fiction.* Blackwell Companions to Literature and Culture. Hoboken: Wiley-Blackwell, 2005. Print.

Seltzer, Sarah. "Hunger Pangs: Hunting for the Perfect Heroine." *Bitch Magazine* 51 (Summer 2011): 38–42. Print.

Sisk, David W. *Transformations of Language in Modern Dystopias.* Westport: Greenwood, 1997. Print.

Springen, Karen. "Are Teen Novels Dark and Depraved — or Saving Lives?" *Publishers Weekly.com.* Publishers Weekly, n.d. Web. 9 June 2011.

Sullivan, C. W., ed. *Science Fiction for Young Readers.* Westport: Greenwood, 1993. Print.

Trites, Roberta. *Disturbing the Universe: Power and Repression in Adolescent Literature.* Iowa City: University of Iowa Press, 2004. Print.

Urbanski, Heather. *Plagues, Apocalypses and Bug-Eyed Monsters: How Speculative Fiction Shows Us Our Nightmares.* Jefferson: McFarland, 2007. Print.

Weaver, Roslyn. *Apocalypse in Australian Fiction and Film: A Critical Study.* Jefferson: McFarland, 2011. Print.

Wilson, Leah, ed. *The Girl Who Was on Fire: Your Favorite Authors on Suzanne Collins' Hunger Games Trilogy.* Dallas: Smart Pop-BenBella, 2011. Print.

Yampbell, Cat. "Judging a Book by Its Cover: Publishing Trends in Young Adult Literature." *Lion and the Unicorn* 29.3 (2005): 348–72. Print.

About the Contributors

Leisa A. **Clark** has a master's degree in women's and gender studies from the University of South Florida, where she is finishing further graduate work in humanities and cultural studies. Her areas of expertise include young adult literature, dystopian fiction, and food studies. She has published and presented on Harry Potter, Carrie Ryan's *The Forest of Hands and Teeth,* and *Doctor Who/Torchwood.*

Bill **Clemente** is a professor of English at Peru State College, where, among other courses, he teaches nonwestern literature, science fiction literature and film, and children's literature. In addition to articles on Canadian and Caribbean literature, he has also published on the dystopian fiction of Suzy Charnas, James Tiptree, and Nalo Hopkinson.

Helen **Day** is a senior lecturer in children's literature at the University of Central Lancashire in Preston, England. She holds a Ph.D. and is course leader of the M.A. Writing for Children Program, specializing in crossover fiction and narrative theories. Her research explores lying and unreliable narrators in young adult and crossover fiction.

Rodney M. **DeaVault** is pursuing a master's degree in children's literature at Simmons College. His academic areas of interest include feminism in Victorian children's literature and popular culture, and children in theater. He has presented papers at the International Conference on the Fantastic in the Arts and at the national meeting of the Popular Culture Association.

Max **Despain** is an associate professor of English at the U.S. Air Force Academy and a lieutenant colonel in the Air Force. She teaches food literature, including a class on "Metaphors of Meals." In recent conference presentations, she has considered the social and cultural implications of food in Willa Cather's novels. She is also interested in questions of memory and identity in literature.

Catherine R. **Eskin** is an associate professor of English at Florida Southern College, where she teaches Shakespeare and rhetoric. As archivist for Temple

Emanuel in Lakeland, Florida, she works on Jewish oral history in the American South. Her interests in the social implications of architecture, rhetoric, and service learning have led her to investigate how pedagogies can be used to expand cultural knowledge while exploring community politics.

Amanda **Firestone** is a Ph.D. candidate in the Department of Communication at the University of South Florida. She received her master's degree from Sussex University in Brighton, England, where she focused on gender studies and media. Her doctoral dissertation focuses on the *Twilight* saga.

Valerie Estelle **Frankel** is the author of *From Girl to Goddess: The Heroine's Journey in Myth and Legend* (McFarland, 2010) and *Buffy and the Heroine's Journey* (McFarland, 2012). She is working on a project on fandom called "Harry Potter: Still Recruiting and Teaching with Harry Potter." Once a lecturer at San Jose State University, she is now a frequent speaker on fantasy, myth, pop culture, and the heroine's journey.

Tammy L. **Gant** is an assistant professor of English at the United States Air Force Academy and a captain in the Air Force. She has a master's degree from Wright State University and has taught at West Point. She is pursuing an M.F.A. in the Children's Literature Program at Hollins University, where her focus is middle-grades fantasy fiction.

Tina L. **Hanlon** is an associate professor of English at Ferrum College and the Hollins University Summer Graduate Program in Children's Literature. She is coeditor of *Crosscurrents of Children's Literature* (2006) and director of the website AppLit: Resources for Readers and Teachers of Appalachian Literature for Children and Young Adults (www.AppLit.org). She teaches courses on Appalachian literature, combining literature and writing with sociology and environmental science.

Holly **Hassel** is an associate professor of English and chair of the University of Wisconsin Colleges Women's Studies Program. She is the coauthor of *Critical Companion to J. K. Rowling* (Facts on File, 2010), and her work has appeared in the journals *Pedagogy, Teaching English in the Two-Year College, Feminist Teacher, Women's Studies,* and *College English.*

Sharon D. **King** is an associate at UCLA's Center for Medieval and Renaissance Studies. She holds a Ph.D. in comparative literature from UCLA. Her publications include *City Tragedy on the Renaissance Stage in France, Spain, and England* and a translation of J. Prevost's 1584 *Clever and Pleasant Inventions: Part One.* She translates and performs short late-medieval comic plays with her troupe *Les Enfans Sans Abri.*

Gretchen **Koenig** is an instructor of English and fine arts at the United States Air Force Academy. Her doctoral dissertation, in progress, is on the aesthetics of fear in the Age of Revolution (1765–1815) in Transatlantic literature. She is interested in examining how fear presents itself in literature of all ages.

Ellyn **Lem** is an associate professor of English and women's studies at University of Wisconsin–Waukesha and is the Honors Program coordinator. She has published essays on *Like Water for Chocolate,* Arthur Miller, women's cookbooks, and interdisciplinary approaches to teaching war. Her teaching and research interests include food studies, children's literature, and women in popular culture. She has received two Arthur Kaplan fellowships for outstanding contributions to education.

Jennifer **Mitchell** completed her dissertation in English literature at the CUNY Graduate Center. At Hunter College, she teaches children's and Victorian literature. She serves on the executive board of the Center for Lesbian and Gay Studies (CLAGS), which promotes scholarship, activism, and discourse about LGBTQ issues. She is working on a project about the intersections of masochism, sexology, and Victorian and modern British fiction.

Amy L. **Montz** is an assistant professor of English at the University of Southern Indiana. Her research and teaching interests include 18th through 21st century British literature, young adult literature, feminism, and fashion. She is working on a project analyzing the way Victorian novels and culture construct women as English or non–English through their clothing, and the way fashion becomes a symbol of national allegiance, power, or resistance.

Shannon R. **Mortimore-Smith** is an assistant professor of English education at Shippensburg University, where she teaches adolescent literature and conducts research on multimodal, twenty-first-century, and new media literacies. She is an advocate for teaching literature for social justice and is interested in critical inquiry related to comics, graphic novels, Japanese manga, and video role-playing games.

Sarah Outterson **Murphy** is a Ph.D. student in English at the City University of New York, where she studies reader-response theories of early modern drama and contemporary speculative fiction. She has published in *Utopian Studies* and teaches at Hunter College.

Anthony **Pavlik** has a doctorate in children's literature and teaches in the Faculty of Education at Boğaziçi University in Istanbul. He has published articles on fantasy literature, ecocriticism, and maps in children's literature.

Mary F. **Pharr** is a professor emeritus of English at Florida Southern College. Coeditor (with Leonard G. Heldreth) of *The Blood Is the Life: Vampires in Literature,* she also edited *Fantastic Odysseys: Selected Essays From the 22nd International Conference on the Fantastic in the Arts.* She holds a doctorate from Vanderbilt, and her publications include essays on the work of Stephen King and J. K. Rowling.

Guy Andre **Risko** is a Ph.D. student at Binghamton University, specializing in New Americanist studies and children's literature. He has specialized in methods of research in topics ranging from legal and policy studies to literary analysis and critical theory.

Kelley **Wezner** is an assistant professor in the Department of English and Philosophy at Murray State University and is director of institutional assessment. Her research interests are in Restoration and 18th-century print culture, as well as how literature of any period embodies and interrogates power. Her research examines gaze and gender in 18th-century women's drama and the intersections of gender and power in modern genre fiction.

Katheryn **Wright** is an assistant professor in the Core Division at Champlain College. She holds a Ph.D. in interdisciplinary humanities from Florida State University, where she specialized in television and new media studies. Her research focuses on digital aesthetics, critical theories related to the body, and the "screenscape" in popular culture.

Index